SO-ACM-438

587 $10.00

Foreword

The world is shrinking—politically, if not physically. Communications and transportation have progressed to the point where nearly every corner of the world is readily accessible to every other corner of the world. Each nation has become the "next door neighbor" of all nations. As a result, domestic policies adopted by one country may well impact on the affairs of many.

This cross-fertilization process, called "interdependence" by social scientists and economists, is particularly apparent in the field of agriculture, where it has wrought many, sometimes massive, changes.

Essentially, the 1985 Yearbook of Agriculture is about agricultural interdependence and its attendant issues, both present and future. Although the primary focus is on U.S. agriculture, other nations are probed as well.

Experts from a variety of disciplines examine such critical factors as the relationship between domestic policies and international trade practices, the conflict between consumer and farmer interests, government participation in production and pricing policies, changing production patterns around the world, the impact of technology, barriers to international trade, and much more.

This Yearbook addresses many of the problems that confront the agricultural community today and that will confront it tomorrow. Yet, its interest quotient reaches beyond the farmer, the economist, the student, the agribusinessman, and the policymaker. It has value for every individual concerned about his or her standard of living, because a solid agricultural foundation is essential to a nation's success.

John R. Block
Secretary of Agriculture

Preface

By Larry B. Marton
Yearbook Editor

This 1985 Yearbook of Agriculture borders on the unique in two respects; it is the first one in many years that was developed without Jack Hayes sitting in the editor's chair, and it is the first one in memory that explores U.S. agriculture in a worldwide context.

Jack Hayes retired this year after more than three decades of meritorious service to USDA and its constituents. Although he has left the premises, Jack's standards of excellence remain behind to guide his successor.

As for the focus of the 1985 Yearbook, the nature of agriculture has changed so much so rapidly as to make an examination of its new dimensions between these covers mandatory.

Be cautioned, however. Not all of our authors agree about what has happened and what will happen. What's more, several authors using identical statistical bases come up with different sets of numbers because their timeframes and their perceptions vary.

This Yearbook will be particularly valuable to economists, teachers, students, farmers, agribusinessmen, and decision-makers—here and abroad. And it will be especially interesting to anyone concerned about the United States and the world food supplies, now as well as in the future.

Deep appreciation is expressed to the Yearbook Planning Committee that contributed much time and expertise. The Committee consisted of:
Ovid Bay, *Extension Service*
Ben Blankenship, *Economic Research Service*
Wallace Lindell, *Foreign Agricultural Service*
Sally A.S. Michael, *World Agricultural Outlook Board*
Victor E. Muniec, *Office of International Cooperation and Development*
M. Ray Waggoner, *Agricultural Stabilization and Conservation Service*

We are grateful to Robert Thompson, assistant secretary for economics, for his thoughtful suggestions, and to John M. McClung, director of the Office of Information, for his guidance.

Contents

Page

Page

For sale by the Superintendent of Documents, U.S. Government Printing Office
Washington, D.C. 20402

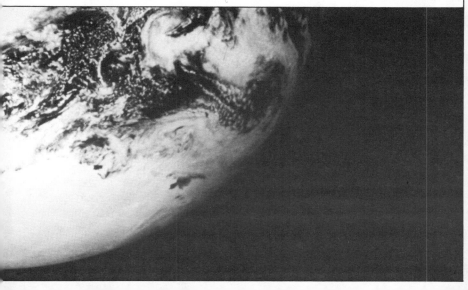

Part I.
AGRICULTURE
IN A CHANGING
WORLD

The Challenge of Change

By Wayne D. Rasmussen,
*historian, Agriculture and Rural
Economics Division, Economic
Research Service*

Change is inevitable. Everyone can think of times—the good old days—when change seemed to take place slowly compared with today. Yet at almost any time in human history the people living then thought that they were in a period of major change.

Forty-five years ago, the theme of the Yearbook of Agriculture was *Farmers in a Changing World.* It began with a summary which said, in part: "The year 1940 marks the end of a decade that has seen more swift and far-reaching changes in agricultural viewpoints and policy than perhaps any other decade in the history of the United States. . . . we do face profound changes and we must do something to adjust ourselves to them." These words foretold one of the greatest changes in agriculture the world had ever seen—the tremendous increase in agricultural productivity after World War II.

By 1961, the foreword to the Yearbook of Agriculture, *Farmer's World,* stated that "At no time in thirty centuries has world agriculture faced greater problems, greater challenges, and greater opportunities. And at no time has American agri-

Smithsonian Institute

culture been so closely con-
nected as now with world
agriculture."

Farming in the Old World

There have, of course, been
many periods of major change
in the past. Civilization itself
began some 10,000 years ago,
or perhaps considerably earlier,
when people first planted seeds
and tamed animals. Agriculture
spread slowly and steadily
through most of the world,
with perhaps separate places of
origin in some of the continents. Over the centuries our
farming ancestors accom-
plished feats that farmers today

*Ancient Egyptians tamed wild stock,
the forerunners of domestic animals
grown today. The early farmers accom-
plished feats that modern farmers have
not yet duplicated.*

have not yet duplicated. Draw-
ing upon wild stock, they developed all the major food
plants and domestic animals
grown today. When agriculture
appeared in written history in
the time of the Egyptians,
Greeks, and Romans, and even
earlier for the Chinese, it was
already a highly developed art,
backed by years of progress
based on observation and trial
and error, and was one of the

important bases of international trade.

Although Roman and other agricultural writers urged improvements in farming and some were made, these mostly disappeared during the Middle Ages. During the 18th century, a number of large farmers and agricultural reformers in western Europe, particularly in England, demonstrated that farming could be improved. More efficient plows, grain drills, and threshing machines were invented even though they were not widely adopted. Former open-field farms in England were enclosed, with much arable land being converted into pasture. Livestock were improved and more productive crop varieties introduced. Many small farmers and laborers, however, were forced to leave agriculture.

Farming in the New World

Meanwhile, English colonists had settled in Jamestown, Virginia, and Plymouth, Massachusetts. They survived mainly because they learned from the Indians how to grow corn. As more settlers arrived and moved west, they learned to cope with the new environment. At the time of the Ameri-

can Revolution, most farming methods and tools differed little from those of 2,000 years earlier.

After the Revolution, settlers continued the westward movement, but farming changed slowly. One exception came with the invention of the cotton gin by Eli Whitney in 1793 and the consequent spread of cotton growing across much of the South. Other machines, such as an iron plow, a horse-drawn grain reaper, and a corn planter were invented, but farmers were slow to adopt them.

First American Agricultural Revolution

The Civil War, with its unlimited demands, labor shortages, high prices, and patriotic appeals to produce brought major changes to agriculture. Congress passed four important agricultural reform laws in 1862. The Homestead Act granted 160 acres of western land to persons who would live on it for 5 years. The Morrill Land Grant College Act gave every State unclaimed western land to be used for founding colleges to teach agriculture and engineering. The Department of Agriculture was established, and land and funds were appropriated to build a transcontinental railroad.

As the war continued, more and more farmers turned to horse-drawn machinery to replace the young men in the armies. Some farmers then bought more land because, with the new machines, they could crop larger areas. As the war ended, most farmers had changed from the old hand agriculture to the new horse-powered machinery.

This change, sometimes called the first American agricultural revolution, turned American farmers from self-sufficiency to commercial production. And by the 1880's, American exports of cotton, meat, and wheat were dominating world markets.

Agricultural Changes Elsewhere

The United States was not alone in increasing its total volume of agricultural exports after 1865. Argentina, Australia, Canada, and New Zealand became competitive in shipping grain and livestock products to Europe, although commercial agriculture began about a generation later than in the United States.

Japan turned to the United States to help modernize its ag-

riculture in 1871, when it persuaded Horace Capron, head of the newly established Department of Agriculture, to leave that post and lead a developmental mission to that nation. Despite difficulties, the mission had much to do with paving the way for better farming in Japan. Russia, Japan's rival in the Far East during the second half of the 19th century, liberated its serfs in 1861 and gave them allotments of land, a change that did much to encourage agricultural productivity.

Change in agriculture continued in the more advanced nations up to World War I. U.S. agriculture reached a balance with the rest of the economy. The growing industrial cities of the United States and Europe were absorbing farm products from many parts of the world. So far as agriculture was concerned, there was a virtual worldwide equilibrium between supply and demand.

World War I Leads to Overproduction

World War I upset this equilibrium in a number of ways. Pushed by patriotism and pulled by high prices, U.S. farmers increased their produc-

DRHEAD 1879
TEN PHOTO

USDA

tion beyond anything that world markets could absorb after the war and European production returned to normal. Farmers saw prices decline by half between 1919 and 1921, the immediate postwar years. Over the next decade, farm prices and land values declined steadily, eventually dragging the United States into the Great Depression.

Great Depression

The depression became world-wide in the early 1930's and world trade in farm products virtually came to a halt. During the 1930's, a series of laws in the United States provided price supports for major farm products in return for farmers cutting back on acreage planted. Other laws provided for farm credit, rural rehabilitation, rural electrification, soil conservation, and the distribution of surplus food to the needy. Many other industrialized nations also undertook programs to aid their farmers. Prosperity returned slowly to farmers in most nations during

Horsedrawn farming triggered the first American agricultural revolution and changed agriculture from self-sufficiency to commercial production. (Minnesota, grain elevator.)

the 1930's. Then World War II brought major changes.

Second American Agricultural Revolution

During the war, the demand for farm products seemed to be unlimited and, in most nations, price controls rather than price supports were emphasized. U.S. farmers were guaranteed high supports for 2 years after the end of hostilities.

Demand, high prices, and labor shortages led to what has been called the second American agricultural revolution, a change which has affected the farms of much of the world. During and just after the war, farmers completed the changeover from animal to mechanical power.

New machines were only one aspect of the second agricultural revolution. Mechanization and many other changes constituted a package of practices, or what has been called the application of systems analysis to farming. These other changes included the controlled application of lime and fertilizer, adoption of soil conservation techniques, irrigation where necessary and possible, the creation and use of improved varieties of plants and breeds of animals, the adoption

USDA

of hybrid corn (developed in the twenties to yield much more than varietal strains traditionally being planted), the formulation of carefully balanced feeds for livestock and poultry, the more effective control of insects and diseases, and the use of chemical weed killers and defoliants.

The effects of these practices on agricultural output were dramatic. Both production and productivity reached heights never before thought possible. In many respects rural life was affected just as profoundly because of the consolidation of farms and the sharp decline in the farm population. These changes were most noticeable in the 1950's and 1960's, but

Increased demands during World War II put U.S. agriculture into the motorized era and with it came sweeping changes which have made U.S. agriculture what it is today. (Alabama, shipping shed.)

continued on a lesser scale into the 1980's.

U.S. Assistance to Other Countries

As high price supports and adoption of new technology brought about increases in production in the early 1950's, surpluses developed. In 1954, the Agricultural Trade Development and Assistance Act, better known as Public Law 480, was approved. The Act provided for selling the surpluses to developing nations for "blocked currency," that is, money that could be spent only within the nation making the purchase, and for donating surpluses to nations suffering disaster.

The law had two purposes: to dispose of surpluses that were overhanging the market, and to aid developing nations in improving their agriculture. Helping other nations improve their agriculture—an activity that had many precedents—was not seen as encouraging competition with American farm exports, but as helping nations develop sound agricultural bases that would enable them first, to develop and maintain their independence and second, to become customers for American industrial and agricultural products. While all the hopes of the proponents of the legislation have not been realized, many have. Even before Public Law 480 was passed, the United States helped Italy, West Germany, and Japan, for example, restore their agriculture, and today they are among our most important trading partners. Later, under Public Law 480, the United States helped Israel, South Korea, Formosa, Morocco, and Egypt, for example, develop their agriculture. Now

these nations buy both our agricultural and industrial products.

The United States cooperated with foundations and international organizations in the 1960's in alleviating drought-induced starvation in India and in modernizing Indian agriculture. Millions of Indians were saved from starvation. Today, India is essentially self-sufficient in the production of wheat, importing small quantities in some years and exporting in others with year-to-year weather being an important factor.

Other nations in South Asia, notably Pakistan, Sri Lanka, and Bangladesh, have increased agricultural production over the past two decades through the adoption of the newly developed high-yielding strains of wheat and rice. The same thing is true of several nations in Southeast Asia, with corn becoming more important in Thailand.

Conservation Projects

Just as improved grains and livestock have changed world agricultural production, people have been changing the face of the earth. Crossing the western United States by air, we can see large circles where pivot irrigation is being carried on, while alternating strips of brown and green testify to soil conservation. Egypt's Aswan Dam on the Nile, although controversial, permits a controlled use of the former flood water.

The usefulness of a full-scale conservation project is seen in the Snowy Mountains Project of Australia, the world's driest continent, where three river systems have been diverted to convert hundreds of miles of arid but fertile plains to productive land. Intensive soil conservation methods have been undertaken, and grazing is controlled to prevent silting of the reservoirs and damage to slopes. The two main products of the plan are power for new industries and irrigation water for agriculture, with recreation and a tourist industry as important byproducts.

Weather Still a Problem

Weather is the greatest question mark faced by world farmers, most evident in sub-Saharan Africa. Some years ago, improved seeds and methods were introduced into several of these nations, but continued drought has made bare survival, not increased production, the goal.

Harvests in the U.S.S.R. vary substantially from year to year, mainly because of weather variations. Shifts in agricultural policies by the central government also may account for some of the shifts in production.

EC Formed

Changes in the agricultural policies of many Western European nations came about with the organization of the European Community (EC). Not all EC nations adopted identical policies. For example, France attempted to preserve the small family farms, while some nations encouraged consolidation where that was most productive. Emphasis on improving farming methods, combined with subsidies and the opening of broader markets, led to substantially increased EC production which, in turn, resulted in surpluses of some commodities, with determined efforts by EC nations to increase exports. This marked change in European agriculture over the past two decades has meant fewer markets and more competition for U.S. farmers.

Although the United States also has emphasized exports during the 1970's and 1980's, this is not a true change but a

Tim McCabe

return to the situation from colonial days to World War I when many U.S. farm products dominated world markets. A change has come, though, in one respect—we now think in terms of world production and world trade.

Changes Ahead

What will be the changes that influence U.S. agriculture over the next three or four decades? First, exports will be even more important than they are today as communications improve and nations lower their trade barriers. Second, U.S. farms will be large, commercial, family-operated enterprises. Third, additional mechanization will further reduce farm drudgery.

The family farm is increasingly a large commercial enterprise. New technology will reduce drudgery. Careful use of water, soil, biotechnology and computer science will increase productivity. (Maryland, family farm.)

Fourth, productivity will continue to increase by the more careful use of soil and water, by the adoption of crops and animals modified through research in biotechnology, and by the application of computer science to farm operations. Finally, the farmer and his family will enjoy virtually all the amenities of the city dweller while still having the feeling of being a group apart that works with soil, water, and seed to provide food to people throughout the world.

What Global Inter-dependence Means to Agriculture

By G. Edward Schuh, *director of Agriculture and Rural Development, The World Bank*

Since the end of World War II, gradual and significant integration of the global economy has occurred. At the end of the 1940's the international economy could best be described as a collection of individual national economies tied together with a relatively small amount of international trade. By the beginning of the 1980's, however, an interdependent world economy had emerged with the economic significance of national boundaries greatly weakened and the meaning and efficacy of national economic policy seriously called into question.

The last 20 years have witnessed a series of changes in the structure of the international economy. These developments have changed the way that monetary and fiscal policy affect agriculture, to its detriment, while at the same time greatly changing the economics of agriculture. Domestic policies and programs no longer affect it in the same ways. Let us now look at some of these changes and their implications for agriculture, particularly that of the United States.

Dana Downie

World Trade Grows

International trade grew faster than world gross national product (GNP) throughout the post-World War II period (only 3 years being exceptions). In the 1970's, the growth was remarkable. U.S. agricultural trade, as well as trade for the U.S. economy as a whole, doubled from 1970 to 1979. If the period is extended back 5 years, trade for the U.S. economy as a whole tripled from 1965 to 1979. By the beginning of the

International trade has grown faster than the world's GNP since World War II and U.S. agricultural trade has more than tripled since 1965. (Imported U.S. produce being unloaded from a truck in Hong Kong.)

1980's, the U.S. economy was as dependent on trade as Western Europe or Japan. This was a surprising development for an economy that had traditionally been self-sufficient and independent. The U.S. economy has become increasingly a part of the larger international economy, and affected by its forces.

International Capital Market Emerges

At the end of World War II, there was no international capital market. Capital was transferred from one country to another, but it was on a government-to-government basis and called foreign aid. During the 1960's a Eurodollar market emerged as banks in Europe started lending their dollar deposits. This market grew rapidly, eventually evolving into a Eurocurrency market.

In the 1970's the large increase in petroleum prices gave rise to large amounts of what were called petrodollars, since petroleum was (and still is) paid for in dollars. Commercial bankers were enjoined by the United States and international agencies such as the International Monetary Fund to reloan or recycle these dollars to keep the international economy from collapsing. This they did to a fault, giving rise to what later came to be known as the international debt crisis.

This international capital market is now very large. By the beginning of the 1980's the credit outstanding in the Eurocurrency market alone has been estimated at approximately $1.7 trillion, roughly

commensurate with the total amount of international trade. Moreover, almost all countries use this capital market, and it connects the respective economies of the world together including the U.S. economy in ways as important as international trade.

From Fixed to Flexible Exchange Rates

At the end of World War II, the international community agreed to establish a system of fixed exchange rates among national currencies. The reason for this was a belief that the severity of the Great Depression of the 1930's was caused in part by competitive devaluations of national currencies as individual countries tried to dump their domestic economic problems abroad.

The fixed exchange rate system served the industrialized countries of the world quite well for about 30 years. The system fell into disrepair in the late 1960's, however, as the United States tried to fight the Vietnamese War and finance the programs of President Johnson's Great Society without raising taxes. The resulting inflation caused the dollar to become increasingly overval-

```
TRAVELERS   CHEQUES  AVAILABLE

AMERICAN  EXPRESS      U.S. DOLLARS
CITICORP

AUSTRALIAN  DOLLARS              SPANISH  PESETAS
CANADIAN  DOLLARS               GERMAN  MARKS
ENGLISH  POUNDS                 JAPANESE  YEN
FRENCH  FRANCS                  SWISS  FRANCS

RATES   OF   EXCHANGE
CHECK  AND  TRANSFER    WE BUY       WE SELL
RATES ONLY

CANADA   (CAN. $)      $ .7325      $ .7535
ENGLAND  (POUND)       1.3885       1.4395
FRANCE   (FRANC)        .1105        .1210
GERMANY  (D. MARK)      .3465        .3575
SWITZERLAND  (S.F.)     .4215        .4325
SWEDEN   (KRONOR)       .1150        .1255
NETHERLANDS  (GUILDER)  .3070        .3180
JAPAN    (YEN)          .00418       .00429
IRELAND  (POUND)       1.0785       1.1300
SPAIN    (PESETA)       .005795      .006405

·THE RATES POSTED ARE CHEQUE RATES.·

WE ALSO BUY AND SELL ALL MAJOR CURRENCIES

RATES  EFFECTIVE  JULY  18   1985
```

Ed McCrossan

Fixed currency exchange rates ended in the 1960's. Today's system of bloc floating major currencies demonstrates flexibility.

ued. After unsuccessfully trying to negotiate revaluations of the Japanese yen and the German mark, President Nixon finally devalued the dollar in 1971. Since this didn't bring the expected adjustment, the dollar was devalued again in 1973 and eventually floated, a tacit recognition that international capital flows had grown so large that exchange rates could no longer be sustained at fixed rates.

The system that has evolved might best be described as bloc-floating since each of the major currencies has a number of other currencies tied to it. This system demonstrates a great deal of flexibility, however; as the values of the major currencies shift relative to each other, so too do the values of the currencies tied to them. Roughly 85 percent of international trade takes place across flexible exchange rates.

Dramatic Changes in Interest Rates

Interest rates and general monetary conditions were quite stable during the 1950's and 1960's, with interest rates in particular showing only modest changes over time. Starting about 1968, this stability in monetary conditions changed. National money supplies began to vascillate dramatically, and with them interest rates. Perhaps the extremes are best indicated by the large negative real rates of interest in the late 1970's, and the record high rates of interest in the early 1980's. This increase in monetary instability was especially significant in light of the emergence of a well-integrated international capital market and the shift to flexible exchange rates.

A New World Food and Agriculture System

The growth in agricultural trade has given us a global food and agricultural system for the first time in history. Among other things, this system has greatly increased food security for the world as a whole since it makes food available through trade on demand. As a consequence, there have been no major famines in the post-World War II period except in those cases in which national governments didn't want the world to know about them, or in which the problem was made known at such a late date that logistic problems made it impossible to respond in sufficient time. These conditions describe the present African situation.

The emergence of this food and agriculture sector is a major accomplishment. It has tremendously reduced human suffering, and prevented numerous deaths at times of production shortfall in individual countries.

Domestic Policies Lose Effectiveness

National economies increasingly dependent on international trade are increasingly beyond the reach of domestic economic policies, a logical consequence of the increased openness of the domestic economy. It also is the source of a great deal of frustration with economic policies as old policies no longer affect the economy the way they once did.

The cost of agricultural commodity programs, for example, has been very large in recent years, but farmers continue to have severe income problems. Domestic commodity programs are being swamped by developments in the international economy. As long as the economy remains as open as it now is, we can continue to expect domestic commodity programs to be ineffective and even counterproductive.

Commodity Programs Counterproductive

Commodity programs have been a part of U.S. agriculture ever since the 1930's. So long as trade was relatively unimportant to U.S. agriculture or important only to a few sectors, and so long as we had fixed exchange rates and virtually no international capital market, these programs could be managed reasonably well to meet their intended objectives.

That no longer is the case.

USDA

With flexible exchange rates, the prices of U.S. commodities are often reflected abroad with little or no basis in underlying conditions of demand or supply. The result may be to price U.S. commodities out of foreign markets, add greatly to domestic stocks, and thus add greatly to the costs of Government programs. Given that changes in the exchange rate may be driven by conditions in international capital markets, the ability to compete in foreign markets may have little to do with the underlying com-

USDA Secretary John R. Block testifies before a congressional committee about the costs of Federal commodity programs.

petitive potential of U.S. agriculture.

Since 1980, the U.S. dollar experienced an unprecedented rise in foreign exchange markets. As the dollar rose, U.S. commodities became less and less competitive in foreign exchange markets. This was translated into lower prices in U.S. markets as foreign sales declined. Eventually, the prices fell to the loan levels, which

Dana Downie

provided a prop under the market. From that point on, U.S. prices were projected abroad at ever higher levels. In this circumstance, the foreign demand for U.S. commodities declined, production was stimulated in other countries, and the U.S. loan level became an umbrella under which other exporters could undercut U.S. exports. It would be difficult to design a better system to lose market shares!

Growth in trade has given the U.S. a global agricultural system. In 70 countries USDA's Foreign Agricultural Service represents U.S. agricultural interests. The Agricultural Trade Officer (left) in Singapore at work.

The problem was exacerbated because supplies that could not be sold abroad were moved into Government stocks or Farmer-Owned-Reserves. This buildup in stocks eventually led to the Payment-In-Kind program and the idling of some

70 million acres of this Nation's most productive land.

It is doubtful whether commodity programs with fixed price provisions can be made to work effectively as long as we have a flexible exchange rate system and large monetary disturbances. A great deal more flexibility in price provisions is now needed, but that flexibility will change the characteristics of the programs.

Adjusting to Monetary and Fiscal Policy

In the 1950's and 1960's, U.S. agriculture was almost completely isolated from the effects of monetary and fiscal policy. Now, changes in monetary and fiscal policy induce changes in the value of a nation's currency and thus cause the trade sectors to bear the burden of adjustments to these changes. A tight monetary policy, for example, causes interest rates to rise and this induces an inflow of capital. This bids up the value of the dollar, which, in turn, makes exports less competitive and induces an inflow of low-priced imports. Hence, export sectors such as agriculture and those that compete with imports (e.g., steel, automobiles, and textiles) bear the

burden of adjustment. The reverse occurs when an easy monetary policy is pursued.

In this changed setting, the increase in monetary instability creates a great deal of instability in commodity markets, as it did for agriculture in the 1970's and early 1980's.

Direct Link Between Financial and Commodity Markets

Although large stocks of commodities in government hands have often masked it, a weak link has always existed between financial markets and commodity markets. The rate of interest is an important cost of carrying stocks and thus influences the rate at which production is fed into the market or added to stocks.

The change in the structure of the international economy, however, has established a more direct relationship. Changes in interest rates now can have a significant effect on the capital flows among countries and this, in turn, has an effect on the value of a nation's currency. The value of a nation's currency influences the competitiveness of the economy in international markets and is reflected in commodity markets. In fact, a realignment in exchange rates tends to be reflected first in changes in commodity prices and only later in trade flows and domestic consumption and production. We now have a direct link between financial markets and commodity markets.

Frustrations of U.S. Agricultural Policies

Responsibility for U.S. agricultural policy is in the hands of House and Senate agricultural committees, and these committees have virtually no authority over domestic monetary and fiscal policy, trade policy, exchange rate policy, and conditions in international capital markets. This disjunction in the U.S. policy apparatus creates a great deal of frustration for those interested in the welfare of U.S. agriculture. It causes U.S. agricultural policy to be counterproductive in furthering the interests of U.S. farmers and has contributed to the problems agriculture now faces.

International Institutions Important to Farmers

With U.S. agriculture now part of an international economy, the institutions that regulate

and influence that international economy are now probably more important to U.S. farmers than U.S. institutions and commodity programs. The rules that influence international capital markets, foreign exchange markets, and international trade now matter to U.S. agriculture. Large monetary disturbances and large swings in currency values have an enormous influence on U.S. farmers. Similarly, U.S. markets in the future will be largely influenced by the ability of foreign countries to export other products to the United States, and by policies such as the Common Agricultural Policy of the European Community. Reforming institutional arrangements to more nearly conform to the changes in the international economy must now be high on the U.S.'s policy agenda headed by reform of international monetary arrangements to provide more monetary stability for the international economy.

Efforts to create a prosperous U.S. agriculture must be focused even more on the international economy and international institutional arrangements than on domestic policy and the domestic economy.

Agricultural Trade Is Vital

By William E. Kost and
Cathy L. Jabara,
agricultural economists,
International Economics Division,
Economic Research Service

Agriculture in the United States plays a central role in global interdependence. It is in the best interest of the world and of the United States to continue that role and to pursue more open trade in agricultural products.

Gains From Trade

International trade involves the exchange of goods or services between at least two countries. Since it is voluntary, countries must perceive a potential for self-benefit for the exchange to take place. Trade occurs because countries can trade their goods or services relatively more cheaply for those they desire but could only produce themselves at a higher cost. The so-called gains from trade arise from the real opportunities that low foreign prices provide.

With each country having different endowments of land, labor, capital, and management, trade allows a country to specialize in the production of those goods it best produces. In some cases it is either impractical or impossible to produce an item locally, and, consequently, it can only be obtained from the international market. In other cases, it can be pro-

Dana Downie

duced locally, but because of high production costs, it is better to buy it from foreign sources. A country is better off using its resources to produce those goods for which it is particularly suited, and buying from other countries the goods they more efficiently produce. Trading and production specialization permit higher living standards and real income than would otherwise be possible and permit more goods to be produced from a given set of resources. Both allow a more efficient allocation of resources.

Many people view international trade as somehow different from interregional trade within a country. Interregional trade is implicitly considered to be beneficial, and international

Consumers in Manila, Philippines buy U.S. agricultural products. Trade occurs when it is cheaper to import, impossible to produce, or better to specialize in products for which resources are best available.

trade harmful. Complications such as different currencies, languages, distances, and national policies may exist, but, with the exception of different currencies, the other factors can exist within a country, particularly a large one like the United States. There is little difference between someone in Illinois selling soybeans in order to buy oranges from Florida or automobiles from Michigan and someone in Iowa selling corn to buy coffee from Brazil or televisions from Japan. The logic is identical.

Imports Benefit The United States

The United States is the second largest importer of agricultural products in the world ($19 billion in 1984) after West Germany ($21 billion). Without these products the U.S. diet and level of living would be lowered. Every time American consumers have a cup of coffee, a glass of iced tea, a banana split, a chocolate candy bar, or add vanilla, cinnamon or pepper to their food, wear silk shirts, or buy rubber tires, they are benefiting from agricultural trade. These, and many other agricultural products consumed in the United States, are produced elsewhere.

Ed McCrossan

Coffee drinking is an American institution but where would it be if it were not for international trade? The United States is the world's second largest importer of agricultural products.

Value of U.S. Imports, Selected Years

	1960	1970	1980	1984
	Million $			
Nonagricultural commodities	11,486	32,627	223,590	297,754
Agricultural commodities, all	4,010	5,592	17,276	18,898
Supplementary[1]	1,979	3,451	9,924	12,220
Complementary[1]	2,031	2,141	7,351	6,678
Total all commodities	15,496	38,219	240,866	316,652

[1]Supplementary agricultural import products consist of all products similar to agricultural commodities produced commercially in the United States, together with all other agricultural products interchangeable to any significant extent with such U.S. commodities. Complementary agricultural products include all others, about 90 percent of which consist of rubber, coffee, raw silk, cacao beans, wool for carpets, bananas, tea, spices, and vegetable fibers.

SOURCE: *Agricultural Statistics*, various issues and *Foreign Agricultural Trade of the United States, 1984*

Without imports, these products would be unavailable.

The United States also imports products such as cheese, processed beef, wool, sugar, strawberries, tomatoes, tobacco, and wine, that compete with domestically produced goods. If these products can be imported for less than domestic output costs, the American consumer will be better off. To the extent that these imports allow for resources to be transferred to the production of commodities for which American resources are more suited, producers also benefit. These imports also allow the American consumer to purchase year-round the commodities produced only seasonally in the United States. Both these complementary and supplementary imports give American consumers lower prices and more varied diets throughout the year.

Exports Benefit The United States

The United States is an industrial nation; however, agriculture accounted for 18 percent of total exports in 1984. The United States is the world's largest exporter of agricultural products ($38 billion in 1983 compared to $208 billion for the world) selling 69 percent of

its wheat, 41 percent of its corn, 59 percent of its soybeans and soybean products, more than 50 percent of its cotton, and 37 percent of its tobacco overseas in 1983. The production from one out of about every 2.5 acres of cropland harvested was exported. The United States exports more of the relatively low-valued, raw material products, such as grains, oilseeds, tobacco, and cotton, in contrast to exports of high-valued, processed products which accounted for $9 billion or 25 percent of U.S. agricultural exports in 1983.

Its relative efficiency in production of agricultural products has given the United States an important role in supplying food and feed products to others through world trade. It has a natural resource base large enough to produce substantially more food than it can consume. For example, the United States has only a small portion of the world's population, yet it produces about half of the world trade in grain. More specifically, in 1983 U.S. farmers supplied about 37 percent of world wheat exports, about 56 percent of coarse grain exports, about 86 percent of world soybean exports, and 21 percent of world rice exports.

U.S. exports provide increased income to farmers, as well as to those employed in industries that supply purchased inputs to farmers, and assemble, process, and transport agricultural exports to foreign countries. In 1983, approximately 23 percent of farm income, or about $1 out of every $4.26 received from the sale of farm products, was derived from exports.

Because of the dispersion of U.S. agricultural production and the variety of products exported, all regions of the country benefit from our agricultural exports. Agricultural exports account for a third to a half of total farm income in 16 States: Arkansas, Illinois, Indiana, Iowa, Kansas, Louisiana, Minnesota, Mississippi, Missouri, Montana, Nebraska, North Carolina, North Dakota, Ohio, Oklahoma, and South Carolina.

More than a million people in the United States work in agricultural export-related jobs. Of these, about half a million U.S. farm workers could be considered as producing for export with the remainder employed in nonfarm, export-related industries. In addition, every dollar's worth of U.S. commodities exported generates an additional $1.05 in eco-

Ed McCrossan

U.S. farm exports generate income that spreads throughout the national economy. Jobs are created in many nonfarm sectors.

nomic activity in such areas as financing, transportation, warehousing, and the production of farm supplies.

Without foreign markets, American producers would have been burdened with even larger surpluses than has been the case. This excess production would have been dumped into the domestic market or forced into government stocks. Prices would have been severely depressed and farm income drastically lowered. More farmers would have lost money and been forced out of production. Consumers might have initially benefited from the depressed food prices; however, as producers left and excess stocks were depleted, food supplies would dwindle and prices would go back up—up to even

higher levels than before.

Without agricultural trade, far fewer farmers would be producing for a smaller domestic market, benefits would be substantially reduced due to economies of scale, and prices would be significantly higher than they are when trade is allowed. In the long run, even consumers would be hurt by lack of trade.

The United States earned $38 billion from agricultural exports in 1984. Only from export earnings or borrowing from foreigners can the United States earn the foreign exchange necessary to purchase overseas goods. Exports of agricultural products help the American consumers buy foreign cars, televisions, video and stereo equipment, cameras,

Value of U.S. Exports, Selected Years

	1960	1970	1980	1984
	Million $			
Nonagricultural commodities	14,591	34,337	169,846	170,014
Agricultural commodities, all	4,519	6,958	40,481	38,027
Grains	1,617	2,341	18,261	17,303
Oilseeds	342	1,120	6,794	6,234
Other	2,560	3,497	15,426	14,490
Total all commodities	19,110	41,295	210,327	208,041

SOURCE: *Foreign Agricultural Trade of the United States,* various issues.

FAO

and many other products in addition to agricultural imports. Historically, the agricultural export surplus has helped to offset a continuing deficit generated by the nonagricultural sector. A country must export in order to import.

U.S. Exports Benefit Others

Agricultural exports are also desirable for humanitarian reasons. Many parts of the world are incapable of producing enough food to feed their people. Others can produce the food, but only at a prohibitively high cost. Since the United States is a more efficient producer of food, it can help.

Peruvian school feeding programs, supported by the World Food Program to which the United States is a major contributor, encourage parents to send children to school and improve their diets. Many of Peru's children under the age of 6 suffer from malnutrition.

Countries with limited resources can buy food from the United States at prices substantially below their cost of production.

The United States operates the world's largest food aid program to needy countries, shipping in 1984 more than 5.6 million tons of food aid to about 70 countries under the Food for Peace Program. Close to 90 percent of this volume was grains. In addition, since 1982, a substantial amount of dairy products has gone to low-income countries under other programs. This food aid can pave the way for U.S. commercial exports. For example, in 1956–58 the United States food aid to 17 overseas markets was $3.1 billion, and commercial sales of all goods were $3.6 billion. Two decades later, food aid from the United States to these same countries was only $756 million, and commercial sales had grown to $43 billion.

In addition to feeding starving people, there are beneficial side effects to the world, to this country in general, and to U.S. agriculture. Providing adequate diets improves a country's ability to develop and grow. As economic growth takes place in developing countries, they are more able to purchase the food they need and also more likely to want more and higher quality food as their incomes rise. Since the United States is a major producer of agricultural products, it is in our best interest to promote world economic growth. Economic growth increases the size of our future markets for products, including agricultural products. This growth in foreign demand is one of the driving factors underlying U.S. economic growth.

Opposition To Freer Trade

The arguments supporting trade hinge heavily on arguments for economic efficiency and maximizing national and global production from given global resource bases. These arguments are of the form "the bigger the pie the better!" They do not address how this larger pie gets divided among countries or individuals within a particular country. Who gets what is the real policy question that must be answered.

Opposition to freer trade is strong in certain segments of most economies, including the United States. Some people or groups are hurt by trade. U.S. beef producers can be hurt by Argentine beef exports. The U.S. automobile industry can be hurt by European and Japanese automobile exports. European grain producers can be hurt by U.S. grain exports. Pressure for protection from these groups is understandable.

Most of the arguments for protection stem from special interest groups wanting help. Arguments usually range from national security, balance of payments protection, the offsetting of unfair policies of other countries, protection of domestic economic policies, revenue

USDA

generation, protection of national health, market differentiation, to infant industry protection. Protecting an industry until it can develop enough to exploit economies of scale and compete may be appealing at first glance. But if the industry has enough influence to get such protection, it also may have enough political influence to maintain it way beyond the point where it is needed.

U.S. agricultural commodities being negotiated with a developing country importer. A growth in foreign demand for U.S. farm products is one of the factors underlying the economic growth of the United States.

Decisionmaker's Perspective

The economists generally respond to these questions of equity among market participants by saying that the gainers from trade will gain enough to compensate the losers and still have more than they did before trade was allowed. Everyone can still be better off with trade. Any protectionist argument should be evaluated in the context of who gains at

whose expense? Once you have identified the winners and losers, you can ask whether you really want those groups to win or lose. Viewing protection issues in this context focuses attention on the proper issues.

With this focus, many recognize the need to maintain flexibility under conditions of continued economic growth and change. An economy cannot remain static under conditions of change. Protectionist policies tend to foster the maintenance of the status quo. Policies that minimize the pain of transition for resources that cannot easily move or adjust may be better pursued than policies that protect and isolate.

Factors Affecting U.S. Production in A.D. 2000

By Don Paarlberg, *professor emeritus, Purdue University, West Lafayette, Indiana*

The best known example of successful long-range prediction of agricultural production is that of Joseph in Egypt, 3,500 years ago. According to the Book of Genesis he predicted, accurately, 7 years of abundant crops to be followed by 7 years of dearth. Subsequent forecasters, less favored than he in their information sources, have done less well. Nevertheless, let us try to foresee production patterns for U.S. agriculture between now and the year 2000 by looking at a dozen of the elements that contribute to the level of agricultural production.

Weather Forecasts Still Uncertain

Long-range weather forecasting has not yet reached a useful stage. Changes in climate can be identified in retrospect, but given present knowledge they cannot be anticipated with sufficient accuracy to be useful in decisionmaking. The cycle of drought years predicted for the mid-1970's did not come about. Nor did the cooling phase expected by some, nor the warming trend feared by others.

It is true that recent weather has increased in variability.

Average variation in 1979–83 U.S. corn yields was 13 percent, up from 8 percent in 1964–68. Wheat variability rose from 3 to 6 percent and soybean yields likewise increased in fluctuations, from 5 to 9 percent. Whether such increased variability will continue is conjectural.

Uncertain weather means that the agricultural plant must have a margin of safety to meet the contingency of crop failure as well as the capability to handle excess bumper crops.

New Technology Can Hurt

Perhaps the broadest and most recent effort to assess the prospect for agricultural technology comes from a 1985 Office of Technology Assessment (OTA) study. New biotechnology, information systems, and disease controls are expected to increase agricultural production significantly. OTA calculates a needed annual production growth rate of 1.8 percent in U.S. farm output over the rest of the century if supply and demand are to be balanced. Assuming the continuation of forces that have shaped development in the past, this increase is expected. In an en-

NOAA

A weather balloon carrying a radio-sonde will send back information on temperature, humidity, pressure, and winds aloft.

Estimates of U.S. Crop Yields and Animal Production Efficiency

	1982	No-New-Technology Environment		Baseline Environment		More-New-Technology Environment	
		1990	2000	1990	2000	1990	2000
CORN bu per acre	115	117	124	119	139	121	150
COTTON lb per acre	481	502	511	514	554	518	571
RICE bu per acre	105	105	109	111	124	115	134
SOYBEAN bu per acre	30	32	35	32	37	33	37
WHEAT bu per acre	36	38	41	39	45	40	46
BEEF							
Pounds meat per lb feed	0.070	0.071	0.066	0.072	0.072	0.072	0.073
Calves per cow	0.90	0.94	0.96	0.95	1.0	0.95	1.04
DAIRY							
Pounds milk per lb feed	0.94	0.94	0.95	0.95	1.03	0.96	1.11
Milk per cow per year (thousand lb)	12.3	13.7	15.7	14.0	17.6	14.2	19.3
POULTRY							
Pounds meat per lb feed	0.44	0.52	0.53	0.53	0.57	0.53	0.58
Eggs per layer per year	245	255	260	258	275	257	281
SWINE							
POUNDS meat per lb feed[a]	0.165	0.167	0.17	0.17	0.176	0.17	0.18
Pigs per sow per year	14.4	14.8	15.7	15.2	17.4	15.5	17.8

[a]The value shown for swine feed efficiency for 1982 is the average of national feed efficiencies for the 10 years prior to 1982. The national aggregate linear trend of swine feed efficiency is slightly negative and gives a value of .157 in 1982.

SOURCE: Office of Technology Assessment.

Tim McCabe

Soil erosion poses a serious problem to our cropland. Only through improved production technology has U.S. agriculture been able to overcome it on remaining good land.

vironment of more new technology, production would increase at 2.2 percent a year and we would be struggling with surpluses. In the unlikely event that significant new technology fails to develop and if associated factors are unfavorable, the rate of growth could be as low as 1.1 or 1.6 percent. Food might then be short in supply and high in price.

On the whole, lack of new technology is not likely to be a constraint on agricultural production.

A Reserve Land Base

The Soil Conservation Service has estimated the U.S. crop-land base to be 413 million acres, of which 387 million acres were either planted to crops or summer-fallowed in 1982. In addition to the 413 million acres, 127 million acres could be converted to cropland in one or two decades if prices were attractive. These additional acres would not be as productive as those presently in use and would be more erosive. But we are far from using our land with real intensity, as anyone knows who has seen the agriculture of Europe or the Orient.

We convert about 675,000 acres of cropland to urban and other nonagricultural uses each year, one-fifth of 1 percent of our cropland. Although this may be disruptive locally, it poses no real threat to our food production.

Soil erosion is more serious. On one-fourth of our cropland the rate of erosion is sufficiently great to cause some decline in productivity. Up to now this loss has been more than offset by improved production technology.

During the past century the agricultural land base has been little changed. Production increases have come primarily from advancing technology. This condition probably will continue, but a reserve is there if needed.

Little Hope From Irrigation

Irrigated agriculture accounts for about one-fourth of the value of the Nation's crops and one-seventh of the cropland. From 1945 to 1974 irrigated acreage doubled, contributing significantly to the overall increase in agricultural production.

Surface water use in western irrigation peaked at 88 million acre-feet in 1955 and since then has been fluctuating at a somewhat lower level. New surface water irrigation projects are likely to be few; nearly all favorable sites have been developed.

Ground-water irrigation, concentrated in the Great Plains, came from virtually nothing in the early thirties to 39 percent of total withdrawals for irrigation in 1975. Much of the ground-water irrigation is a mining operation, withdrawals exceeding recharge. Overdrafts in the High Plains are estimated at 14 million acre feet per year. As the water table declines, pumping costs increase and on some lands irrigation is no longer profitable. Nevertheless, there are some not as yet exploited opportunities for ground-water irrigation.

Prospects for further overall production increases from irrigation appear dim. In some areas, as in the Southern Great Plains, irrigation water use is projected to decline by 3 percent between 1985 and 2000. Reduced supplies of water and the likely higher costs will cause farmers to economize on water, reducing the impact on crop production.

Tim McCabe

About 25 to 35 percent of the irrigated lands of the West are estimated to have some kind of salinity problem, and the difficulties are getting worse. Farmers in affected areas face decreasing crop yields, increased leaching requirements, and higher management costs.

In summary, irrigation, which gave agricultural production a major boost during the past 50 years, is unlikely to provide much, if any, incre-

Irrigation as U.S. farmers have known it for the past 50 years is decreasing. Reduced water supply and high costs will cause farmers to economize on water and decrease crop production.

mental increase during the remainder of the century.

Fewer Farmers Not Critical

From 1930 to 1974, 33 million people left the land. The farm population, which stood at 15 percent of the total only three decades ago, is now down to less than 3 percent. Some people think we may run out of farmers and that agricultural production will be thus reduced. This is an unwarranted concern. The number of young people reaching working age on farms still exceeds the number of needed farmer replacements.

Input Items Costly

Major production costs for farmers are interest, machinery costs, fuel, fertilizer, pesticides, and hired labor. Formerly, the farmer supplied many of these items himself. Now most of them must be purchased. Their cost and availability have much to do with the prospect for agricultural production.

High interest rates on $212 billion of borrowed money are a major present drag on agriculture and an investment inhibitor. Whether this burden will be eased depends largely on how the Government handles its fiscal and monetary problems.

During the energy crisis of the midseventies, concern arose about the future availability of nitrogen fertilizer, which is dependent on petrochemicals for feedstock. Easing of the energy crisis reduced this concern, but the low-cost nitrogen and motor fuel of 15 years ago are unlikely to return.

In good times farmers increase their borrowing and their purchases of machinery, fertilizer, and pesticides with production-boosting consequences. When times are bad, they reduce these purchases and so curtail production. Agribusiness firms stand ready to supply as much of these input items as farmers want. Constraints on their use are their unit costs and the incomes of farm people, not physical limitations.

Efficiency Increasing

Changes in the productivity of agriculture, sometimes referred to as efficiency, are measured by changes, through time, in overall output per unit of input, the inputs being land, labor, capital, and management. Efficiency has been rising irregularly for the past 60 years at a rate of about 1.5 percent a year. By improving efficiency, agriculture has been able to

High interest rates are the major problem with U.S. agriculture. Whether this will change depends largely on how the government handles its fiscal and monetary problems.

Ed McCrossan

supply increasing amounts of
food with approximately the
same total input. The input
mix has changed greatly, however. We use the same amount
of land, much less labor, and
much more capital. This increased efficiency, which has
permitted agriculture to supply
consumers with better food for
a reduced share of their disposable income, should continue
to rise in the years ahead.

Government's Fiscal Behavior

By macroeconomic policy is
meant the fiscal and monetary
behavior of the Federal Government. These are the actions
that result in inflation and de-
flation, rising and falling interest rates, a strong or a weak
dollar, and international policies that encourage or inhibit
farm exports.

Presently, agriculture is experiencing the adverse effects
of anti-inflationary macroeconomic discipline intended to
correct the excesses of a decade earlier. These conditions
seem to be temporary and
likely to change. The recent
past is not the new normal. Financial stress in agriculture is
likely to affect ownership and
tenure on a number of farms
but is not likely to have much

effect on overall volume of
production.

Changed Domestic Farm Policy

Domestic farm policy has given
contradictory production signals. On the one hand, high
price supports have signaled
increased output. On the other,
acreage limitations have called
for production cutbacks.

There is growing disappointment with these programs. A
change—perhaps modest—in
the direction of more reliance
on the market seems in prospect during the next 15 years.
This would reduce the incentives for high production associated with past price policies
and open more market opportunities.

Loosened Trade Constraints

U.S. farm exports as of 1985
are reduced, both in total and
as a percentage of world trade,
from the high levels reached a
few years ago. Causes of this
reduction are multiple: the
high exchange value of the dollar, high price supports, economic slack in other countries,
third-world debt, and unfair export policies of other nations.
So long as these obstacles ex-

ist, production will be held substantially below its potential. Some of these constraints will be lifted in the years ahead, either as a result of deliberate policy or as a consequence of natural events.

Continued Development Policies

Agricultural development is underway throughout the world, most of it a result of actions by the developing nations themselves but some of it with U.S. help. In certain cases, this development inhibits export of American farm products (e.g., tobacco production in Africa). More often economic development means increased farm exports (e.g., wheat to South Korea, feed grains to Taiwan). On balance, agricultural development abroad means increased production and export opportunities for American agriculture.

Price Is the Key

Whether the future holds excessive agricultural output or tight supplies depends in major degree on our price policy. If farm prices are held substantially and continuously above competitive levels, production will be stimulated while consumption is curtailed and sur-

pluses will appear, regardless of all else. If, on the other hand, farm prices are held down in an effort to benefit the consumer or to suppress inflation, production will be discouraged while consumption is increased. Shortage will then be a problem, even though the potential for agricultural production is great.

The effectiveness of the price adjuster is attested by the fact that from the beginning of our country until 1933 food supplies were kept reasonably in line with need, accommodating the changing food requirements of a population that increased to 30 times its earlier level. Since 1933, supplies and demands of the unregulated farm products—beef, pork, poultry, fruits, and vegetables—have been kept in fairly good balance. That experience is better than the recent record of the controlled products: corn, wheat, cotton, rice, peanuts, and tobacco.

If prices received by farmers are allowed to seek their own level (with perhaps some means of reducing the amplitude of fluctuations), the resources necessary to supply our needs will be drawn into use, and a reasonable balance will ensue.

Why People Eat What They Eat Around the World

By Gene A. Mathia, *deputy director,* and
Larry Deaton, *agricultural economist, International Economics Division, Economic Research Service*

"**Y**ou are what you eat." It may not be factual, but it does provide a basis for discussing food consumption patterns. It is a fact that quality of life, work habits, and productivity relate directly to the quantity and quality of the diet. In many cases, the diet is so rich in substance and volume that people get fat and suffer for it. In other cases, people get enough to eat, but are grossly short of essential nutrients to keep them healthy and productive. Finally, some diets are simply inadequate to live on, resulting in malnutrition and death. The rather elusive concept of a balanced diet consumed in the appropriate amount is a stated goal of most people, but many diets fall short for various socioeconomic, political, cultural, and educational reasons.

In most environments, a balanced diet is a moving target with its composition heavily dependent on a particular individual's needs, the geographic and seasonal availability of foods, and a market which sets values based on both the demand and supply of foods and related marketing services. In some countries, diets are developed from a few staple foods. In others, the variety of foods is

great. The flexibility of combining foods to construct a balanced diet is apparently great.
Generally, particular tastes and
preferences can be accommo-
dated in a market economy
without greatly sacrificing diet
quality. In many centrally
planned economies, the variety
of products depends on government intervention policies, but
usually, enough products are
available for people to have
wholesome diets. Foods also
compete with many nonfood
and industrial products for consumers' incomes.

The proportion of consumers'
budgets spent on foods and
food-related services varies
greatly among countries. In the
United States, less than 20 percent of a person's income is required to purchase about 1,425
pounds of food annually. The
protein and calorie levels resulting from this food package
are very high and of generally
high quality.

At the other extreme are
some African countries. There,
the volume and quality of food
are extremely low, but it takes
a large share of one's income
anyway. This situation typifies
about 70 countries which get
substantial amounts of food
aid. Food aid is an important
factor in determining their con-

sumption patterns.

A step higher on the eco-
nomic ladder are higher income countries that have to
buy much of their food elsewhere. They are influenced
heavily by changes in world
commodity and financial
markets.

In all these cases, a country's
exchange rates, the extent of
its debts to others, and world
commodity prices become important in determining food
consumption levels and
patterns.

Varied Eating Patterns
Regional differences in food
consumption are great both in
terms of types and quantities of
food consumed.

Cereals. As the most important food source for most consumers around the world, cereals exemplify both changing
patterns and regional differences. Per capita cereal consumption has changed only
slightly since 1970. Most of
this growth came from in-
creased livestock feeding of
coarse grains in the developed
and centrally planned regions
and increased food grain consumption in the developing
regions.

The importance of each cereal varies greatly from region

to region. For example, wheat is the predominant food grain in the temperate zones, rice holds this position throughout most of Asia, corn takes over in the subhumid tropics of Latin America and Africa, while sorghum and millet are the main staples in the arid regions. In other regions, roots and tubers take the place of grains. Cassava, for example, is the principal crop in parts of Africa, Latin America, and Oceania, where climate and prevailing rainfall patterns hinder cereal production.

Meat and Poultry

Consumption of selected animal products has grown the most in recent years. In particular, per capita consumption of poultry has climbed steadily and shows few signs of abating. Pork consumption likewise grew rapidly until 1980, then began to wane. Just as for the grains, there are major regional differences in the consumption of animal products. Beef consumption is greatest on a per capita basis in developed countries and a few developing countries, e.g. Argentina. On the other hand, pork consumption, at least on a per capita basis, has been falling in many developed countries, while ris-

ing in the Eastern bloc, China, and parts of Latin America and Asia. Poultry consumption has grown rapidly in most countries, but actual levels of consumption vary greatly. For example, we eat 64 pounds per capita in the United States. Those in North Africa and the Middle East average less than 4.4 pounds.

Recent changes in the consumption of other food products vary greatly from commodity to commodity. For example, the use of oilseeds, such as soybeans, grew rapidly during the 1960's and 1970's. Much of this happened when people ate more animal products, boosting usage of oilmeals in mixed feedstuffs in the production of livestock products.

Sugar is a far different story. World per capita consumption of sugar—an important product in many countries simply because of the calories it contributes to diets—climbed only 1 percent annually. Finally, people cut down on some products, especially traditional foods such as roots and tubers and pulses, because they were able to switch to other foods.

Processed Foods. Foods themselves have undergone major transformations in recent decades. In particular, more

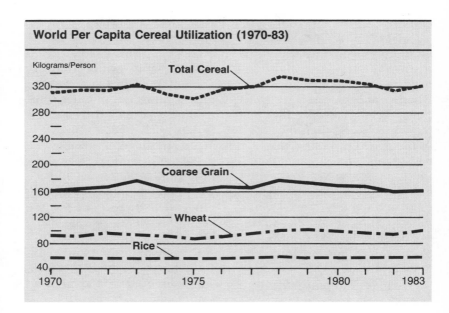

World Per Capita Cereal Utilization (1970-83)

Kilograms/Person

Total Cereal

Coarse Grain

Wheat

Rice

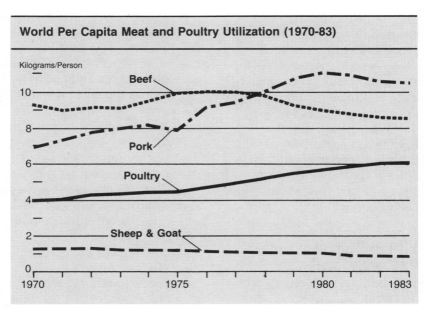

World Per Capita Meat and Poultry Utilization (1970-83)

Kilograms/Person

Beef

Pork

Poultry

Sheep & Goat

and more consumers in the developed countries are eating away from home more often. In many countries—rich and poor—foods that are eaten, whether at home or in restaurants, receive considerably more processing than they did in the past. Processing gives consumers who can afford these services a way to spend less time preparing food. With more and more women—even in developing countries—working outside the home, such foods take on an added importance in the diet.

Processed and prepared foods, however, are only available if there is an infrastructure that supports their production and distribution. This is certainly the case in the developed countries, most of the European centrally planned countries, and increasingly in the urban areas of the developing world. In these cities, not only have processed and prepared foods replaced many of the traditional foods, but Western-style fast food restaurants are coming in, too.

Why Different Patterns Exist

Why do consumption patterns and levels vary so greatly from country to country? The answers rest in differences in economic, political, and sociological characteristics. Here are several: individual commodity prices, the prices of other commodities, particularly those of closely related goods, the level and distribution of incomes, population characteristics, tastes and preferences, and a wide range of institutional arrangements to regulate political, economic, or sociological behavior.

It has long been known how these factors relate to consumption of foods and other commodities. The principles apply in those countries where consumers exercise freedom of choice as well as in most centrally planned countries where choice is restricted. Economists are busy refining and estimating the relationships implied by these well-conceived principles. Let's examine a few.

Prices. The price of any product is inversely related to the quantity consumed. The amount of food products consumed, however, will not change as much as the amount of nonfood products in response to a given change in price. In fact, for few agricultural commodities will a price change cause a proportionate

Les Shepard

Consumers substitute one commodity for another when prices change. When the price of one goes up, the consumption of others tends to rise.

or greater change in quantity consumed.

On the other hand, the relative prices of many foods do affect each other greatly. Consumers will substitute one commodity for another as the price relationships change. When the price of one goes up, the consumption of the others

goes up, unless the foods are normally served together.

The wide variety of commodities to choose from in developed countries results in higher response relationships than in most developing countries. In the latter, consumers depend on a few essential commodities, such as rice in Asia and corn in Africa. So they cannot easily switch if prices change. In the centrally planned countries, where prices are rigidly controlled, consumers may protest government-announced price increases, but consumption of other products is usually not greatly affected when the price of one product changes.

Income. For most agricultural commodities, higher incomes lead to more consumption. The strength of this relationship declines as per capita incomes increase. The consumption of meats, fruits, and many vegetables usually changes more in response to income changes than the consumption of most cereals.

Over the last several years, the quantity of marketing services demanded by consumers has been particularly responsive to income changes and is one of the reasons for the rapid growth of convenience foods

and eating out, particularly in the richer and faster growing countries.

The distribution of income within a country is also an important determinant of consumption. Adequate food to ensure at least a minimum diet is considered an essential household expenditure in all societies. In industrialized countries, income is sufficient to ensure adequate purchasing power for foods. In a country like the United States, where only about 15 percent of income goes to purchase foods, distribution is not as important as in the developing countries,

The quantity of marketing services demanded by consumers has been responsive to income changes and is one of the reasons for the rapid growth of convenience foods and eating out.

where a much higher proportion of income is used to purchase foods. In the latter, income for food is not only low, but also distributed disproportionately. Therefore, the actual purchasing power of most households is very low. Finally, growth in incomes in recent years has lagged in the developing and centrally planned countries, undoubtedly a major constraint to growth in their food consumption.

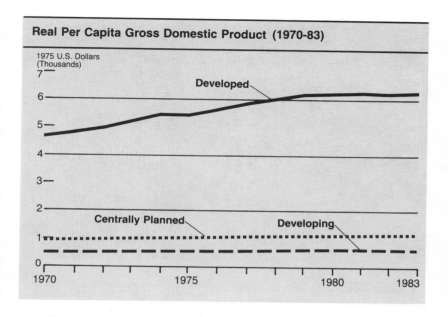

Real Per Capita Gross Domestic Product (1970-83)

1975 U.S. Dollars
(Thousands)

Developed

Centrally Planned   Developing

1970   1975   1980   1983

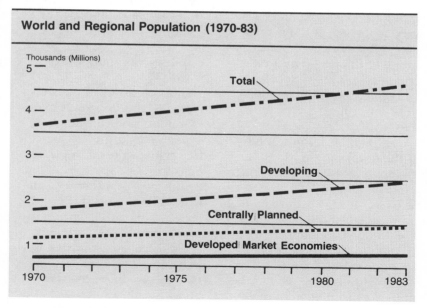

World and Regional Population (1970-83)

Thousands (Millions)

Total

Developing

Centrally Planned

Developed Market Economies

1970   1975   1980   1983

FAO

Population. Increases in population are directly related to increases in total food use. Per capita food consumption does vary as the age of the population shifts by either an increase in the birth and survival rates or a change in life expectancy. Per capita consumption tends to be lower for the very young and the elderly.

The high birth rates of most of the developing world have greatly increased populations in these countries. This growth also has effectively lowered the average age of the population and whetted the demand for specific foods like dairy products and selected cereals. The net result has been an increase in total consumption in those

The increase in a country's population directly relates to the amount of food consumed. China, with the world's largest population, has made spectacular agricultural progress since 1978.

countries with purchasing power.

Characteristics of the work force are also important in determining food consumption. Type of employment (blue-collar versus white-collar occupations, rural versus urban, and the dictates of a country's climate) affect consumption patterns. Many developing countries are in the semitropical and tropical zones, with a large agricultural base. Consumption of home-produced foods is great. Surpluses of foods, after meeting at-home consumption needs, are low, thereby expanding the need to import many commodities as the urban population expands. In many developing countries, the urban population is growing rapidly, and domestic agricultural production cannot keep up with domestic food needs.

An additional consideration is the rapid growth of the percentage of women working outside the home. This, in itself, is an important force underlying the rapid increase in demand for food marketing services in the form of prepared meals and restaurant services.

Tastes and Preferences.
Just as food consumption levels differ among regions of a particular country and among countries, tastes and preferences may also differ because of religion, family living patterns, employment, education, age, and other socioeconomic factors.

Obviously, relationships also exist between the foods consumed and the adaptability of products to local growing conditions. For example, tropical fruit consumption per capita is greater in the tropical zone than elsewhere. But the relationships may not be as obvious as they appear. The de-

gree to which tastes and preferences adapt to the products locally produced and to which they, themselves, determine the available products remains largely unknown.

In other countries, some foods are not commonly eaten because of religious beliefs. Beef in India and pork in many Middle Eastern countries come to mind. Vegetarian diets are becoming common in many countries, including the developed countries. Such diets demonstrate how health concerns have altered consumption patterns—the red meats, eggs, and dairy products are examples of recent losses due to consumer health concerns.

Institutional Policies and Other Factors. Food consumption patterns have been affected by many government interventions in most, if not all, countries. In the United States, the interventions have taken on many different forms including food safety and quality regulations, food stamp and other food assistance and surplus disposal programs, school lunch programs of various types, and a variety of research and extension education programs designed to help in the preparation, preservation, and presentation of foods. Food ad-

Dana Downie

Yuen-Gi Yee

A grader with USDA's Agricultural Marketing Service monitors oranges being processed at a plant in Florida's citrus belt.

vertising and promotion activities are common in many countries.

Such programs are present in many developing countries, where consumers are also subsidized by institutionally controlled prices below market clearing levels, particularly for staple products like bread, rice, sugar, and cooking oils. While this may be beneficial to urban consumers, farmers and marketing agents are discouraged with prices unfavorable for ex-

Tastes and preferences are important determinants of consumption. For example, tropical fruit consumption is greater in tropical zones than elsewhere. A consumer purchasing tropical produce in Singapore.

panding production. Consequently, shortages of locally produced foods develop. Foreign exchange is often needed to finance imports and relieve food shortages that could have been averted at far less cost.

Consumers in the developing countries also suffer from the low turnover volume and wastes of primitive marketing systems. Marketing costs of moving the product from the producer to the consumer are high and have a major effect on reducing the food choices of these consumers.

Why People Eat What They Eat

Feeding the Developing World

By Charles E. Hanrahan, *senior analyst for International Food and Agricultural Policy, Congressional Research Service, Library of Congress.*

Despite modest improvements in the world food situation over the past two and one-half decades, many people, especially in the developing countries, still suffer from hunger and malnutrition. Present-day concern about food availability focuses mainly on sub-Saharan Africa where large numbers of people are facing famine caused by drought of continent-wide proportions. Africa is not the only region in the developing world with serious food problems. In both Asia and Latin America, where food production performance has been markedly better than in Africa, there are large numbers of malnourished people.

The Food Situation

Production. Over the past two and one-half decades, food production in the developing countries has increased, but it has barely kept up with the pace of population growth. Food production in those countries during 1960–84 grew at the rate of 2.7 percent a year, but population grew at the rate of 2.6 percent. While total food production grew more rapidly in the developing than in the developed countries, per capita food production grew more rapidly in the developed countries. Rapid population growth in the developing countries nearly overwhelmed their substantial gains in total food production.

Although total and per capita food production increased in the developing countries as a group, considerable regional variation existed. East Asia (excluding Japan and China) experienced the most rapid increases in food production—1.3 percent a year—and the largest percentage change. In South Asia, with 65 percent of the developing world's population, increases in food production per capita were a more modest .5 percent a year. Gains in food production in South Asian countries, especially India, were associated with the Green Revolution—the introduction

and widespread adoption of high-yielding grain varieties together with the expansion of irrigated area and fertilizer use beginning in the late 1960's. China also has made gains in food production per capita. Its growth rate in per capita food production is slightly higher than that for the developing countries as a group.

In Latin America, food production per capita increased by .9 percent a year during 1960–84. The countries of South America made more rapid gains than did the Caribbean or Central American countries.

In contrast to the moderately successful food production record in most parts of the developing world, sub-Saharan Africa has experienced large and troubling declines in per capita

Indices of Total Food Production, Selected Years

Region	1960	1970	1980	1984	Compound Rate of Growth
	— 1976–78 = 100 —				Percent
Developed countries	77	89	105	113	1.7
Developing countries	61	82	107	120	2.7
Centrally planned countries	60	84	101	117	2.8
World	66	85	105	116	2.4

SOURCE: World Indices of Agricultural Production, 1975–84, U.S. Dept. of Agr., Econ. Res. Serv., Statis. Bul. No. 730, Wash. DC, June 1985.

Indices of Food Production Per Capita, Selected Years

Region	1960	1970	1980	1984	Compound Rate of Growth
	— 1976–78 = 100 —				Percent
Developed countries	91	94	103	107	.7
Developing countries	91	97	100	102	.5
Centrally planned countries	81	95	98	108	1.1
World	92	97	99	103	.4
East Asia	83	89	102	112	1.3
South Asia	95	101	96	103	.3
South and Central America	83	94	105	103	.9
Middle East	88	92	95	94	.3
Africa	113	106	99	93	−0.8

SOURCE: World Indices of Agricultural Production, 1975–84, U.S. Dept. of Agr., Econ. Res. Serv., Statis. Bul. No. 730, Wash. DC, June 1985.

food production for more than two decades. Total food production has even declined in some African countries. Slow and stagnant growth in total food production combined with the developing world's fastest rate of population growth—almost 3 percent per year—account for Africa's poor food production record.

Because most food is produced under rainfed conditions, droughts, whose frequency seems to have increased over the last 15 years, are a major contributor to Africa's periodic food crises.

But the roots of Africa's food problems are much deeper. Africa's traditional food production system has not been able to produce sufficient food for the region's burgeoning population. Breakthroughs in food production technologies have been few, and high-yielding crop varieties developed elsewhere have been difficult to transfer to Africa. A widely held view is that policies of many African governments have neglected, or worse, discriminated against the agricultural sector in favor of more politically powerful urban

FAO

constituencies, and created strong disincentives for farmers to produce marketable food surpluses.

Compounding these weaknesses in the food production system are widespread civil and international disturbances and political instability which disrupt food production, complicate food distribution, and create large refugee movements that put added strains on the food supplies of the individual countries, neighboring countries, and international food donors.

Africa's food production suffers from many problems, weather being one of them. Because most crops are grown under rainfed conditions, droughts are a major cause of its food crises. (Ethiopia, farm before plowing.)

Imports. Food imports have become an increasingly important source of food supplies for the developing countries. Their imports of grains, the major traded food staple, increased more than sixfold, from 10 to 67 million metric tons from the early 1960's to 1983/84.

The developing countries as

Total Grains: Production, Consumption, and Net Exports, Selected Years

Region	1960/61–1962/63 Production	Consumption	Net Exports[1]	1969/70–1971/72 Production	Consumption	Net Exports[1]	1983/84 Production	Consumption	Net Exports[1]	Rate of Growth of Net Exports
				— Million Metric Tons —						Percent
Developed	316	300	20	403	377	32	459	417	120	8.8
U.S.	168	140	33	209	169	40	206	180	96	5.2
Canada	24	15	10	35	22	15	48	25	28	5.2
EC	70	91	−22	93	111	−17	124	118	−11	11.9
U.S.S.R. & East Europe	180	179	—	237	340	−2	283	318	−34	22.0
Others	54	54	−1	66	75	−6	82	95	−16	16.9
Developing	210	220	−10	285	305	−19	449	510	−67	9.3
East Asia	20	23	−4	30	38	−9	15	27	−12	6.9
South Asia	98	99	−2	126	128	−2	256	255	−5	5.0
South & Central America	42	42	−1	64	61	−3	92	95	−3	6.5
Middle East	30	35	−4	39	49	−9	49	87	−38	9.5
Africa	16	17	−1	21	23	−2	37	47	−9	12.0
World	806	801	—	1,051	1,051	—	1,483	1,545	—	—

[1]Numbers with a minus sign are imports.

SOURCE: U.S. Dept. of Agr., *World Agricultural Situation*, various issues.

a group were net exporters of grains from the mid-1940's to the mid-1950's but since the 1950's their grain imports have grown steadily and now account for a substantial part of grain consumption. Grain imports which accounted for 4.7 percent of consumption in developing countries in the early sixties had increased to 13.1 percent by 1983/84.

Imports grew most rapidly in sub-Saharan Africa, the Middle East (including North Africa), and East Asia. While the developing countries were increasing their grain imports, the U.S.S.R. and Eastern Europe were also rapidly expanding their grain imports which amounted to 34 million metric tons in 1983/84.

The increase in grain imports is a response to both growing populations and income in the developing countries. Growth in incomes, especially in the middle- and high-income developing countries, has created an effective demand for grain imports. The desire of higher income consumers in these countries to consume more livestock products has increased the demand for grains used in animal feeding. Most of the increased grain imports have come from the United States, which increased its net grain exports from an average of 33 million metric tons in the early 1960's to 109 million tons in 1981/82.

Consumption and Nutrition.

Aggregate data compiled by the United Nations Food and Agriculture Organization (FAO) and the U.S. Department of Agriculture (USDA) indicate that food consumption increased in the developing countries since the early 1960's but because of the rapid rates of population growth, the improvements were modest. These improvements can be attributed more to increased imports of staple foods than to increased food production. Per capita food consumption has fallen in sub-Saharan Africa.

According to FAO's food balance assessments, the nutritional situation in these countries has not changed much since the 1960's when the average per capita food availability provided 2,130 calories or 93 percent of the minimum daily requirement. Despite deficiencies underlying national food balance assessments—national aggregates say nothing about how food is distributed to households or individuals, averages conceal considerable variations in actual food consumption, and energy requirements are only imprecisely determined—they support the view that food consumption in many parts of the world is inadequate and that undernutrition and malnutrition are continuing, serious problems. No one knows how many people suffer from inadequate food intake, but FAO and World Bank estimates indicate a range of 500 million to a billion malnourished people in the developing countries.

Current World Grain Production and Food Need Estimates

World grain output is likely to rise again in 1985/86 as it did in 1984/85. World grain stocks are forecast by USDA to increase to 248.8 million metric tons in 1985/86. Recent USDA estimates of the food needs of low-income countries provide a perspective on the amount of food required both to maintain consumption at recent, but admittedly nutritionally inadequate, levels and to meet internationally defined minimum nutritional requirements. USDA's food needs assessment indicates that during 1985/86 developing countries will require 11.4 million tons of food,

in the form of grains, above expected levels of commercial imports. To meet minimum nutritional requirements, the countries—69 past and likely recipients of food aid—would need an additional 19.4 million tons. The largest needs for both maintaining consumption and attaining minimum nutrition are in sub-Saharan Africa—6 and 9.2 million tons respectively. While these estimates may seem large, they could be amply covered by existing or anticipated global grain stocks. USDA expects that 1985/86 food aid allocations by donors will exceed its estimates of status quo consumption needs. Even the nutrition-based food need is only 8 percent of the volume of global grain stocks forecast for 1985/86.

Increasing Food Supplies

Meeting the food needs of people in the developing world requires both increasing the supply of food in developing countries as well as enhancing the ability of their people, especially the poor, to purchase an adequate and nutritious diet. Because of the interaction of supply and demand factors in increasing food supply in these countries, no single approach is likely to be effective in improving the food situation.

Major Considerations. Two points about the nature of the world food situation should be underscored. First, the food problem of the developing countries is not a global lack of food. More than enough food is produced and stored in the world to provide people everywhere with adequate diets. In times of food crises, countries have the capacity to respond quickly with food and other needed supplies to alleviate hunger and suffering. Unfortunately, political differences within and between countries and logistics sometimes impede the efforts to save lives, as in the current food crisis in sub-Saharan Africa.

Second, the food problem is not primarily one of global resource scarcity, although population pressures on limited land area in the developing countries means that future increases in food production must come from technological advance rather than from putting more land into production. The conclusion of USDA's decade-old study, *The World Food Situation and Prospects to 1985* (1974), is still valid: "The availability of (resources and inputs)—the underlying major determinants of the world's ability to produce more food—does not appear to be an impediment to future increases in production. . . . Basic imbalances in world food production and consumption which produced surpluses in developed countries, growing imports in developing countries, and malnutrition among some groups remain uncorrected, however."

Food aid, food trade, and more domestic food production are three ways to increase the food supply in the developing countries. None of these approaches will necessarily contribute to improved nutrition unless they are explicitly linked with efforts to increase the food available to low-income people.

Food Aid. The United States and other developed countries with food surpluses, such as members of the European Community, make food available to the developing countries as concessional sales (sales financed with long-term credits at low interest rates) or donations. The United States provides food under both auspices, while most other donors' food aid is in the form of donations. Some countries that are not surplus food producers, such as Japan, make cash

FAO

Although sufficient food is produced and stored in the world, political differences and logistical problems prevent sufficient food reaching some of the hungry and suffering. (Gambia, millet farm.)

available through international organizations to finance food aid shipments to the developing countries.

Food aid can augment the food available to people in developing countries if it is a net addition to domestic supplies and not merely a replacement for commercial food imports. If food aid is to increase the food available to the poor or low-income consumers, however, its distribution must often be subsidized and targeted to needy groups, or it must be used in conjunction with projects to increase employment, such as rural construction, where food paid as wages to workers in such projects represents an increase in their incomes.

Two widely supported purposes of food aid are to meet emergency food needs such as those that many African countries are currently experiencing and to meet the special nutritional requirements of pregnant and nursing women, infants, and young children. Food aid for emergency relief not only can meet the food needs of the disadvantaged but also can contribute a measure of stability to food supplies by compensating for crop shortfalls. Food aid used to build or rebuild depleted stocks also contributes

to stability. Some view food made available in special feeding programs, especially to children, as a form of investment in human resources with longer run economic development payoffs.

Supporters of food aid hold that, in addition to meeting emergency and special feeding needs, food aid provided in substantial quantities over several years also can contribute to economic and agricultural development and in the process increase the food available to both low-income producers and consumers. To be used effectively in this way, food aid must be linked with efforts that generate employment and income such as the food-for-work projects, and it must be accompanied by both technical and financial resources that promote development. Food to supply workers with energy is only one of the inputs needed to build roads or bridges in developing countries.

Critics of using food aid for other than emergency relief and special feeding programs argue that food aid has a disincentive effect on local food production because it depresses prices for domestically produced foodstuffs and encourages governments to neglect policies that would increase domestic food production. Proponents of using food aid for development argue that such disincentive effects are not inevitable if governments give priority to agricultural development including food production, pursue price and investment policies that stimulate agricultural and economic growth, and use the food aid in ways that generate employment and income, thereby strengthening the demand for domestically produced as well as imported food.

Trade. Trade is a more important way of increasing domestic food availability than food aid for consumers with purchasing power. The growth in food imports, however, raises for developing countries the issue of food self-sufficiency versus dependence on international trade for some portion of their food supplies. In the 1970's, perceiving greater instability in world grain markets, many developing countries adopted policies to increase food self-sufficiency and reduce dependence on imported foodstuffs. In large measure because of these policies, many developing countries and China too have become self-sufficient in grain production, and some

have even become net grain exporters. In the 1980's, surplus grain production and mounting stocks are exerting downward pressure on prices and may encourage the developing countries to purchase more of their food supplies in the world market. Future grain purchases will depend largely on how stable world grain supplies will be.

Financial difficulties and an inadequate system for receiving and distributing food imports constrain the growth of trade. The large debt service burden has forced many developing countries to reduce all imports including food. Weak global demand for their exports also has reduced their foreign exchange earnings and slowed the growth of food imports. The cereal import arm of the International Monetary Fund (IMF), which lends to countries short of foreign exchange to finance food imports, can help to overcome some of the current financial difficulties as can credit or credit guarantees from food exporters.

An inadequate distribution system is probably a more important constraint to the expansion of food imports by low-income than higher income developing countries. Improved

World Bank

transportation networks can contribute to economic growth and development generally as well as increase the import capacity of countries. Such networks also can enhance the capacity of countries to export products that earn foreign exchange.

Trade is, however, a two-way street. The developing countries must have access for their

Jamaica's potato production is an example of the country's move towards agricultural improvement. Jamaica now produces its total potato requirement and exports as well.

exports to the markets of developed countries to earn the foreign exchange to pay for imports. The conditions of access to these markets are mixed. Many primary product exports face low or negligible tariffs and few, if any, quantitative barriers. Manufactures, including processed and semiprocessed food and agricultural products, however, face higher tariffs and many more quantitative restrictions. While there is broad agreement that improved market access for developing countries' exports would enhance their purchasing power, protectionist pressures in the developed countries are strong to maintain or increase the barriers to imports that compete with their domestic products.

Increasing Food Production.
In the final analysis, the developing countries will have to produce most of the food they consume. Food aid and food trade may still play important roles but will meet only a part of the food need.

What then can countries do to increase domestic food production? The experience of those that have successfully increased food and agricultural production suggests the following fundamental requirements: 1) agricultural research leading to the development and application of new knowledge; 2) a transportation network that links farms to markets; 3) a broad-based educational system; 4) an effective input-delivery system; and 5) a coordinated mix of price, investment, and trade policies that provide incentives for farmers to produce marketable surpluses of food and agricultural products.

But developing countries run the risks of increasing their food output, even substantially, without contributing to increased food availability for low-income people unless they follow a development strategy that increases food production and, at the same time, generates employment and income among low-income people. Paradoxically, with effective demand for food created by additional employment and income, such a strategy also can spill over into faster economic growth, increased demand for food imports with better financing, and more effective use of food aid.

The developing countries will have to underwrite most of the effort to increase food production. Nevertheless, significant roles exist for bilateral donors such as the United States and multilateral agencies such as the World Bank in providing financial and technical assistance in support of strategies to increase food availability and promote economic development and growth.

FAO

Reason for Hope

Many people are inclined to despair that anything can be done to substantially increase food availability for the poor and malnourished in the developing countries, and consider that, at best, countries will end up as permanent recipients of food aid from surplus-producing countries. The same despairing views were expressed about India during the 1960's, yet today India is a surplus producer of grain, will be a net exporter in 1985, and has even pledged food aid shipments to drought-affected African coun-

India, once a major food aid recipient, has become an exporter. To minimize losses from rodents and the elements, the government is producing metal grain storage containers to sell to farmers.

tries. No one would argue that food self-sufficiency has solved all of India's problems of hunger and poverty, but after nearly a quarter century of effort, India is in a much better position to feed itself today than in the 1960's. India's experience gives reason to hope, even expect, that the food situation in Africa and other parts of the developing world also can be improved.

Part II.
AGRICULTURE AROUND THE WORLD

Agriculture in the United States and Canada

By Don Seaborg, *associate deputy administrator, Economic Research Service (ERS)* and
Carol Goodloe, *agricultural economist, International Economics Division, ERS*

Discovery of the New World changed the way people viewed the world for all time. Lost in the initial search for precious metals was the discovery of new foods. Today, it is hard to imagine how life would be without corn, potatoes, tobacco, tomatoes, or turkeys. Along with the new foods came an enormous additional potential to produce food and fiber.

Over the years, North American agriculture has been developed and improved to where farmers in the United States and Canada are among the world's most efficient. They are capable of producing enough food for domestic needs as well as for people who live in other countries with less agricultural potential.

Variety of U.S. Crops and Growing Regions

American farmers produce a wide variety of crops and livestock, reflecting the tremendous variations in climate, soil types, and dietary interests of consumers. In the Corn Belt— the nation's breadbasket— farmers grow an abundance of corn and soybeans to be fed to cattle, hogs, and poultry. But this area also produces a host of fruits and vegetables, food grains, feed grains, and some

Tim McCabe

specialty crops. A prime factor is its long growing season along with deep soils that receive more than 3 feet of moisture each year.

Other areas produce livestock and crops best suited to their soil and climate. West of the Mississippi River, the elevation increases and rainfall diminishes. Wheat, other small grains, and sorghum are the primary crops. The West Coast offers a cool moist climate in

In the Corn Belt, farmers grow an abundance of corn and soybeans which are fed to livestock. U.S. farmers produce a wide variety of crops and livestock. (Iowa, corn harvest.)

the north, but a dry and hot climate to the south. Wheat and barley are typical crops of Washington and Oregon while the Southwest produces crops that do well in warmth and under irrigation—citrus, cotton, and truck crops. The region is

USDA

Livestock populate every State, but the largest concentrations of cattle are in the Southwest because of dry climate and inexpensive land. (Texas, cattle ranch.)

also known for its wine, nuts, and processed fruits and vegetables. The Delta States produce rice, cotton, and sugarcane, as well as many other field crops. Here too, irrigation plays a role in offsetting the shortcomings of the climate.

Farmers in the Southeast grow mostly field crops, but yields are usually lower than in the Corn Belt. Florida produces fruits and vegetables, especially oranges for frozen concentrated orange juice. During the winter, both Florida and California raise fresh produce for consumption in other areas of the country. The Northeastern States have a much harsher climate, but are still able to raise a variety of crops and livestock. These states are important producers of potatoes, fruits, eggs, and milk.

Livestock populate every State, but in general most of the hogs are raised near the biggest supply of corn. Cattle feeding is common in the Corn Belt, but the largest concentrations are in the Southwest because the dry climate and cheap land contribute to efficiencies in production. Beef cattle are found almost everywhere as they make use of forage from land that is not economical for cash crops. The dairy industry is concentrated in areas with an abundance of roughage—the Northeast, Lake States, and the West Coast. Much of the poultry and eggs are produced near a stable feed supply, but the mid-Atlantic States have a large chunk of the production, because this highly mechanized industry allows efficiencies in production to cover the cost of shipping in feed from the Midwest. It also allows efficiencies in marketing since it is nearer the large population centers.

Canadian Production Less Diverse

Unlike the United States, Canada's cropland is small relative to its total land size. Only 4 percent of Canada's area is devoted to crops, with an additional 2 percent in meadows and pastures. Most of its crops are produced in the western "Prairie" provinces of Manitoba, Saskatchewan, and Alberta. The most important crops are grains—wheat, barley, oats, and rye—and oilseeds—rapeseed and flaxseed.

Crop alternatives in western Canada are limited by soil and weather conditions. The Prairies are characterized by a short growing season, limited

USDA

Unlike the United States, Canada's cropland is small relative to total land size. Only 4 percent of Canada's area is devoted to crops. The most important are wheat, barley, oats, rye and oilseeds.

precipitation, and long harsh winters. The growing season must be squeezed in between the last spring frost, which can persist into June, and the first frost of fall, which can occur as early as August. Drought is another and not infrequent event on the Prairies. Severe droughts occurred in 1980 and 1984.

Conditions are milder and rainfall more abundant in eastern Canada and British Columbia, allowing a greater variety of crops to be grown. Ontario produces corn and soybeans. Fruit and vegetable production, mostly apples and potatoes, is located primarily in Ontario, Quebec, and British Columbia. The Maritime provinces of Prince Edward Island, New Brunswick, Nova Scotia, and Newfoundland are small agricultural producers, but potatoes are important. Forestry and fisheries are also significant industries in British Columbia and the Maritimes.

Cattle, hogs, dairy, and poultry are significant enterprises, accounting for about half the value of Canada's farm output. Alberta, Saskatchewan, and Ontario have about 70 percent of the cattle, while two-thirds of the hogs are located in Ontario and Quebec. These two

provinces are also the main dairy and poultry producers.

Decline in Farm Numbers

Canada has 25 million people, but only 4 percent live and work on farms. This percentage, however, varies greatly by province—from only 2 percent in the Maritimes to almost 20 percent in Saskatchewan. Both the farm population and the number of farms have been steadily declining since World War II.

Canada has about 315,000 farms, compared with about 339,000 in 1976, a farm being defined as an agricultural holding with annual sales of at least Can$250. The number and size of farms differs by region. Ontario, with about 82,000, has the most farms, followed by Saskatchewan, Alberta, and Quebec. Farms are largest in Saskatchewan and Alberta, averaging about 975 and 869 acres, respectively. Farms in Ontario and Quebec are much smaller, averaging about 190 acres.

More than half of all U.S. land is used for cropping or for ranges and pastures. Only 3 million farm workers are needed to produce food and other agricultural products for 235 million citizens, as well as

USDA

enough others to make the United States the leading agricultural exporter. Farms and ranches vary in size, even within a particular region. Farm size has been increasing as the number of farms has dropped. In recent years, the largest 12 percent of the farms, those with sales of more than $100,000, produce about 70 percent of the total cash receipts. Most farms are family owned although many are incorporated.

Only 3 million U.S. farm workers are needed to produce food and other agricultural products for the country and what it exports. Most farms are increasing in size as the number of farms decreases. (Michigan, hay baling.)

Wide Variety of Food

Americans and Canadians have similar diets, and many of the same consumption trends are evident in both countries. These trends are affected by the same factors: changing relative prices for different foods; more women in the work force; and an increasing awareness of the link between diet, nutrition, and health.

Americans and Canadians are eating less red meat and more poultry than 5 years ago. In both countries over the last decade, per capita consumption

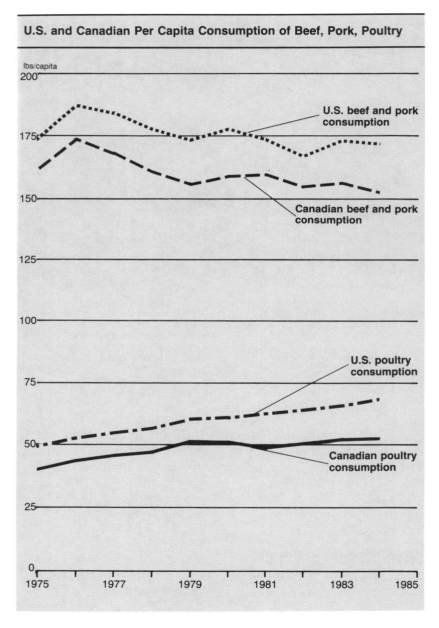

U.S. and Canadian Per Capita Consumption of Beef, Pork, Poultry

lbs/capita

U.S. beef and pork consumption

Canadian beef and pork consumption

U.S. poultry consumption

Canadian poultry consumption

74

of sugar, milk, eggs, and animal fats dropped, while consumption of cheese, yogurt, vegetable fats, and wine increased. Margarine consumption has grown at the expense of butter in Canada, but these items have shown flat trends in the United States. Consumption of fresh fruit has changed little in Canada, but grown significantly in the United States. The composition has changed as more exotic, tropical fruits such as kiwi are being eaten. Fruit juice consumption is on the rise, as is consumption of fresh and frozen vegetables.

Exports and Imports

Exports of agricultural commodities from the United States typically are raw products rather than processed high-valued items. In fiscal 1984, wheat, corn, and soybeans accounted for more than half of the $38 billion in agricultural exports. Exports of other feed grains and rice are also large. Animal fats and hides and skins account for more than half of the $4 billion of animal and products shipments. Other U.S. agricultural exports include fruits, nuts, vegetables, tobacco, cotton, sugar, and seeds.

Imports include a number of products not grown in the United States such as coffee, cocoa, bananas, and spices as well as many items competitive with U.S. commodities such as feeder cattle, meat, fruits, vegetables, and beverages. In fiscal 1984, imports rose to nearly $19 billion, so that the United States enjoyed an agricultural trade balance of $19 billion. The trade balance has been narrowing during the past couple of years as imports continued to rise while exports have fallen.

Although Canada is a small producer relative to the United States and the world, it is a major agricultural exporter. Agricultural exports account for about 10 percent of Canada's total exports, and in recent years have contributed about half of Canada's trade surplus.

Wheat is the single most important commodity export, equal in value to over half of Canada's farm exports. Canada has traditionally been the second largest wheat exporter behind the United States. Barley and rapeseed are Canada's most important coarse grain and oilseed exports. Live animals, meats, dairy products, and hides and furs also are significant. Canada's biggest customers are the United States,

USDA

U.S.S.R., China, Japan, the European Community (EC), Brazil, and Cuba.

Canada's cold climate necessitates large imports of fresh fruits and vegetables—about a third of Canada's total agricultural imports. The United States is the main supplier, with Mexico also providing some fresh vegetables. Like the United States, Canada must

Canada's cold climate necessitates large imports of fresh fruits and vegetables. The United States is a major supplier. (Lettuce harvested in California is shipped by rail to Canada.)

import tropical products such as coffee, sugar, and cocoa, most of which come from Latin America. Canada also imports beef, live cattle, corn, soybeans, and soybean meal from the United States.

Competitors and Customers

The United States and Canada compete in world wheat, coarse grain, and oilseeds markets, but they are also each other's largest trading partners. Agricultural trade, although a small part of total trade, is significant. In 1984, about a third of Canada's agricultural exports went to, and about two-thirds of its imports came from, the United States. Canada is usu-

ally one of the U.S.'s top five customers for farm products. Animal products are the largest category of traded products. Grains and animal feeds also are important.

Although Canada has become more dependent on the U.S. market for both agricultural exports and imports, the U.S. agricultural trade surplus has narrowed in recent years. In 1984, the U.S. trade surplus was only $116 million compared with $850 million just

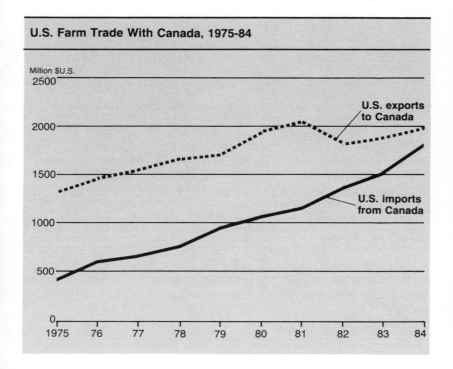

U.S. Farm Trade With Canada, 1975-84

Million $U.S.

U.S. exports to Canada

U.S. imports from Canada

USDA

five years ago. If the trend continues, the United States could soon become a net agricultural importer from Canada.

This declining U.S. trade surplus coincides with a steady erosion in the value of the Canadian dollar, which has given many Canadian products a price advantage over comparable U.S. products. This fundamental alteration of the U.S.-

The United States and Canada share common agricultural goals—maintaining adequate food supplies, supporting farm income, and preserving the family farm structure. (Colorado, feeding the cow.)

Canadian trade balance has been accompanied by various trade policy actions on both sides of the border. A wide range of commodities have been affected—pork and live

U.S. and Canada's Share of World Production and Exports[1]

Commodity	Production			Exports		
	Canada	U.S.	Share of World	Canada	U.S.	Share of World
	Million Metric Tons		Percent	Million Metric Tons		Percent
Wheat	24.8	70.6	19.3	20.0	39.2	58.0
Feed grains	23.1	208.3	30.6	6.0	56.0	65.4
Oilseeds	4.2	59.3	44.1	1.5	24.1	76.7
Beef	1.0	10.7	28.2	0.1	0.1	3.7
Pork	0.8	6.7	14.8	0.2	0.1	11.0
Poultry	0.5	7.2	32.9	0	0.2	12.2
Milk	8.1	62.1	17.2	0	0	0

[1]1982–84 average.

hogs, potatoes, sugar, red raspberries, onions, millfeeds, and rapeseed meal. Trade problems are likely to continue as long as the U.S. dollar retains its strength against the Canadian dollar.

Agricultural Policy and Marketing

The United States and Canada share a common set of agricultural goals. These include maintaining adequate food supplies for domestic needs and exports, supporting farm income, and preserving the family farm structure. The two countries also share common problems: 1) poor current financial conditions of some farms; 2) a decrease in farm populations and numbers; 3) an increase in farm size at the expense of small family farms; 4) excess farm production capacity; 5) deteriorating soil quality; and 6) a loss of farmland to urbanization.

Despite these similarities in goals and problems, Canada and the United States differ substantially in their approach to agricultural policy and marketing. U.S. agricultural policy has been administered by the Federal Government to support farm income by various means of restricting farm output. Canadian agriculture relies exten-

sively on marketing agencies to regulate producer prices, set production or marketing quotas, control licensing, and regulate interprovincial and international trade.

In the United States, major acreage programs for grains, cotton, tobacco, and dairy have existed for many years. Changes in the legislation relating to farm programs occur about every 4 years. The 1981 law will run out following harvest of the 1985 crops, so new legislation that will affect farm decisions for the next 4 years is being debated. In the past, the cornerstone of most farm programs has been an acreage limiting provision that offered participating farmers a support price for their commodity, if they restricted use of their land according to program provisions. More recently, interest is greater in letting markets be a stronger determining factor in farmers' decisions of what and how much to grow.

Canadian marketing boards cover a wide range of commodities—from apples to wool. Over 100 such agencies account for about half of Canada's farm sales. Because the regulation of Canadian agriculture is a shared federal-provincial responsibility, all but five

of the boards are provincial.
The Federal boards regulate
wheat, barley, and oats grown
in the Prairie provinces, and
dairy products, chicken, turkey,
and eggs on a national basis.
These boards function as state
monopolies, controlling the production, pricing, and marketing
of these commodities. The
Wheat Board is the largest (in
terms of the value of sales) and
most influential board in
Canada.

Transportation

Year-round transportation by
rail and truck has benefited
U.S. agriculture and con-
sumers. Good transportation
facilities have encouraged off-
season production of fruits and
vegetables in the southwestern
areas for consumption in the
major population centers.
Without an efficient rail, highway, and inland waterway network, it is unlikely the chain
store movement would have
been nearly as strong. This system depends on large supplies
delivered where they are
needed on a set schedule. Of
course, the efficient movement
of feeds, livestock, and dairy
products has helped determine
the structure of U.S. agriculture. It also helps explain the
large exports of bulk commodities.

In contrast to the United
States, transporting farm products in Canada has been more
difficult because much of Canada's growing areas are located
great distances from population
centers and ports. Whereas the
United States has access to
rail, trucks, and barges, Canada has had to rely almost exclusively on trains. To move
products out of the Prairies,
one must either cross the steep
mountains to the west or the
boggy areas to the east.

Because the mountains in
the west made railway construction difficult, the Government and the railroads struck a
deal almost 100 years ago that
provided land for the railroads
in exchange for fixed freight
rates for farmers. Over time,
these rates covered only a
small portion of the railroads'
costs of moving grains and oilseeds to ports, and rail service
began to deteriorate. These
rates, fixed since 1897, will
now rise to more fully reflect
rail costs, following a change
in the law in 1984. Although
farmers will have to pay more,
the Canadian Government an-
ticipates that grain exporting
capacity will expand, making
Canada even more competitive
in world agricultural trade.

Agriculture in Western Europe

By Reed E. Friend, *branch chief,* and
Ronald Trostle, *leader, Situation and Outlook Section, Western Europe Branch, International Economics Division, Economic Research Service*

Western Europe's population of 350 million people outnumbers the United States' but the gross domestic products (GDP) are about equal. Western Europe is the major region of the world in international trade, accounting for 40 percent of total world exports. The northern tier of Western European countries is highly developed economically and, outside of a few oil-rich middle East countries, ranks among the highest in per capita income in the world. The southern tier of countries—Greece, Portugal, and Spain as well as the south of France and Italy—is less economically advanced.

Agriculture is important to the West European economies. Total gross agricultural product, as a proportion of total GDP, is only about 2.3 percent. The contribution of agriculture to the different national economies, however, varies widely, from 2.1 percent in the United Kingdom to 16.7 percent in Greece. In all countries, the role of agriculture to total economic activity has been declining for a long time.

The major economic grouping in Western Europe is the European Community (EC), established in 1958. Initial members were Belgium, Fed-

Population, Total and Agricultural Labor Force, Western Europe, 1980

Country	Population	Total Labor Force	Agricultural Labor Force[1]	Agriculture as Percentage of Total
	Millions	Millions	Millions	Percent
European Community	270.5	106.89	8.82	8.3
Belgium/Luxembourg	10.2	3.91	.12	3.1
Denmark	5.1	2.50	.21	8.3
France	53.7	21.14	1.86	8.8
Greece	9.6	3.31	1.02	30.8
Ireland	3.4	1.15	.22	19.2
Italy	56.4	20.57	2.93	14.2
Netherlands	14.2	4.67	.28	6.0
United Kingdom	56.3	24.37	.66	2.7
W. Germany	61.6	25.27	1.52	6.0
Other Western Europe	78.4	29.59	4.43	15.0
Portugal	9.9	3.93	1.12	28.5
Spain	37.4	11.25	2.12	13.9
Finland	4.8	2.19	.25	11.5
Norway	4.1	1.91	.16	8.5
Sweden	8.3	4.23	.24	5.6
Austria	7.5	3.07	.32	10.5
Switzerland	6.4	3.01	.22	7.2
Total Western Europe	348.9	136.48	13.25	9.7
United States	227.8	99.30	3.53	3.6

[1]Includes forestry and fishing.

SOURCES: *Population: Main Economic Indicators*, OECD. Jan. 1985, p. 187. *Labor Force: Labor Force Statistics 1969–1980*, OECD. 1982.

Gross Domestic Product and Gross Agricultural Product, Western Europe, 1982

Country	Gross Domestic Product (GDP)	Gross Agricultural Product (GAP)	GAP as Percentage of GDP
	Billion dollars		Percent
European Community			
Belgium	84.3	2.08	2.4
Luxembourg	3.3	—	—
Denmark	56.4	3.00	5.3
France	540.1	—	—
Greece	37.9	6.33	16.7
Ireland	17.6	—	—
Italy	347.4	—	—
Netherlands	137.6	5.83	4.2
United Kingdom	477.4	10.07	2.1
West Germany	658.4	15.21	2.3
Other Western Europe			
Portugal	23.4	—	—
Spain	181.3	11.04	6.1
Austria	66.9	2.59	3.9
Norway	56.2	2.44	4.3
Sweden	99.2	3.25	3.3
Finland	49.1	3.95	8.0
Switzerland	96.5	—	—
Total Western Europe	2923.7	65.81	2.3
United States	3052.1	77.44	2.5

— = Not available.

Totals may not add up because of rounding.

eral Republic of Germany (West Germany), France, Italy, Luxembourg, and the Netherlands. Membership was expanded in 1973 to include Denmark, Ireland, and the United Kingdom and again in 1981 to include Greece. Spain and Portugal are slated to join in 1986.

The EC's Common Agricultural Policy (CAP) supports a complex, highly protected agricultural sector and is based on three fundamental principles—common pricing, community preference, and common financing. The EC, as a result of CAP, has become a major world producer and exporter of agricultural commodities.

Common pricing is intended to eliminate duties and restrictions on trade between member countries and promote the flow of exports from main producing to deficit areas. Community preference provides a preferred market for the products of EC members to the detriment of non-EC suppliers. Common financing refers to sharing the costs of the CAP under the auspices of EC institutions.

The European Free Trade Association (EFTA)—a much less formal combination of countries than the EC—was established in 1960 as a regional trade group. Membership in EFTA currently includes Austria, Norway, Portugal, Sweden, and Switzerland with Finland as an associate member. Although EFTA countries have eliminated tariffs on manufactured goods originating in their countries and traded among themselves, agricultural products are not generally included in the schedule for tariff reductions.

Structure of Agriculture

Agriculture in Western Europe used to be characterized by small, fragmented holdings operated by peasant farmers. Originally, Europe's land inheritance laws required that landholdings be divided equally among all surviving children. Small farms, often consisting of widely scattered plots, led to a high-cost, inefficient agriculture.

The structure of agriculture has changed markedly over the past several decades. Migration from agriculture, particularly strong in the EC during the 1960's and 1970's, helped to enlarge farm size and increase per capita farm incomes.

Farms in the EC averaged 38 acres in 1975, less than a tenth as large as in the United

States, with wide variation in farm size among countries. In the United Kingdom, where inheritance laws have not required the division of land among all heirs, average farm size is 170 acres. Countries with the lowest averages, less than 20, are Italy and Greece. Farm size also varies significantly within countries. For example, in the highly commercialized agricultural areas of the Po Valley in Italy and the Paris Basin in France, farms are much larger than elsewhere in each country.

Part-time farming in the EC is widespread, particularly in some countries. In West Germany, for example, more than 50 percent of the farmers are part-time. Frequently, nonfarm income outweighs farm income, and the farm enterprise is viewed largely as a desirable place to live and as an investment. Most part-time farms depend largely on farm family labor.

Number and Size of EC Farms, Selected Years

Country	Number of Farms			Average Size		
	1960	1970	1980	1960	1970	1980
	1,000			Acres		
European Community[1]	7,272.0	5,722.0	5,670.0	29.8	38.3	38.8
Belgium	198.7	130.4	91.2	20.3	28.7	38.1
Luxembourg	10.4	11.9	4.7	33.1	48.0	68.2
Denmark	193.7	143.4	116.3	39.5	51.0	61.7
France	1,773.5	1,420.9	1,135.0	42.0	51.8	62.8
Greece	877.6	810.8	731.7	10.0	10.6	10.6
Ireland	281.0	270.3	223.3	39.5	43.8	55.8
Italy	2,756.3	2,173.5	2,191.9	16.8	19.1	18.3
Netherlands	230.3	181.8	129.2	24.5	29.6	38.5
United Kingdom	443.1	312.5	249.2	79.1	141.7	169.8
West Germany	1,358.3	1,083.1	797.4	22.9	28.8	37.8
United States	3,962.5	2,954.2	2,427.8	297	373	429

[1]Excludes farms of less than 2.5 acres

Western Europe

85

Pertti Maen Tila

Agricultural Production

Diversified farming character-
izes agricultural production in
northern European countries.
Dairying is the most widespread livestock activity and
a mainstay in the income of
many farmers. Unlike pork and
poultry production, which tend
towards large enterprises, dairy
herds are relatively small averaging 14 cows per farm in the
EC. Although some beef production is specialized, approximately 80 percent of the EC's
beef production is a byproduct
of the dairy industry.

*Dairying is the most widespread live-
stock activity and a major source of income among northern European farmers. (Denmark, dairy farm.)*

Field crop production in
northern Europe consists
largely of grains, sugar beets,
oilseeds (rapeseed and sunflowerseed), and potatoes.
Wheat is the major grain, followed by barley and corn.
Sugar beets, produced under a
quota system in the EC, provide an important source of income to many producers. Oilseed production, particularly
sunflowerseed, is gaining favor

while potato production is in a long-term decline.

Although fruits, vegetables, and wine are part of northern European agriculture, they carry an especially heavy weight in the agriculture of Mediterranean countries. Fruit production is largely citrus in this region compared with deciduous in the north. Olive oil is an important crop in Spain, Portugal, Greece, and southern Italy. Grain and livestock also constitute important parts of the agriculture of Greece, Portugal, and Spain but much less so than in northern Europe.

The three major sheep producers are Spain, France, and the United Kingdom, and goat herds are concentrated in Greece, Spain, and Portugal where they provide significant meat, milk, and cheese.

Agricultural production in Western Europe rose in the decades of the 1960's and 1970's and is continuing this trend in the 1980's. The increased production is largely due to expanded use of higher yielding varieties of seeds, improved breeding stock, and better management practices. In the EC, for example, wheat

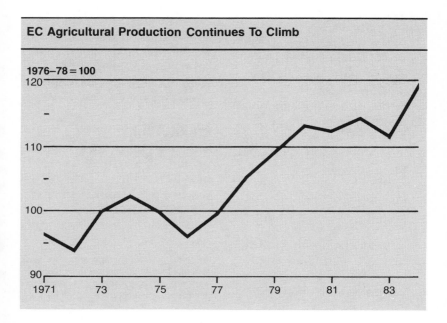

EC Agricultural Production Continues To Climb

1976–78 = 100

and coarse grain yields in the last decade rose an average 2.8 and 1.9 percent a year, respectively. Milk per cow climbed 1.9 percent a year, and the number of slaughtered pigs per sow increased about one-third. The incentives to increase agricultural production include high support prices and a stable agricultural policy which reduces risk and encourages investment.

Surpluses and Self-Sufficiency

Western Europe emerged from World War II numbed by food shortages. Today it is burdened with surpluses. This situation is now particularly evident given the world's relatively low level of economic growth and general oversupply of agricultural commodities.

The EC has major agricultural surpluses of dairy products (particularly dry milk powder and butter), soft wheat and barley, sugar, and beef and veal. Surpluses of pork, eggs, and poultry also arise from time to time. EC market intervention tends to be minimal for these products, however, with market forces bringing supply and demand back into balance. Surpluses of wine and some fruits and vegetables are

commonplace, but the EC uses producer groups to regulate the marketing of these commodities, withholding excess supplies for conversion to industrial alcohol. Products for which the EC has consistently showed a deficit include rice, corn, high-protein feedstuffs, sheepmeat and goatmeat, fresh deciduous fruit, citrus, and vegetable fats and oils.

Increased emphasis on self-sufficiency by numerous non-EC countries in Western Europe also has generated surpluses. Sweden has become a consistent annual exporter of up to 1 million tons of grain and Austria a frequent grain exporter. Spain produces a large surplus of olive oil which would even be greater if consumption subsidies on olive oil were curtailed or consumption quotas on soybean oil removed.

Marketing

The marketing, processing, and retailing of agricultural commodities and foods have reached a relatively high level of sophistication in most coun-

In some countries cattle and hog sales are made directly on the farm, while in Denmark all hogs and most cattle are sold to slaughterhouses. (Austria, hog farm.)

B. Michal

tries of Western Europe. But considerable differences exist between countries and sometimes between commodities.

Marketing of grains through cooperatives is quite important in France, West Germany, the Netherlands, and the Scandinavian countries. Private trade is the strongest competitor of cooperatives and is particularly important in the United Kingdom. Direct sales by farmers to the processing industry are much less important.

In some countries, most cattle and hog sales are made directly on the farm, as in France, while in Denmark all hogs, except for sows, and a large proportion of cattle are sold directly to slaughterhouses. Livestock marketing cooperatives also are an important marketing channel.

Food retailing has changed dramatically in Western Europe over the past two decades. The trend has been toward concentration and modernization of food retail trade with a proliferation of self-service stores and supermarkets. Concentration of the food distribution system is not nearly as advanced in the Mediterranean countries as in the northern European countries, especially West Germany and Sweden.

Agricultural Trade

Western Europe is a major importer and exporter of agricultural commodities with a net trade deficit continuing through 1984. However, with increased productivity in agriculture and slow growth in domestic demand, agricultural exports are rising much faster than agricultural imports, particularly for the EC.

Agricultural exports as a share of total exports varies widely among Western countries—the share exceeds 30 percent for Greece and Denmark but is less than 5 percent for Finland, Norway, and Switzerland. Agriculture's share of total exports and imports has long been dropping in Western Europe as it has in the United States.

Western Europe imported a wide range of agricultural commodities during 1981–83. Major commodities were fruits and vegetables; meat and meat preparations; coffee, tea, cocoa, spices; cereals and cereal preparations; animal feeds; and oilseeds. Major agricultural commodities exported during this period, some of which were also major imports, included dairy products and eggs, fruits and vegetables, meat and meat preparations, cereal and cereal

Dana Downie

preparations, and beverages. Many of these commodities are traded among Western European countries.

The United States is a major agricultural trading partner with Western Europe. The value of U.S. agricultural exports to this region, however, has dropped sharply in recent years because of its increased agricultural self-sufficiency and low level of economic growth. A sharp rise in the value of the U.S. dollar—making our com-

Western Europe is a major importer of a wide range of agricultural commodities including lemons from California. (Netherlands, produce importer.)

modities more expensive to European consumers—also contributed to lower U.S. exports. On the other hand, the value of U.S. imports of agricultural commodities from Western Europe has risen in recent years. Consequently, the U.S. net agricultural trade position with Western Europe has declined.

Western Europe still ac-

Western Europe

Agricultural and Total Imports and Exports of Western Europe, 1973 and 1983

Item	Unit	Total Western Europe		European Community		Other Western Europe	
		1973	1983	1973	1983	1973	1983
Imports							
Total	Bil. $	270	723	218	585	52	138
Agricultural	Bil. $	48	95	41	82	7	13
As % of total	Pct.	18	14	19	14	14	10
Exports							
Total	Bil. $	254	693	211	570	43	123
Agricultural	Bil. $	27	74	24	67	3	7
As % of total	Pct.	11	11	11	12	7	6
Net Trade							
Total	Bil. $	−16	−30	−7	−15	−9	−15
Agricultural	Bil. $	−21	−21	−17	−76	−4	−6

counted for 23 percent of total U.S. agricultural exports in 1984. Recent year declines in exports to the EC have, however, been greater than to the other areas of Western Europe. Major individual country markets for the U.S. in 1984 were Netherlands ($2.2 bil.), West Germany ($1.3 bil.), and Spain ($1 bil.).

Major U.S. agricultural exports to Western Europe have traditionally been grains, oil-seeds, and oilseed products, the commodities that have declined the most in recent years. Animal and animal products; fruits, vegetables, and nuts; and tobacco are other commodity groupings of major value to the United States. U.S. imports of agricultural commodities from Western Europe are concentrated in beverages, primarily wine; dairy products, primarily cheese; and meats and preparations, primarily pork.

U.S. Agricultural Exports to and Imports from Western Europe, 1975, 1980, and 1984[1]

Country	U.S. Agricultural Exports			U.S. Agricultural Imports		
	1975	1980	1984	1975	1980	1984
	Million dollars					
European Community	5,653	9,818	6,717	1,082	2,037	3,153
Belgium/Luxembourg	292	645	836	28	30	55
Denmark	89	217	122	192	249	486
France	485	832	510	191	400	606
Greece	129	273	82	42	61	87
Ireland	30	75	118	22	55	95
Italy	839	1,329	770	146	390	532
Netherlands	1,721	3,515	2,227	234	388	590
United Kingdom	602	1,060	790	100	134	174
W. Germany	1,466	1,872	1,260	127	330	528
Other Western Europe	1,540	2,809	2,547	316	468	701
Portugal	281	594	702	40	42	58
Spain	813	1,463	1,026	157	201	223
Finland	47	101	44	22	57	102
Norway	120	189	119	25	44	42
Sweden	88	137	110	24	24	51
Austria	15	26	18	16	33	44
Switzerland	164	280	311	32	61	104
Other countries	12	19	217	1	6	77
Total Western Europe	7,193	12,627	9,264	1,398	2,505	3,854

[1]Fiscal years. Includes transshipments through Canada.
SOURCE: Bureau of the Census.

Dana Downie

Consumption Patterns

Consumption in Western Europe varies substantially from country to country, but differs the most between southern and northern regions. Caloric intake is higher in the north than in the south, but both are below the average for the United States. The percentage of personal disposal income spent on food varies significantly within Western Europe and is highest for the countries with the low-

Because of costly agricultural policies in Western Europe, consumers have become accustomed to high food prices. (Norway, family at breakfast.)

est per capita incomes (Portugal, Greece, and Spain).

Consumption of cereals (excluding rice) averaged 185 pounds per person per year in the EC during 1980/81–1982/83 but consumption in Italy and Greece was double the Netherlands. Per capita con-

Percentage of Private Consumption Expenditures for Food and Beverages, West European Countries and the United States, 1982

Country	Expenditures for Food and Beverage[1]
	Percent
European Community	
Belgium	22.4
Denmark	21.7
France	20.0
Germany, West	22.8
Greece	41.7
Ireland	[2]37.9
Italy	28.6
Luxembourg	[3]18.8
Netherlands	17.6
United Kingdom	17.5
Other Western Europe	
Austria	22.4
Iceland	[4]25.5
Finland	25.2
Norway	24.5
Portugal	[2]35.8
Spain	[5]31.2
Sweden	22.0
Switzerland	[5]27.7
United States	14.4

[1]Percent of total private consumption expenditures excluding food and beverages purchased in hotels, as well as most institutional purchases. [2]1981. [3]1980. [4]1973. [5]Includes tobacco.
SOURCE: OECD.

sumption of potatoes in Ireland was triple that of Italy with the EC averaging 168 pounds. Consumption of fresh milk products (other than cream) averaged 220 pounds per person annually. Per capita meat consumption in the EC averaged 176 pounds; France led with 220 pounds and Greece had the least, at 145 pounds.

The longer run consumption trends in Western Europe show reduced per capita intake of cereals, potatoes, and butter but rising use of fresh fruits and vegetables and meats. Per capita consumption of beef and veal seems to have stabilized (or possibly slightly declined). Gains have occurred for pork and poultry meat. Both the Scandinavian countries and the Mediterranean countries have higher per capita fish consumption than other Western European countries.

Domestic Policies

Western Europe is characterized by costly agricultural and food price policies, particularly the EC and the Scandinavian countries. Consequently, consumers have become accustomed to high food prices and the generous income transfers to the farm sector implicit in these policies. Spain and Portu-

Per Capita Consumption of Food Products, EC and United States, 1983

Item	EC	United States
	Pounds per person per year	
Cereals (excluding rice)	185	150
Rice	7	10
Sugar	77	136
Potatoes	168	91
Vegetables (including preserves)	231	206
Fruit (including preserves and fruit juices)	194	145
Citrus fruit	62	32[1]
Wine (litres/capita)	46	
Vegetable oils and fats	26	58
Milk (fresh products other than cream)	220	216
Butter (fat)	14	5
Cheese		21
Meat (excluding offal)	176	223
beef/veal	55	108
pigmeat	82	66
poultrymeat	30	47
sheep and goat meat	9	2
Eggs (including processed products)	31	39

[1]Fresh only.

SOURCE: EC Based on data presented in *The Agricultural Situation in the Community—1984 Report*. Commission of the European Communities, Brussels. 1985. U.S. data from *Agricultural Statistics, 1984*. USDA.

gal have traditionally had a policy of food subsidies for consumers and lower price support levels for farm commodities, but these policies are being changed in anticipation of EC membership.

The Rome Treaty establishing the EC set forth several objectives for its common agricultural policy:

1) Increase agricultural productivity through technical progress;
2) Ensure a fair standard of living for the farm population;
3) Stabilize markets;
4) Guarantee regular supplies; and
5) Ensure reasonable prices to consumers.

In practice, the EC has given top priority to the improvement of farm income and has subordinated other objectives. Politically powerful farmer organizations backed by a large farm population have kept EC member country politicians keenly aware of agricultural interests.

The EC has established detailed production and marketing regulations for practically every commodity in its farm sector. Target, threshold (minimum import) and intervention (support) prices are decided annually by the EC Agricul-

tural Council consisting of the agricultural ministers of all member states. Actual prices tend to range between the intervention price and the target price with surplus commodities tending towards the bottom of the price range and deficit commodities towards the top.

The largely open-ended guaranteed high prices by the EC have stimulated farmers to make capital investments in new technology leading to the agricultural surpluses of today.

Concomitant with this development were sharply rising agricultural program costs by the EC, amounting to an estimated 19 billion European Currency Units (ECU) or $15 billion in 1984. Practically all the EC's agricultural expenditures support agricultural prices leaving little money for structural changes in agriculture. The monies for structural change must be used on EC-approved projects and in conjunction with funds from the national governments.

International Policy
The EC's agricultural policies have traditionally been inward looking with little regard for their international implications. When world prices are below the threshold (minimum im-

Agricultural Expenditures by the EC, Selected Years

Year	Guarantee Fund	Guidance Fund	Total Expenditures		ECUs Per Dollar
	Million ECU			Million dollars	ECU
1972	2,258	167	2,425	2,720	1.193
1975	4,523	325	4,848	6,015	1.241
1980	11,315	592	11,884	16,578	1.392
1981	11,141	695	11,884	13,268	1.117
1982	12,406	801	14,121	13,834	0.980
1983	15,920	846	16,700	14,866	0.890
1984	18,401	619	19,020	15,006	0.789

SOURCE: Various issues of the EC's: *The Agricultural Situation in the Community*, and annual financial reports.

port) level, they impose a variable levy on imports. On those rare occasions when world prices rise above EC prices, they can impose a variable export levy to keep the commodities from moving into world markets. Consequently, EC policies destabilize world markets rather than contribute to needed supply and demand adjustments.

One of the disconcerting aspects of EC policy to the United States and other agricultural exporting countries is the heavy export subsidization of agricultural commodities. Since EC prices are above world market prices, export subsidies are needed to move commodities into world markets. These export subsidies have increased over time and totaled 6.4 billion ECU ($5.3 billion) in 1984. Thus, one-third of CAP expenditures are for export subsidies. Major expenditures are for dairy products, grains, sugar, and beef and veal.

Prospects

Western Europe will remain a major producer, exporter, and importer of agricultural commodities. Some countries, including those in the EC, are expected to push self-sufficiency even more, so that agricultural exports will continue to grow faster than imports. Technological improvements in agriculture will result in increased productivity.

The EC is not expected to make any significant changes in its CAP in the foreseeable future. Continued agricultural surpluses, in combination with budgetary limitations, may lead to greater use of supply management tools, such as the quotas currently imposed on sugar. However, those issues are currently under study in the EC.

U.S.-EC agricultural trade issues are expected to remain in the forefront of trade relations. The EC's past policy of largely externalizing resolution of surplus problems (rather than exercising greater price support restraints, imposing other types of supply management controls, or adjusting stocks) has brought the United States and other traditional suppliers face to face with the EC in world markets. The widespread commodity supply-demand disequilibrium that prevails throughout world markets, modest economic growth, and the burdensome debt situation facing many countries point to a continuation of slow growth in effective world demand and continued strong competition.

Both the United States and the EC face difficult obstacles to improving trade relations between them. U.S. macroeconomic policies have resulted in a stronger dollar and caused many of our commodities to be more expensive to EC consumers. The financial crisis in the U.S. farm sector, low commodity market prices, the possibility of additional losses in world commodity market shares through EC export subsidies, and the threat of additional action by the EC to squeeze imports (such as the import quotas on corn gluten and the consumption tax on fats and oils) have created problems and anxieties in the United States.

Obstacles faced by the EC in bringing agricultural surpluses under control include a large politically strong farm sector; small, inefficient farms; extremely slow economic growth leading to a high rate of unemployment that severely hampers the migration out of farming; and an ineffective EC-decisionmaking process resulting in tradeoffs favorable to all member countries rather than the making of solid economic decisions with useful international dimensions.

Agriculture in Eastern Europe and the U.S.S.R.

By Edward Cook, *economist,* and Robert Cummings, *agricultural economist, International Economics Division, Economic Research Service*

Opinions about the health of the agricultural economies in Eastern Europe and the U.S.S.R. are often shaped by the region's most striking disparities. Tremendous Soviet grain imports, food rationing in Poland and Romania, and private farmers struggling for legal guarantees in Poland contrast with flourishing farm exports from Hungary, competitive per capita food consumption levels in the German Democratic Republic (GDR), and an accepted, dominant private farm sector in Yugoslavia. The result is often confusion over the state of agriculture.

But the region does have commonalities that present a truer picture of agriculture's development and place in the economy. In the past 20 years gains in crop and livestock production and meat consumption have been impressive. Agriculture has been mechanized, although less so than in the United States and Western Europe, and basic research capabilities are quite advanced.

The gains have come at great cost. Growth required large agricultural and capital imports and extensive domestic investment. The U.S.S.R. can continue these policies in part because it can earn hard cur-

Interfoto MTI

rency through energy exports. Foreign loans, however, financed Eastern Europe's growth in imports. A debt crisis ensued that caused economic recession, slashed agricultural imports and consumption, and stimulated a nearly single-minded drive by the governments for increased food self-sufficiency.

Agriculture in Eastern Europe and the U.S.S.R. has been mechanized although less so than in the United States and Western Europe. (Hungary, spraying herbicides.)

Socialistic Farming

The U.S.S.R. and countries of Eastern Europe have developed their agricultures within a socialist framework. Even in Poland and Yugoslavia, where private farming represents roughly 70–80 percent of agri-

cultural production and arable land, the farms must function within a rigid socialist rather than a market-oriented economy.

Much of the U.S.S.R.'s agricultural land is in marginal climatic areas. The average socialized farm in the U.S.S.R. is roughly 25,000 acres, while in the Eastern European countries it is about one-third as large. These socialized farms permit the introduction of specialized technology and the probable advantages of size in crop production.

The socialized farms are assigned annual targets for the sale of key commodities to the state. Farm prices set by the state are held constant for at least 1 year and often longer. Investment funds are provided either by the state or are allocated from the farm's own revenue. Credit policies are lenient, with interest rates about 2 or 3 percent and debts frequently forgiven. Although credit terms are easy, farm managers receive extensive interference from local, regional, and national authorities in running their farms.

In all countries of the region, farm service organizations, producers and distributors of machinery, fertilizer and other farm supplies, and food purchasing and processing organizations are state-run monopolies. These organizations' lack of responsiveness to farm and consumer needs is often cited as a factor limiting improvement in agricultural production.

Private agriculture plays an important role nevertheless. Although these operations are tiny, private plots in the U.S.S.R. produce 25 percent of all agricultural and 30 percent of livestock production. In Hungary and Bulgaria the shares are even higher. In most countries farm workers are entitled to tend a private plot which can be as large as an acre or slightly more. This is where production of labor intensive crops such as fruits, vegetables and potatoes are concentrated. They are also entitled to own and tend a limited number of livestock depending heavily on feed supplied by the socialist sector. Private plot production is largely for local consumption, but some also is brought to collective farm markets and sold to state purchasing organizations at state-set prices.

Under socialized agriculture the state attempts to reduce differences in profitability among farms by assigning varying plan targets, purchase prices, taxes, and subsidies. They shore up unprofitable farms with direct grants and easy credit. State budgetary grants, subsidies, and priority access to centralized investment funds also artificially support agriculture in marginal farming areas at the expense of development of the more productive regions. The tendency to equalize income extends to individual workers, who generally get paid according to the number of acres they plow or cows they milk, not for how well the work is done.

What's Produced. The U.S.S.R. and Eastern Europe account for a significant share of world production of wheat, rye, barley, oats, potatoes, sunflowerseed, and sugar beets. The U.S.S.R. is the world's largest producer of potatoes, barley, rye, oats, sunflowerseed and sugar beets. It is second in wheat production and roughly equal with the United States in second place in cotton production. Except for southern por-

tions of the region, the growing season is too short for corn and soybeans. Crops yields per acre are generally highest in Czechoslovakia, the GDR, Hungary, and Bulgaria and lowest in the U.S.S.R.

The U.S.S.R. and Eastern Europe also are major producers of livestock products. The U.S.S.R. is the world's largest milk producer and is third behind the United States and China in meat production. Poland, Czechoslovakia, and the GDR rank high in per capita production of milk, and Hungary ranks very high in per capita production of meat.

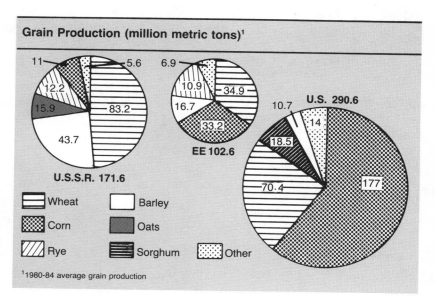

Grain Production (million metric tons)[1]

U.S.S.R. 171.6 — 11, 5.6, 12.2, 15.9, 83.2, 43.7

EE 102.6 — 6.9, 10.9, 34.9, 16.7, 33.2

U.S. 290.6 — 10.7, 14, 18.5, 70.4, 177

Wheat · Barley · Corn · Oats · Rye · Sorghum · Other

[1] 1980-84 average grain production

Interfoto MTI

Livestock productivity comparisons with the West are less favorable than for crops with much more feed expended per unit of meat or milk production. Poor quality, protein-short feeds, and socialized agriculture's difficulty providing adequate around-the-clock animal care are primary reasons.

What's Consumed. East European and Soviet diets have improved greatly in the last 20

The U.S.S.R. and Eastern Europe also are major producers of livestock products. The U.S.S.R. is the world's largest milk producer and third in meat production. (Hungary, state dairy farm.)

years. Consumption of some foods in several countries now approaches developed Western levels. Meat consumption is the region's benchmark for dietary progress, and per capita consumption expanded greatly

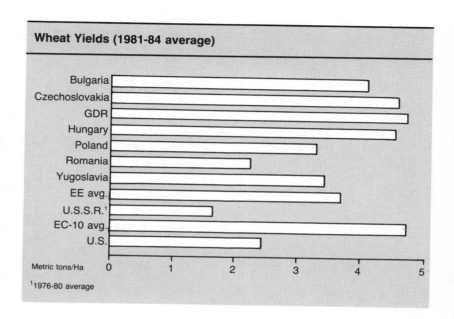

Wheat Yields (1981-84 average)

Bulgaria
Czechoslovakia
GDR
Hungary
Poland
Romania
Yugoslavia
EE avg.
U.S.S.R.[1]
EC-10 avg.
U.S.

Metric tons/Ha   0   1   2   3   4   5

[1]1976-80 average

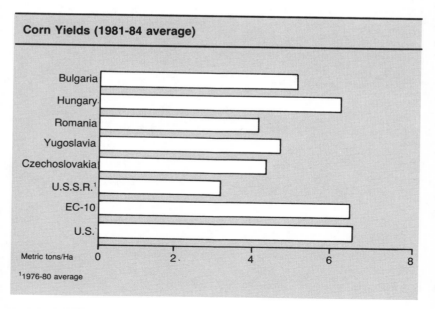

Corn Yields (1981-84 average)

Bulgaria
Hungary
Romania
Yugoslavia
Czechoslovakia
U.S.S.R.[1]
EC-10
U.S.

Metric tons/Ha   0   2   4   6   8

[1]1976-80 average

Per Capita Consumption of Selected Foods

	Bulgaria	Czechoslovakia	GDR	Hungary	Poland	Romania	Yugoslavia	U.S.S.R.	EC	USA
				Kilograms per capita						
Meat[1]										
1975	60.6	(87.5)	82.9	(91.4)	70.3	45.7	48.3	57	—	(97.6)
1980	64.9	91.6	95.1	93.6	74.0	60.0	54.2	58	—	(104.5)
1983	73.8	90.5	97.6	98.3	58.3	[2](58)		58	—	(104.7)
Milk[3]										
1975	198	(402)	494	(177)	432	NA	97	316	—	151
1980	234	416	516	212	451	NA	110	314	—	147
1983	253	440	536	234	424	NA	[4]102	309	—	137
Eggs[5]										
1975	146	297	269	274	209	214	166	216	[6]308	349
1980	204	316	289	317	223	270	190	239	[6]308	345
1983	225	328	301	320	200	(270)	[4]187	253	[6]308	330
Grain (in flour equivalent)										
1975	162	108	95	112	120	189	183	141	[6]83	66
1980	160	107	95	115	127	172	179	138	[6]83	68
1983	154	108	97	112	122	(173)	[4]174	136	[6]84	68
Potatoes										
1975	23	96	142	67	173	96	66	120	[6]80	39
1980	27	76	143	61	158	71	61	109	[6]78	41
1983	30	79	144	60	154	(100)	[4]61	110	[8]76	41
Vegetables										
1975	127	74	90	85	109	113	87	89	[6]99	90
1980	125	66	94	80	101	140	97	97	[6]103	92
1983	138	71	91	78	103	(170)	[4]96	101	[6]105	94
Sugar										
1975	33	38	37	39	43	20	33	41	[6]38	[7]54
1980	35	38	41	38	41	28	37	44	[6]36	[7]60
1983	36	38	39	36	45	NA	[4]34	44	[6]35	[7]62

NA = Not applicable. ( ) = Estimate. — = Comparable data not available.
[1]Includes offals, meat products and fat. For the United States, per capita consumption is estimated at 5 kilograms.
[2]Includes fish.
[3]Includes milk products in fresh milk equivalent.
[4]1982 data.
[5]Units.
[6]Three-year averages as follows: 1974–76, 1978–80, 1981–83.
[7]Includes other sweeteners such as corn sweeteners and syrups.
SOURCE: Statistical yearbooks of the respective countries, various editions. Vestnik statistiki, various editions.

Agriculture Around the World

since 1965. Hungarians now consume only slightly less meat than Americans do, with the GDR close behind.

People in the region still eat much more grain and potatoes than West Europeans and Americans do, however. In every country, food quality is poor particularly of perishable products, consumer choices are few, and shortages are common.

Higher Production and Consumption Costs

The achievements in agricultural production and consumption during the 1970's came at a heavy cost. For most countries, extensive retail price subsidies that increasingly strained government budgets encouraged relatively high levels of food consumption. Agriculture accounted for a large share of labor and investment in comparison with the developed West. Furthermore, to maintain consumption growth they had to import more and more feed and food, almost all purchased with scarce hard currency.

Price Subsidies. Extensive retail food price subsidies coincided with rising household income to fuel the expansion in meat and livestock product consumption. Stable retail

prices are a hallmark of Soviet-style economies, and this is particularly true for food. The cost of these subsidies has skyrocketed over the years because of rising production costs. The Soviet budget for retail food subsidies increased from $15 billion in 1970 to $38 billion by 1980. In late 1981, a market basket of food worth $100 in Czechoslovakia contained $40 worth of subsidies.

Despite the subsidies, consumers spend much of their income on food. The price subsidies have stimulated excess demand, and the inadequate supply of nonfood consumer goods channels income into food purchases. Additionally, declines in real income in Yugoslavia and Poland have increased food's share in income expenditures.

Inputs. Agricultural production gains in this region have cost much in labor and capital resources. Despite advances in mechanization of crop and livestock production, agriculture accounts for a much larger share of the labor force in the U.S.S.R. and most Eastern European countries than in developed Western nations, and labor intensity per 250 acres of arable land remains high. Likewise, the share of national

TASS

investment devoted to agriculture also is large, particularly in the U.S.S.R., where it exceeds 25 percent of all investment.

In almost all these countries, agricultural production costs rose sharply during the 1970's. Input prices were driven up primarily by higher material and energy costs. The policy of trying to make agricultural incomes catch up with industrial incomes allowed wage increases to exceed growth in labor productivity in agriculture, driving up unit labor costs.

Despite subsidies, consumers spend much of their income on food. The price subsidies have stimulated excess demand, and the inadequate supply of nonfood consumer goods channels income into food purchases. (Moscow, family dining.)

Furthermore, central planners in most countries had trouble coordinating resource use in their increasingly complex, modern agricultural sectors.

Increased Agricultural Trade

All countries relied heavily on agricultural imports to increase

Expenditures on Food and Beverages as a Percentage of Household Total Disposable Income

Country and Type of Employment	1975	1980	1983
		Percent	
Bulgaria:			
Industrial workers	43	48	48
Professionals	39	45	44
Collective farmers	45	52	49
Czechoslovakia:			
Industrial workers	30	27	26
Professionals	27	24	25
Collective farmers	28	26	25
GDR:[1]			
Industrial workers and professionals, total	37	36	35
Collective farmers	37	37	34
Hungary:[2]			
Industrial workers	41	43	42
Professionals	33	35	NA
Collective farmers	43	46	42
Poland:			
Industrial workers and professionals, total	40	39	46
Peasants	49	43	48
Romania:			
Nonagricultural workers	NA	46	NA
Collective farmers	NA	63	NA
Yugoslavia:[1]			
Four-person household	34	32	40
U.S.S.R.:			
Industrial workers	33	32	30
Collective farmers	37	36	34
EC:[1]			
Total households	27	23	22
United States[2]	19	19	18

NA = Not available.
[1]Includes tobacco.
[2]Per capita food expenditures divided by per capita disposable income.
SOURCES: Statistical yearbooks of the respective countries.

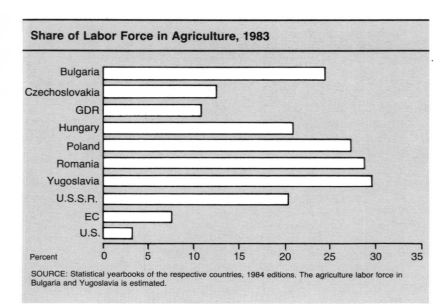

Share of Labor Force in Agriculture, 1983

SOURCE: Statistical yearbooks of the respective countries, 1984 editions. The agriculture labor force in Bulgaria and Yugoslavia is estimated.

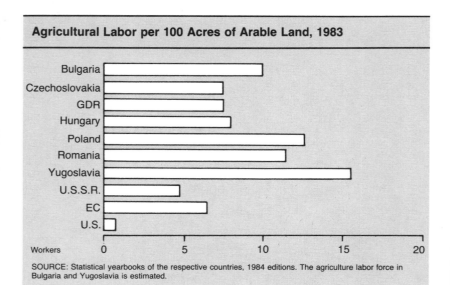

Agricultural Labor per 100 Acres of Arable Land, 1983

SOURCE: Statistical yearbooks of the respective countries, 1984 editions. The agriculture labor force in Bulgaria and Yugoslavia is estimated.

TASS

consumption. In Eastern Europe, large feed imports allowed the livestock sector to expand during the late 1970's. Although little corresponding growth occurred in the U.S.S.R's livestock sector, grain imports for food and feed were nonetheless substantial, and the already large meat imports increased greatly.

Between 1975 and 1980, the value of agricultural imports increased 71 percent for Eastern Europe and 88 percent for the

Although producing a significant share of the world's wheat and grains, the U.S.S.R. continues to import food and feed grains. (U.S.S.R., collective grain farm.)

U.S.S.R. The increases in Eastern Europe were largest in Poland, Romania, and Yugoslavia. Total imports also rose, leaving agriculture's share unchanged, 12 percent for Eastern Europe and 23–24 percent in the U.S.S.R.

Increased purchases of grain and oilseeds, and oilseed meal accounted for the higher farm

Agricultural Trade

	Bulgaria	Czechoslovakia	GDR	Hungary	Poland	Romania	Yugoslavia	Eastern Europe	U.S.S.R.
				Million dollars					
Exports									
1975	840	383	267	1,398	917	862	482	5,149	2,427
1980	1,436	688	554	1,990	1,107	1,374	1,074	8,223	2,712
1983	1,241	540	374	2,032	801	830	1,114	6,932	2,302
Imports									
1975	539	1,304	1,552	809	1,585	694	769	7,252	9,146
1980	616	2,093	2,484	1,100	3,098	1,393	1,641	12,425	17,232
1983	712	1,775	2,066	790	1,334	889	1,117	8,683	17,732
Balance									
1975	301	−921	−1,285	589	−668	168	−287	−2,103	−6,719
1980	820	−1,405	−1,930	890	−1,991	−19	−567	−4,202	−14,520
1983	529	−1,235	−1,692	1,242	−533	−59	−3	−1,751	−15,430

SOURCE: Statistical yearbooks of the respective countries, various editions.

Imports of Selected Agricultural Commodities

	Bulgaria	Czechoslovakia	GDR	Hungary	Poland	Romania	Yugoslavia	Eastern Europe	U.S.S.R.
				1,000 metric tons					
Grain									
1975	659	970	3,422	189	4,025	1,230	22	10,508	15,909
1980	692	1,980	4,465	153	7,811	2,277	1,417	18,795	27,913
1983	204	779	3,770	85	3,339	(1,196)	406	(9,778)	33,949
Oilseeds									
1975	1	132	112	1	125	20	4	395	424
1980	6	91	84	15	279	(273)	233	(981)	1,155
1983	—	(90)	63	10	192	(333)	303	(991)	1,422
Oilseed Meal									
1975	218	616	875	505	948	273	150	3,585	NA
1980	184	753	943	620	1,361	385	148	4,394	NA
1983	272	701	1,167	836	446	(185)	188	(3,795)	2,411
Meat and Meat Products									
1975	19	32	23	12	16	3	8	113	515
1980	5	31	31	16	52	90	70	295	821
1983	6	27	112	17	58	21	48	289	985

NA = Not applicable. ( ) = Estimate. — = No information reported or amount less than 1,000 tons.
SOURCE: Statistical yearbooks of the respective countries, various editions.

imports. Eastern Europe's grain imports went from 10.5 to 18.8 million tons between 1975 and 1980, and Soviet imports rose 75 percent to 27.9 million tons. Imports of oilseeds—the raw material for vegetable oil and high protein meal—more than doubled for Eastern Europe and nearly tripled for the U.S.S.R. Soviet imports of meat jumped 59 percent. Although Eastern Europe's purchases more than doubled, the region remained a substantial net meat exporter.

The United States benefited greatly from the import surge. The U.S. share of the grain, oilseed, and oilseed meal import markets increased in all countries. The U.S. share in the Soviet market, however, fell in 1980 after rising steadily because of the U.S. sales suspension.

The rise in farm imports took place within a larger East European and Soviet expansion of trade ties with the West. Improved East-West political relations, regional efforts to improve economic performance and living standards, and ample foreign credit underlay the expansion. The availability of credit was particularly important for Eastern Europe. By 1981, net foreign debt was

U.S. Market Share of Selected Agricultural Imports, Eastern Europe and U.S.S.R.

	Eastern Europe	U.S.S.R.
Grain		
1975	44	46
1979	NA	66
1980	55	21
1983	17	22
Oilseeds		
1975	36	0
1979	NA	100
1980	75	15
1983	73	40
Oilseed meal		
1975	30	0
1979	NA	39
1980	39	0
1983	20	0

NA = Not applicable. Data for 1979 are used for the U.S.S.R. because U.S.–U.S.S.R. trade in 1980 was constrained by the U.S. Sales Suspension (commonly referred to as the grain embargo).

SOURCE: Statistical yearbooks of the respective countries, various editions; Bureau of the Census, U.S. Dept. of Commerce.

Net Hard Currency Debt

Country	1981	1984
	Billion dollars	
Bulgaria	2.2	.9
Czechoslovakia	3.4	2.5
GDR	12.3	7.7
Hungary	7.0	6.1
Poland	24.7	26.8
Romania	9.8	6.8
Yugoslavia	16.3	17.0
U.S.S.R.	12.5	10.9
Total	88.2	78.7

SOURCE: Eastern Europe Outlook and Situation Report, USDA/ERS, June 1985.

$88.2 billion, $75.7 billion of that owed by Eastern Europe.

1980's East European Agriculture

The extensive foreign borrowing of the 1970's proved unsustainable, however, and the major borrowers—Poland, Romania, and Yugoslavia—became unable to service their mounting debt. The social and political unrest in Poland surrounding the Solidarity Union and martial law periods also contributed to the near elimination of new credits for the whole region. Agriculture suffered and major changes in farm management, consumption, and trade resulted. Officials slashed imports, investment, and consumption and called on agriculture to produce more food with less inputs and financial help. Farm policy is now dominated by a minimal reliance on imports and a greater reliance on expanded domestic output.

Management Style Changes.

All countries increased producer prices in an effort to raise production by improving farm profitability. Moreover, several countries have either made or continue to make changes in the Soviet style of

agricultural management which predominates in all but two of the countries. The most extensive changes are occurring in Hungary, Bulgaria, and the GDR where local farm organizations are being given a greater voice in decision-making.

All countries also are searching for new sources of inputs beyond traditional channels of central government allocation. This is largely responsible for the more favorable treatment of private producers in most countries. In so doing, officials hope to increase food output without having to spend more in the socialized farm sector. Current policies call for more emphasis on small-scale machinery, better access to grazing land on state and collective farms, favorable credit, and allocations of needed chemical and mechanical supplies previously reserved for the socialized sector.

Socialized agriculture is not being abandoned, however. The private sector maintains an uneasy presence, and all officials in countries where socialized agriculture predominates are strongly committed to the status quo. Even in Poland, where the dominant private sector has specific constitu-

TASS

tional protections, policy still calls for the socialization of agriculture.

Food Prices Increase. Retail food prices also have been raised to control demand and consumption. Prices have gone up almost annually and substantially since 1980 except in the GDR. They went up approximately 35 percent in Romania, over 100 percent in Poland in late 1981 and early 1982, and 54 percent in Yugoslavia in 1983. Only the GDR, bolstered in part by its special economic and trade links with the Federal Republic of Germany, remains unwilling to increase prices despite rising production costs.

Retail food prices have been raised to control demand and consumption. Prices have gone up almost annually. (Moscow, supermarket shopping.)

Consumption Suffers. Improvements in food consumption have suffered with the economic retrenchment. Meat consumption has either fallen or stabilized everywhere from the 1980 and 1981 peaks. A severe economic downturn since 1981 in Poland has forced meat rationing and left consumption 21 percent below the 1980 high point. Romanian citizens also face rationing, and consumption will barely rise soon in other countries.

Imports Down. Agricultural imports have plummeted with

the credit crunch. The absence of credit reduced Eastern Europe from a $12.4 billion import market in 1980 to an $8.7 billion market in 1983. Agriculture's share of all imports for Eastern Europe fell from 12 to 9 percent between 1980 and 1983. Grain imports dropped to 9.8 million tons in 1983, approximately one half of 1980's purchases. Oilseed meal imports also declined, although not as steeply.

Planners have adjusted livestock inventories downward to match better the domestic feed base and have targeted the crop sector for higher output. Many countries are now unwilling to return to extensive feed imports even if financially possible.

Exports from the United States have suffered accordingly. An export market worth $2.3 billion in 1980—exceeding that of all Africa and slightly smaller than the South American market—dropped to $757 million in 1984. The value of two major U.S. export items, grain, and soybean cake and meal, fell 85 and 56 percent respectively, accounting for much of the decline.

The successes of the East European governments in adjusting consumer expectations and revitalizing domestic agricultural production make it unlikely that these countries as a whole will again become large net importers of agricultural commodities any time soon. Despite recent signs of improvement in the last couple of years in their economic situations, the current level of foreign debt remains a tremendous burden, and priority for hard-currency imports has shifted to industrial items.

1980's Soviet Agriculture

Returns on investment declined and costs of production grew strongly in Soviet agriculture in the 1970's, paralleling the experience of most East European countries. The ability of the U.S.S.R. to earn hard currency primarily from oil exports, however, meant that as agricultural imports increased, dependence on foreign credit did not. The U.S.S.R. is not faced with the immediate credit crisis that overhangs Eastern Europe, but a longer term problem of declining do-

The Druzhba oil pipeline, through which the U.S.S.R. exports petroleum to Western Europe, is an important means of earning hard currency to import agricultural products.

TASS

mestic agricultural performance. As a result, Soviet consumers have not had to
sacrifice to the extent of those
in Eastern Europe. Rather than
contracting, Soviet agricultural
imports were at record large
levels in 1981–85. At the same
time, the promise of stable retail food prices has not been
abandoned. To keep this promise, though, the cost of retail
price subsidies roughly has
doubled since 1980 and exceeds $70 billion a year.

Reforms Needed. Even with
these moves to maintain price
and supply conditions in Soviet
food markets, the need for reform in the agricultural sector
has been clearly recognized.
The Soviet Food Program, a
major document on agricultural policy, was announced in
May 1982 and extends to 1990.
It calls for an upturn in agricultural production growth
rates at the same time that the
growth in agricultural investment resources is slowing no-
ticeably. This is to be achieved
through greater local control in
economic decisionmaking,
more direct ties between
worker performance and pay,
large farm price increases for
unprofitable or barely profitable
farms, and better coordination
of farm activity with service,

input, and food purchasing and
processing organizations.

Although most of these ideas
make sense, the Food Program
fails to take serious enough
steps to insure their realization.
Instead, traditional policies of
centralized decisionmaking and
equalization of economic results remain virtually intact. In
fact, the increase in purchase
prices for poorly performing
farms, though improving the
ability of these farms to cover
their own expenses at least in
the short run, would seem to
act as a disincentive for improved productivity by again
cutting the tie between economic performance and
returns.

Imports Continue. The
U.S.S.R. will remain a major
net agricultural importer for
the rest of the decade. Its recent policy adjustments are not
likely to improve significantly
domestic agricultural performance. At the same time, the
Food Program emphasis is on
increased meat consumption,
which should result in further
growth in feed demand. Soviet
grain imports in some recent
years have reflected poor
weather conditions. Assuming
more normal weather in coming years, grain imports may
not be as high.

Agriculture in Asia and the Pacific

By Carmen O. Nohre, *chief, Asia Branch, International Economics Division, Economic Research Service*

When Americans think of Asian agriculture, rice paddies usually come to mind. Rice does remain Asia's dominant crop, but farmers on that vast continent have diversified their crop production considerably in recent decades. Livestock production has become increasingly important, particularly in East Asia. Such changes have been encouraged as growing real incomes have allowed consumers in most countries to expand and diversify their diets.

Australia and New Zealand have ranked among the advanced countries of the world for many years and have modern agricultural sectors. Their economic and agricultural evolution has been quite different from that of their Asian neighbors.

Economic Growth Since World War II

At the end of World War II, most countries in Asia were mired in poverty. Since then, several have achieved phenomenal economic progress, while many others have made impressive gains. Incomes remain low in some countries, including several of the largest, but even most of these have significantly improved. The world-

FAO

Rice is Asia's dominant crop. In Thailand rice seedlings are bundled together and carried to the rice fields for planting.

wide recession in the early eighties caused some slowdown, but, with few exceptions, Asian countries maintained higher growth rates than other countries in the world, both developed and developing.

Economic growth has been accompanied by changes in consumption, production, and trade in agricultural products. Increasing affluence has permitted consumers to increase their food consumption and to upgrade their diets to include more preferred foods. With over 60 percent of the world's population, Asia (excluding the Middle East and Soviet Asia) has long been recognized as having vast potential for increased food consumption. Economic growth has begun to unleash that potential. As food demand has increased, farmers have found expanding markets for their products and have gradually shifted from subsistence agriculture to production for commercial markets. Since

World War II, agricultural production has kept pace with population growth. Agriculture is an important sector in almost all Asian economies, in some dominant.

Agricultural production growth in Asia has compared favorably with that elsewhere in the world. Part of this increased production has been exported. Many countries that have increased their agricultural exports have also imported more of other farm products as well. In other countries, particularly in East Asia, consumer demand has outpaced production, leading to increased imports of food and other agricultural products. Asia's role in world agricultural trade has gradually expanded.

U.S. farm exports have gained a substantial share of the growing Asian market during the last three decades. Asian countries have purchased between 30 and 35 percent of total U.S. agricultural

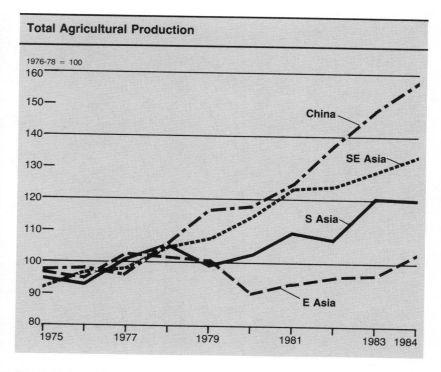

Total Agricultural Production

1976-78 = 100

Selected Indicators for Asian and Pacific Countries[1]

	Population 1984 Mid-Year	Gross Domestic Product (GDP) Per Capita 1984	GDP Growth Rate 1975–84	Ag. Prod. Index 1984 (1976–78=100)	U.S. Ag. Exports 1984 Calendar Year
	Million	Dollars	Percent		Million dollars
China	1,030.5	350	7.3	158	613
East Asia					
Hong Kong	5.6	5,550	12.4	NA	411
Japan	119.6	9,651	4.4	100	6,782
North Korea	19.6	923	NA	NA	—
South Korea	40.6	1,998	6.4	118	1,650
Taiwan	18.8	3,003	8.0	108	1,458
Southeast Asia					
Brunei	0.2	NA	NA	NA	2
Burma	38.7	166	6.0	148	—
Indonesia	162.2	518	6.7	150	395
Kampuchea	6.1	NA	NA	NA	1
Laos	4.1	184	NA	NA	—
Malaysia	15.2	2,089	7.4	135	123
Philippines	53.4	601	4.0	108	318
Singapore	2.5	7,242	9.1	NA	145
Thailand	50.5	831	6.6	132	164
Vietnam	58.3	272	NA	126	—

Selected Indicators for Asian and Pacific Countries[1]

	Population 1984 Mid-Year	Gross Domestic Product (GDP) Per Capita 1984	GDP Growth Rate 1975–84	Ag. Prod. Index 1984 (1976–78 = 100)	U.S. Ag. Exports 1984 Calendar Year
	Million	Dollars	Percent		Million dollars
South Asia					
Afghanistan	14.2	NA	NA	84	—
Bangladesh	95.9	130	4.2	114	229
Bhutan	1.1	116	NA	NA	—
India	733.3	258	3.5	122	264
Nepal	16.2	139	2.9	119	1
Pakistan	94.1	317	6.2	129	310
Sri Lanka	15.9	378	5.6	110	53
The Pacific					
Australia	15.6	9,431	2.5	116	144
New Zealand	3.2	7,040	0.6	106	34
Papua New Guinea	3.4	NA	NA	NA	1

NA = Not available. — = Zero or less than $500,000.

[1] These indicators convey a sense of the size and variability of Asian countries in terms of population and income, economic and agricultural growth in the last decade, and importance as markets for U.S. agricultural exports.

exports in recent years. Their purchases include a variety of products, with four categories—food grains, coarse grains, soybeans, and cotton— accounting for over 70 percent of U.S. agricultural exports to Asia.

China

China's emphasis on developing heavy industry resulted in one-sided growth for most of the postwar era. This led to a

growing industrial sector but allowed only limited growth in production and consumption of consumer goods. Agricultural production dropped sharply in the late fifties, then recovered, but leveled off for about a decade before the spectacular growth following policy changes in 1978.

Priorities changed sharply in 1979. China's new economic policies favor improved living standards, greater balance be-

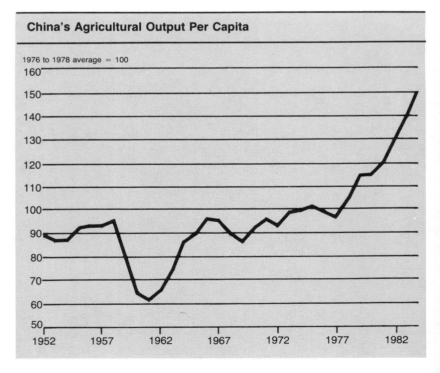

China's Agricultural Output Per Capita

1976 to 1978 average = 100

tween agriculture and industry, and greater reliance on economic incentives rather than political exhortation. These policies have given farmers the opportunity to improve their incomes in return for increased production. They have also contributed to the rejuvenation and phenomenal growth of China's agriculture.

Farm Prices and Production Up.

Farmers' prices leaped nearly 50 percent between 1978 and 1983. Moreover, the nation's collective production system has been progressively dismantled and the land parceled out to individual households, helping link each farm family's income to its production efforts. Farmers are now allowed to retain or sell production above the amounts set in annual contracts with the Government, so they can benefit directly from increased output and higher prices.

These changes are helping transform rural China. Total agricultural output has grown 54 percent since 1978, a gain of 43 percent per person. Farm production has grown steadily, with no down years since 1977. Crop output has risen 50 percent. Crop area has dropped as

Agricultural Production in China			
Commodity	1982	1983	1984
		1,000 tons	
Wheat	68,470	81,390	87,680
Rice	161,600	168,870	178,090
Corn	60,560	68,210	72,340
Cotton	3,598	4,637	6,077
Soybeans	9,030	9,760	9,700
Rapeseed	5,656	4,287	4,194
Peanuts	3,916	3,951	4,810
Tobacco	18,850	19,380	1,650[1]
Tea	397	401	411
Sugarcane	36,882	31,141	39,662
Sugar beets	6,712	9,182	8,284
Pork	12,718	13,161	14,315

[1]USDA estimate.

FAO

land has been withdrawn for other uses and as multiple cropping has declined, but yields have improved dramatically. Meat production, nearly 95 percent of it pork, has increased 78 percent since 1978. Livestock production remains low, however, despite recent growth, accounting for only 17 percent of total farm output.

Farm Incomes Doubled. As a result of these changes, average farm incomes have more than doubled since 1978. Food consumption has risen sharply, and rural diets are beginning to show greater diversity with a larger proportion of meat, eggs, and fruit. Despite recent improvement, livestock product consumption remains extremely low: in 1983, rural consumers averaged only 7 ounces of red meat and one-half ounce of poultry meat a

China's food consumption has risen sharply and rural diets are showing greater diversity with a larger proportion of meat, eggs, and fruit. Livestock product consumption remains low. (China, family dining.)

week, and only one egg every 2 weeks.

U.S. Imports Reduced. Increased Chinese agricultural production has had important effects on U.S. farmers. China's grain imports have fallen by half since 1982/83, and its corn exports have risen to about 5 million tons a year. China was the world's leading cotton importer 5 years ago, but now exports over 1 million bales annually. China has stopped importing soybeans and soybean oil and has begun exporting increasing quantities of soybeans and soybean meal. The falloff in imports has reduced U.S. agricultural exports

Agriculture Around the World

U.S. Agricultural Exports to China, 1981–84

Commodity Group	Fiscal Years			
	1981	1982	1983	1984
	Million dollars			
Animals & products	14	22	6	11
Grains & feeds	1,511	1,407	536	674
Wheat & products	1,402	1,268	285	674
Coarse grains and				
products	109	139	250	—
Oilseeds & products	176	95	—	—
Soybeans	155	95	—	—
Cotton, ex linters	481	292	3	5
Other	1	2	2	2
Total	2,184	1,819	546	692

— = none or negligible.
SOURCE: U.S. Bureau of the Census.

to China from $2.2 billion in fiscal 1981 to under $300 million during 1985. No significant near-term recovery is likely.

East Asia (Japan, South Korea, Taiwan)

The countries of East Asia have been particularly successful in modernizing. Two decades or more of sustained rapid economic growth have made this region the most highly developed in Asia. Japan, the most advanced Asian economy before World War II, resumed rapid economic growth during the fifties. South Korea and Taiwan emerged from relative stagnation in the early sixties and have grown quickly since. Much of their success is credited to growth in exports of manufactures which generated capital for investment and expanded capacity to produce further exports.

Rice Surpluses. Having suffered food shortages during and after the war, Japan, South Korea, and Taiwan strove to improve food security. All eventually adopted price and income support policies that encouraged maximum production from their limited land area. In all countries, the emphasis was on rice. Responding to high support prices, farmers increased rice production to the point where Japan began to have surpluses in the late sixties, Taiwan a few years later, and South Korea reached approximate self-sufficiency in the mid-eighties. Both Japan and Taiwan have subsidized the use of rice for feed and for export and have adopted land diversion programs to reduce the resulting surpluses.

Livestock Production Growing. Farmers have boosted livestock production rapidly in response to rising demand for

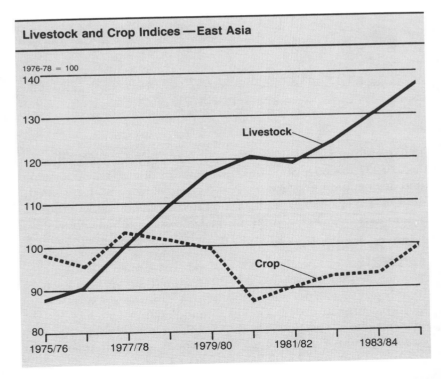

Livestock and Crop Indices — East Asia

1976-78 = 100

     Agriculture Around the World

Agricultural Production in East Asia, 1982–84

Commodity	1982	1983	1984
		1,000 tons	
JAPAN			
Rice, paddy	12,838	12,957	14,848
Pork	1,427	1,429	1,430
Vegetables	13,393	13,355	13,500
Eggs	2,057	2,085	2,111
Milk	6,750	7,036	7,140
Poultry meat	1,080	1,143	1,217
Beef and veal	481	495	535
Citrus fruit	3,625	3,624	2,726
Tobacco	139	137	135
SOUTH KOREA			
Rice, paddy	7,307	7,608	7,970
Vegetables	7,501	6,509	6,720
Beef and veal	83	90	122
Pork	238	295	340
Eggs	248	271	270
Milk	580	712	830
Chicken meat	99	120	121
Apples	527	586	528
Barley	749	815	804
TAIWAN			
Pork	525	591	700
Rice, paddy	3,360	3,369	3,042
Poultry meat	293	352	350
Vegetables	3,044	3,019	3,215
Eggs	153	210	207
Sugarcane	8,275	7,070	6,529
Citrus fruit	391	379	355
Tea	24	24	24

meat, eggs, and milk generated by increased affluence and dynamic economic growth. Currently livestock accounts for 25 percent of gross farm production in Japan, 23 percent in South Korea, and over 20 percent in Taiwan. Rapid growth has occurred in hog and poultry production by the establishment of larger, more modern production units using concentrate feed. Japanese and Korean consumers prefer beef, but limited pastureland severely restricts cattle production in both countries. Import restrictions keep beef supplies low and prices high. None of the countries has an arable land base adequate to produce the feedstuffs to meet the expanded requirements of its growing livestock inventories, so imports of coarse grains and soybeans have risen to high levels. The United States is the major supplier. These commod-

U.S. Agricultural Exports to Middle-Income East Asia, 1981–84

Commodity group	Fiscal years			
	1981	1982	1983	1984
	Million dollars			
Animals & products	326	343	409	543
Grains & preparations	1,731	1,262	1,455	1,384
Wheat & products	504	447	425	425
Rice	506	83	61	0
Coarse grains and products	697	689	925	909
Fruits & preparations	167	138	151	151
Oilseeds & products	485	461	549	697
Protein meal	4	15	17	15
Soybeans	465	423	506	629
Tobacco	81	82	61	82
Cotton, ex linters	665	732	522	674
Other	174	158	151	141
Total	3,629	3,176	3,294	3,632

SOURCE: U.S. Bureau of the Census.

品質を誇るアメリカ食品

US

U.S. QUALITY FOODS

USDA

ities, along with wheat and cotton, are the leading U.S. agricultural exports to the region.

Large Market for U.S. Sustained vigorous economic performance and the resulting growth in demand, combined with production limitations imposed by serious land constraints, (crop production declined somewhat since the late seventies, as scarce land was diverted to nonfarm use) have made East Asia a multibillion dollar market for U.S. agricultural products. In particular,

The East Asian countries are the most highly developed in Asia, and Japan has been America's largest agricultural foreign market for many years. (Tokyo, U.S. food fair.)

Japan has been American agriculture's largest foreign market for many years, with average annual sales of over $6 billion since 1980. South Korea and Taiwan also purchase more than a billion dollars in U.S. farm products annually. In 1984, U.S. agricultural exports to East Asia exceeded those to all of Western Europe.

Asia & the Pacific

U.S. Agricultural Exports to Japan, 1981–84

Commodity group	Fiscal years			
	1981	1982	1983	1984
	Million dollars			
Animals & products	900	856	890	971
Beef	149	209	271	308
Pork	158	117	110	84
Poultry meat	81	68	90	87
Inedible tallow	42	35	25	23
Grains & feeds	3,082	2,286	2,436	3,094
Wheat & products	635	564	579	557
Coarse grains and products	2,437	1,583	1,700	2,343
Feeds & folders	129	127	143	181
Fruits & preparations	282	268	291	289
Nuts & preparations	53	57	59	72
Vegetables & preparations	146	175	128	142
Oilseeds & products	1,319	1,153	1,193	1,348
Soybeans	1,211	1,063	1,127	1,282
Vegetable oils	45	58	39	42
Tobacco	237	290	314	312
Cotton, ex linters	477	534	462	590
Other	114	116	116	117
Total	6,739	5,735	5,888	6,935

SOURCE: U.S. Bureau of the Census.

Southeast Asia (Brunei, Burma, Indonesia, Malaysia, the Philippines, Singapore, and Thailand)

Most of these nations are rich in agricultural resources and are net exporters of farm products. Except for Singapore, however, they have not enjoyed exceptional economic growth like East Asia, but their economic progress has been more rapid than in most other world regions.

While Indonesia, and to a lesser extent Malaysia, benefited from expanding oil revenues in the seventies, and while Singapore specialized in trade and services, the region's agricultural sectors have provided a major impetus to economic growth. Prospects are good for continued economic expansion, although the Philippines' serious debt problem clouds its economic future. Six nations—Indonesia, Thailand, Malaysia, Singapore, the Philippines, and Brunei—are members of the Association of Southeast Asian Nations (ASEAN), working jointly to accelerate economic cooperation and development.

Rice Dominant. As elsewhere in Asia, rice is the dominant crop and the principal food grain, with Thailand the world's leading rice exporter. Burma, an early rice exporter, disappeared from the export scene in the late sixties but has reemerged after adopting policies stimulating production. The Philippines became a rice exporter in the seventies, but bad weather, inappropriate policies, and economic problems have reduced production in recent years, leading to imports. Indonesia was on occasion in the seventies the world's leading rice importer. Crop intensification programs have stimulated Indonesia's production of rice and other food crops with such success that agricultural production has increased 50 percent since 1976–78. In 1985 Indonesia was exporting rice. Only Malaysia appeared content to grow less rice than it consumed.

Corn. Thailand exports large amounts of corn, and uses growing quantities as feed for its expanding livestock sector. Corn is used mainly for food in Indonesia and the Philippines, but use as livestock feed is growing there as well.

Wheat Imports. Wheat is not grown in Southeast Asia. U.S. food aid to many of the countries in past years made

Agricultural Production in Southeast Asia, 1982–84

Commodity	1982	1983	1984
	1,000 tons		
BURMA			
Rice (milled)	8,984	9,000	9,250
Peanuts	550	531	667
Sesame	198	207	231
Pulses	491	600	665
Vegetables	1,150	1,150	1,150
INDONESIA			
Rice (milled)	22,837	24,006	25,825
Cassava	12,988	11,651	14,700
Sugarcane	21,794	24,531	26,500
Rubber	963	899	1,230
Copra	1,711	1,607	1,731
Palm Oil	884	983	1,055
Coffee	273	308	318
MALAYSIA			
Rubber	1,517	1,562	1,580
Palm oil	3,512	3,015	3,712
Meat, eggs, milk	387	399	409
Rice (milled)	1,199	1,171	1,130
Bananas, pineapples	623	658	660
Palm kernels	911	830	1,047
PHILLIPINES			
Rice (milled)	5,025	5,097	5,183
Copra	2,080	2,015	1,337
Sugarcane	24,213	25,384	17,360
Pork	457	500	460
Corn	3,126	3,346	3,373
Pineapple	889	800	869
THAILAND			
Rice (milled)	11,139	12,931	12,045
Cassava	17,788	19,000	20,000
Rubber	576	594	650
Sugarcane	24,400	23,900	23,100
Corn	3,450	4,000	4,500
Tobacco	86	86	86

wheat available, however, and consumers readily accepted it as adding welcome variety to their diets. Wheat consumption has leveled off, but wheat remains a significant import commodity.

Other Crops. Several countries produce cash crops for export. Malaysia, long the world's top exporter of rubber, boosted palm oil production in the last two decades and now leads in its export, holding more than a 70-percent share of the world palm oil market. Indonesia is a leading producer and exporter of rubber, palm oil, and spices, and grows large amounts of coffee and tea. Thailand and the Philippines export sugar and pineapple products, and the Philippines is a leading exporter of coconut products and bananas. Thailand also produces significant quantities of palm oil.

Livestock Production. Most ASEAN countries have the beginnings of a modern poultry sector. Thailand has progressed the farthest and exports poultry meat. The Philippines, Indonesia, and Malaysia have made more modest starts. All import soybeans or soybean meal for poultry feed and, except for Thailand, varying amounts of

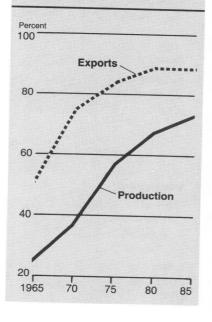

Southeast Asia: Share of World Production and Exports of Palm Oil

corn. Hog production has developed more slowly but will probably grow along with poultry as meat demand increases with rising incomes.

U.S. Sales. U.S. agricultural exports to Southeast Asia have held at about $1.2 billion annually in recent years. Wheat, cotton, oilseeds, and tobacco are the major commodities sold to the region. The availability of corn from Thailand has limited sales of U.S. feed grains.

U.S. Agricultural Exports to Southeast Asia, 1981–84

Commodity group	Fiscal years			
	1981	1982	1983	1984
	Million dollars			
Animals & products	62	73	73	75
Grains & preparations	529	417	466	433
Wheat & products	374	339	354	342
Rice	64	7	21	29
Coarse grains & products	66	48	68	39
Fruits & preparations	53	57	63	60
Vegetables & preparations	23	27	29	22
Oilseeds & products	129	190	195	215
Protein meal	2	34	27	88
Soybeans	103	139	146	93
Oil & waxes	29	16	27	35
Tobacco	116	176	116	108
Cotton, ex linters	209	195	191	235
Other	73	72	66	62
Total	1,193	1,207	1,199	1,210

SOURCE: U.S. Bureau of the Census.

Currently, China is also a strong competitor in soybeans and corn.

South Asia (Bangladesh, India, Pakistan, Nepal, and Sri Lanka)

Agriculture in South Asia depends heavily on favorable monsoons. Expanded irrigation systems, better crop varieties, and improved food grain storage and distribution programs have improved the region's ability to cope with bad crop years. While many South Asians still live on substandard diets, gains in grain production over the last two decades have brought the region to near self-

Agriculture Around the World

FAO

sufficiency in food grains, in sharp contrast to the occasional huge food grain deficits of the past. Policies supporting agriculture have stimulated fuller use of resources leading to solid growth in agricultural production. Moreover, the region's abundant soil and water resources give it vast potential for further production increases.

South Asia remains a region with low per capita incomes, but economic progress in the last decade has improved the situation substantially. All countries in the region use subsidized food distribution

After years of grain shortages India now produces sufficient grain to feed itself. Only during weather-induced production shortfalls is grain imported. (India, sun drying rice.)

schemes to assist lower income groups.

Rice and Other Grains. Rice is the major food grain except in Pakistan, where wheat production is three to four times that of rice. Pakistan generally consumes all its wheat domestically, while exporting one-fourth to one-third of its rice production. Wheat has become increasingly important in India and to a lesser extent in Bangladesh, contributing a substantial share of the overall growth in domestic food grain supplies. Rice is practically the sole food grain produced in Sri Lanka, although wheat is imported. Millet, sorghum, and corn are primarily grown for food in In-

dia, Pakistan and Nepal. Demand for coarse grains as livestock feed in the region is limited.

Grain is now imported by India and Pakistan only to cope with periodic weather-induced production shortfalls. Bangla-

Agricultural Production in South Asia, 1982–85

Commodity	1982–83	1983–84	1984–85 Estimate
		1,000 tons	
BANGLADESH			
Rice	14,216	14,500	14,500
Wheat	1,095	1,198	1,460
Jute	872	932	817
Sugarcane	7,242	6,960	6,700
Tea	41	41	44
INDIA			
Rice	47,116	59,769	59,500
Wheat	42,794	45,148	45,000
Coarse grains	27,752	33,973	31,500
Pulses	11,857	12,655	12,200
Peanuts	5,282	7,284	6,500
Rapeseed	2,207	2,566	2,900
Cottonseed	2,700	2,692	2,758
Other oilseeds	2,430	2,857	3,068
Cotton	7,004	6,086	7,000
Sugarcane	189,506	177,020	165,000
Tea	586	635	650

desh and Sri Lanka still depend on imports, mostly wheat, for a significant share of consumption needs, but their food deficits are shrinking because of steady gains in rice production.

Edible Oil. India is the world's number one importer of edible oil, while Pakistan is consistently among the top five. Both have recently begun to encourage domestic oilseed production, following many years in which policies and resources were focused on expanding food grain production.

Agricultural production in South Asia, 1982–85

Commodity	1982–83	1983–84	1984–85 Estimate
		1,000 tons	
NEPAL			
Rice	1,220	1,836	1,798
Wheat	660	632	540
Coarse grains	864	899	889
Jute	39	25	25
Potatoes	375	376	385
Sugarcane	616	594	610
PAKISTAN			
Wheat	12,414	10,936	11,000
Rice	3,445	3,336	3,458
Coarse grains	1,619	1,637	1,690
Cottonseed	1,648	1,021	2,014
Rape & mustard seed	246	217	210
Chickpea	286	499	522
Cotton	3,750	2,188	4,500
Sugarcane	32,533	34,287	32,958
SRI LANKA			
Rice	1,466	1,688	1,640
Cassava	450	450	450
Copra	174	138	62
Tea	188	179	208
Rubber	125	140	143

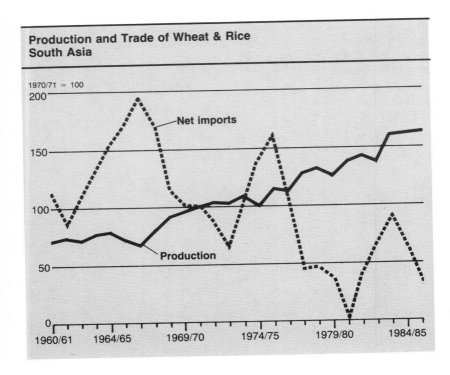

Production and Trade of Wheat & Rice South Asia

1970/71 = 100

Net imports

Production

1960/61   1964/65   1969/70   1974/75   1979/80   1984/85

Pakistan is a major cotton producer and exporter, and cottonseed oil is its principal domestic vegetable oil. Peanut and rapeseed oil, along with cottonseed oil, are India's most important edible oils. Production of nontraditional oilseeds such as soybean and sunflower is expanding in Pakistan and India. Soybean and palm oil make up the bulk of the edible oil imports.

U.S. Sales. Wheat and soybean oil are the main U.S. farm commodities sold to South Asia. Annual wheat exports to India, now almost entirely on commercial terms, vary from negligible amounts to several million tons depending on Indian production and stocks. Bangladesh and Sri Lanka are consistent but variable importers of U.S. wheat, mostly under food aid programs. U.S. soybean oil sales to the region fluctuate considerably depending on prices relative to Brazilian soybean oil and Malaysian

U.S. Agricultural Exports to South Asia, 1981–84

Commodity Group	Fiscal Years			
	1981	1982	1983	1984
	Million dollars			
Animals & products	66	62	63	75
Nonfat dry milk	5	4	7	21
Inedible tallow	55	52	51	49
Grains & feeds	312	421	899	387
Wheat & products	290	386	863	341
Rice	—	15	18	18
Nuts & vegetables[1]	10	10	10	12
Oilseeds & products	155	185	172	293
Vegetable oils	155	185	170	292
Cotton, ex linters	11	26	20	94
Other	44	7	6	6
Total	598	711	1,170	867

— = none or negligible. [1] Primarily almonds and pulses.
SOURCE: U.S. Bureau of the Census.

palm oil. Bangladesh usually purchases some U.S. cotton.

The Pacific (Australia, New Zealand, and Pacific Island Nations)

Australia and New Zealand are among the world's major exporters of agricultural products. With their sparse populations and abundant land resources, they are efficient, low-cost producers in extensive agriculture—beef and dairy cattle, sheep, and grains. Australia is also a leading exporter of cotton and sugar, and New Zealand is rapidly expanding its foreign sales of fruits and vegetables. Both countries are self-sufficient in temperate-zone farm products, and their agricultural imports are confined to tropical products, vegetable oils, tobacco, and items meeting specific consumer preferences.

Cattle and Sheep. Beef cattle in Australia and New Zealand

Australian News Bureau

Australia and New Zealand together raise one-fifth of the world's sheep. (An auction in New South Wales, Australia.)

are raised on pastures, mainly fertilized or improved, rather than in feedlots as in the United States. Cattle herds have declined since the mid-1970's because of periodic droughts and poor profitability to farmers relative to sheep and crops. Still, the two countries account for almost half of world beef and veal exports. The dairy industry continues to have a major role in New Zealand agriculture although dairy exports have been hurt by the European Community's subsidized exports.

Australia and New Zealand together raise about one-fifth of the world's sheep. They export four-fifths of the mutton and lamb and about 85 percent of the wool traded on the world market.

Agricultural Production in the Pacific, 1982–85

Commodity	1982–83	1983–84	1984–85
	1,000 tons		
AUSTRALIA			
Wheat	8,876	21,764	18,699
Coarse grains	3,894	9,330	8,576
Fruits	2,164	2,239	2,289
Vegetables	1,837	1,905	1,933
Sugar (94 nt)	3,535	3,170	3,550
Cotton	101	141	205
Wool	702	728	773
Beef & veal	1,544	1,300	1,224
Mutton & lamb	530	437	491
Pork & poultry meat	551	542	570
Milk	5,673	6,087	6,060
NEW ZEALAND			
Wheat	324	308	300
Coarse grains	594	908	1,009
Apples	192	223	246
Kiwifruit	25	35	64
Wool	371	364	390
Beef & veal	536	461	493
Mutton & lamb	651	636	667
Milk	6,775	6,879	7,637

Wheat. Crop production has been expanding in both countries. Australia supplies about 15 percent of world wheat exports and is a major competitor of the United States in Asian markets.

Tropical Products. The Pacific Island nations have tropical climates and, for the most part, poor soils. Their agriculture is based on production of tropical products for export and small-scale food production for local use. Major exports are sugar, copra, coffee, and spices. Numerous agricultural development projects are underway on the islands, especially to improve livestock production. Several nations are becoming more self-sufficient in poultry meat and eggs, and, in some cases, red meats.

U.S. Agricultural Exports to Oceania, 1981–84

Commodity Group	Fiscal Years			
	1981	1982	1983	1984
	Million dollars			
Animals & products	27	103	36	31
Poultry meat	10	9	9	10
Butter	2	75	9	—
Grain & feed	15	20	13	18
Rice	6	10	4	7
Fruits, nuts & vegetables	56	68	70	78
Oilseeds & products	46	37	43	24
Protein meal	3	2	17	5
Soybeans	14	—	11	4
Vegetable oils	26	30	10	8
Tobacco	38	41	37	35
Other	26	25	25	30
Total	208	294	224	216

SOURCE: U.S. Bureau of the Census.

Agriculture in Latin America

By John E., Link, *leader, Situation and Outlook Section,* and David L. Peacock, *acting branch chief, Western Hemisphere Branch, International Economics Division, Economic Research Service*

Fast growth, heavy debt, rich natural resources, and great diversity . . . that's Latin America today. It has only about 8 percent of the world's population, but one of the highest population growth rates. Its population has nearly doubled since 1960, with the rate before 1970 more than 3 percent a year. Growth since then has slowed down slightly and is now about 2.4 percent. Like most of the developing world, the cities of Latin America have grown rapidly in recent decades and now contain nearly 70 percent of the region's total population.

Latin America (Mexico, Caribbean, Central America and South America) is highly diverse. The countries in the region vary with respect to their stage of development, type of agriculture, level of industrialization, per capita incomes, population growth rates, literacy and education levels. While Spanish is the most common language, more than a third of the people live where Portuguese, French, or English is the official language. Per capita income generally is higher than in many other developing regions of the world, averaging $1,674 in 1983. The range, however, is wide: from $310 in

Haiti to $6,644 in the Bahamas, $3,012 in Trinidad and Tobago and $2,732 in Venezuela. Income distribution within most countries is uneven, too.

Recent Economic Adjustments

The region has been undergoing major economic adjustments during the past few years, with one of the highest rates of gross domestic product (GDP) growth in the world during the 1960's and 1970's. The oil crises in the 1970's and the massive accumulation of international debt in the last few years, have slowed GDP growth rates significantly. Agriculture's share of GDP, for example, decreased from 16 percent in 1960 to 11 percent in 1984. Hardly a country in the region has not suffered. Since 1980 they have tried to realign foreign trade and capital flows. The results have been a drop in imports, including agricultural imports; major devaluations of local currencies; and severe reductions in public and private investment expenditures. These adjustments have increased unemployment, lowered incomes, boosted inflation and reduced purchasing power. The economic recovery in the

Inter-American Development Bank

Although deep in debt, Latin America is rich in natural resources, and agricultural production has been expanding. (Ecuador, banana harvest.)

United States and other industrialized countries is encouraging for the recovery of Latin America, although full recovery will likely take some time.

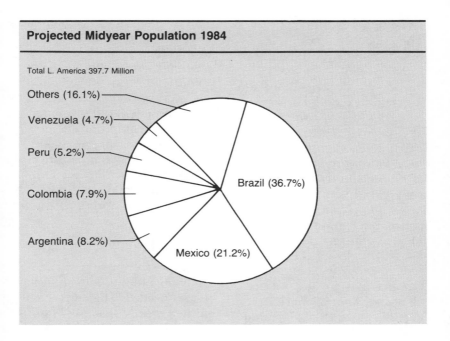

Projected Midyear Population 1984

Total L. America 397.7 Million

Others (16.1%)
Venezuela (4.7%)
Peru (5.2%)
Colombia (7.9%)
Argentina (8.2%)
Mexico (21.2%)
Brazil (36.7%)

National Goals

National economic goals and priorities for most countries of Latin America have focused on inflation, increased employment, more equitable income distribution, reduction of foreign debt, and expansion of agricultural production and exports. Agricultural goals and priorities in practically all countries are concerned with the expansion of agricultural production for both the domestic and export markets, national food self-sufficiency or import substitution, the stabilization of food prices, rural development and employment, and improving nutritional levels. Agricultural policy formulation and its implementation are almost always the responsibility of not one, but a galaxy of ministries and agencies. Unfortunately, these agencies have rarely functioned harmoniously. This working at cross purposes has often resulted in complicated, even contradictory, policies that have contributed little to efficiency and achievement of economic goals.

Resource Base

The region's natural resource base is impressive. Products of mining, lumbering, and fishing provide 35–40 percent of Latin America's exports. For some countries, one or two products of extractive industries dominate foreign exchange earnings. Petroleum and derivatives alone account for 20–30 percent. Oil exports generated about 95 percent of Venezeula's export value and two-thirds of Mexico's foreign exchange in 1984. Bauxite ore is the major foreign exchange earner for Guyana and Jamaica. Yet not all of the countries have large deposits of exploitable natural resources. Many Latin American countries are major oil importers and were hard hit by the petroleum price increases in the 1970's. To reduce its petroleum import costs, Brazil distills millions of gallons of alcohol from sugarcane each year. Over 3.7 million acres of sugarcane annually are devoted to keeping Brazil's vehicles rolling.

Land Most Valuable Resource

For many countries, farm and ranch land is their most valuable natural resource. Despite extensive urbanization, agriculture still plays an important role in most countries, providing employment and foreign exchange. About 15 percent of the world's land area is in Latin America, and it is equal in size to that of Canada and the United States combined. Cultivated land and pasture comprise about 30 percent of the region's land area and 13 percent of the world's cultivated and pasture area. Latin America has an estimated 1,736 million acres of land, based on soil surveys, that could be brought into cultivation if needed. The current cultivated area is about 437 million acres, roughly 90 percent of the U.S. crop area. Only 11 percent of this cropland is irrigated. Consequently, Latin America has only about 5 percent of the world's irrigated area.

Historically, land in Latin America has been abundant relative to population, and some countries still have land that remains unexploited. Not unlike other natural wealth,

Land in Latin America has been abundant, and some countries still have land that remains unexploited. (Nicaragua, crop dusting.)

Inter-American Development Bank

the distribution of good land varies greatly from country to country. Brazil has the greatest potential for increasing its cultivated area, both in absolute and percentage terms. Paraguay, adjoining Brazil, also has ample area to cultivate. At the other end of the spectrum, El Salvador is short of farmland given its rural population, and land is in short supply in Haiti.

Although Latin America has many large farms, farm units are generally characterized by their small size. While the number of farms has increased in Latin America since 1940, the average size has gotten smaller.

Agricultural production has been increasing since 1950, at an average annual rate of 3.3 percent. Within Latin America, Surinam and Venezuela have been the fastest growth areas, with annual output increases of more than 5 percent a year.

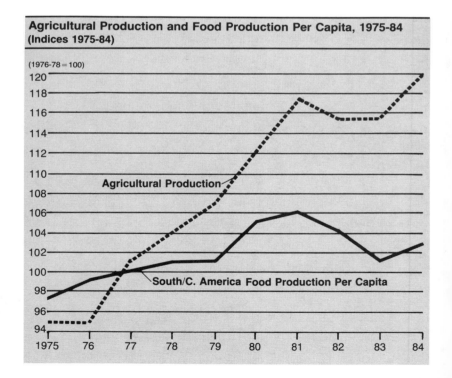

Agricultural Production and Food Production Per Capita, 1975-84 (Indices 1975-84)

Because of high population growth rates in most Latin American countries, however, per capita increases in agricultural output from 1975 to 1984 were not satisfactory, and on a regional basis, per capita output remained about constant. This, combined with improved incomes, resulted in significant increases in food imports in several countries. Mexico, as an example, was an exporter of grains in the 1960's but became a major import market for U.S. grains in the late 1970's and early 1980's.

Grains. Grains accounted for roughly one-fourth of Latin America's agricultural output in the mid-1970's, ranging from as little as 2 percent in Jamaica, and less than 10 percent in Costa Rica and Ecuador, to about 30 percent in Mexico and Argentina, and to a high of 48 percent in Haiti, the only country where grains were the major source of farm output.

Yields per acre vary broadly among Latin American countries. For example, wheat yields ranged from 55 bushels (bu) an acre in Mexico (produced mostly on irrigated land) to 25 bu/acre in Argentina compared to 39 bu/acre in the United States; corn ranged

FAO

Corn is one of Latin America's most valuable crops. It has become an important part of the diet of many people in the Andean region. (Ecuador, corn experiment.)

Latin America

from 39 bu/acre in Brazil to 47 bu/acre in Argentina compared to 81 bu/acre in the United States; and soybeans from 26 bu/acre in Argentina and in Brazil compared to 25 bu/acre in the United States.

Corn, one of Latin America's most valuable crops, was first grown in the Andean region of South America and from there it spread north. It is an important part of the diet of many people in the region and has also been an important feed for the developing poultry industry during the past decade. Production for the region in 1984 was over 52 million metric tons. This output compares with more than 100 million tons produced in the United States on about three-quarters of the area it took to produce corn in Latin America. About 5.6 million tons of corn were exported from the region, nearly all from Argentina, in 1984. At the same time, about 5.5 million tons were imported, mainly by Mexico and Venezuela. The United States supplied about 2.7 million tons of Latin American corn imports during 1984.

Wheat production in 1984 was over 20 million tons, over two-thirds of it in Argentina. Argentina exported over 8 million tons of wheat while the rest of the region imported over 11 million tons. The United States supplied over two-thirds of the imports at 7 million tons.

Livestock. Livestock production accounted for about one-third of Latin American agricultural output. It was the dominant group, however, in only six countries in the mid-1970's. Its share varied from a low of 7 and 9 percent in Guyana and Jamaica to over 50 percent in Uruguay, Venezuela and Chile.

Nongrain Food Crops. Nongrain food crops were almost as important as livestock, accounting for a little over 30 percent of the total. Nongrain food crops were the major production items in 14 of the 22 countries for which data were available. This group accounted for at least 25 percent of output in all but 7 of the 22 countries, for more than 50 percent in 5, and as much as 70 percent in Jamaica and in Trinidad and Tobago.

Malnutrition

Malnutrition is a problem in Latin America although not as severe as in the famine-plagued African Sahel or in the Indian subcontinent. At face value, and in contrast to the

Colombia Information Service

other developing regions of the world, Latin America appears to have enough food to satisfy the dietary energy requirements, of its populace. The most recent information indicates that Latin America had daily per capita food supplies of 2,634 calories, 67.2 grams of protein, and 60.4 grams of fat compared to a world average for 1979-81 of 2,624 calories, 68.5 grams of protein, and 63.4 grams of fat. Rice, beans, and potatoes are important contributors to the Latin America diet, supplying about 20 percent of the total calories, while wheat accounts for about 15 percent and corn 14 percent of total calories.

Livestock production accounts for approximately one-third of Latin America's agricultural output. (Colombia, cattle roundup.)

Exports and Imports

Most Latin American countries depend on trade, with the larger countries having smaller trade sectors—relative to population and GDP—than the smaller countries. The smaller the country, generally, the less diverse are its resources and exports, and the more extensive its imports. The region is a net exporter of minerals, fuels and fish, and a net importer of forest products.

Agricultural exports have historically been a major

FAO

source of foreign exchange earnings. Major agricultural exports include coffee, sugar, cocoa, bananas, soybeans, beef, cotton, maize, and wheat. Coffee exports come from the cooler regions of southern Brazil; the Andes mountains of Colombia, Ecuador, and Venezuela; and the mountainous regions of Central America. Central America and the Caribbean nations have been the major source of sugar exports. Cocoa is exported from Brazil and the tropical zones of Central America. Bananas are important exports of Ecuador, Colombia, and particularly Honduras in Central America. Beef and cotton exports are less concentrated. While soybean exports

Coffee is a major export commodity produced in the cooler regions of southern Brazil, Colombia, Venezuela, and Central America. (Nicaragua, inspecting coffee plants.)

come from Brazil, Argentina and Paraguay in the southern end of the hemisphere, wheat and corn exports are mostly from the temperate region of Argentina.

Major farm imports include wheat, maize, sorghum, soybeans, and soybean products as well as machinery, insecticides, pesticides, and fertilizers.

U.S. and Latin American Trade

The United States and Latin America are important trading partners. The United States traditionally has had a positive balance of total trade with the region, but, on the agricultural side, imports more than it exports. In 1984 the United States imported about $7.2 billion worth of farm goods from the region while exporting $5.3 billion. Major imports from the region are: coffee, about one-third of the total; vegetable products, 29 percent; sugar and products, 12 percent; bananas, 10 percent; animal products, 9 percent; and other, 7 percent. Brazil supplies about 28 percent of farm imports from Latin America, while Mexico and Central America each supply another 20 percent. Major U.S. farm exports to the region are: grains and feeds, 45 percent; oilseed products, 29 percent; animal products, 14 percent; and other, 12 percent. Mexico takes about 37 percent of the U.S.'s farm exports to the region while the

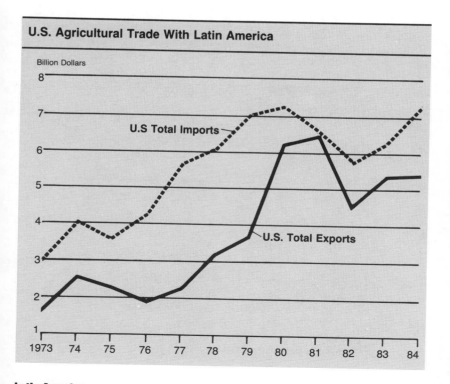

U.S. Agricultural Trade With Latin America

Billion Dollars

U.S Total Imports

U.S. Total Exports

1973 74 75 76 77 78 79 80 81 82 83 84

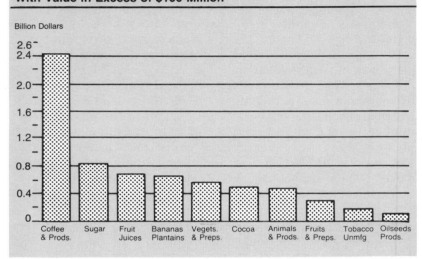

**U.S. Agricultural Imports From Latin America
With Value in Excess of $100 Million**

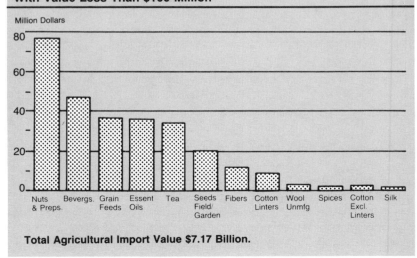

**U.S. Agricultural Imports From Latin America
With Value Less Than $100 Million**

Total Agricultural Import Value $7.17 Billion.

Caribbean takes 16 percent; Venezuela, 13 percent; Brazil, 8 percent; Central America, 7 percent; and other South America, 19 percent.

Region's Potential

The economic potential of Latin America is unquestionable considering its vast underutilized natural and human resources. A resumption of strong economic growth in the late 1980's or early 1990's is a strong possibility. Latin America has an adequate resource base, but the critical issue is resource management. The area of potentially productive land in many countries, other than Brazil, is limited. Agriculture has reached a stage where yield per acre increases are the best means to expand production. The economics of water use also has become an important issue. Still, considerable potential exists for irrigation and hydropower expansion.

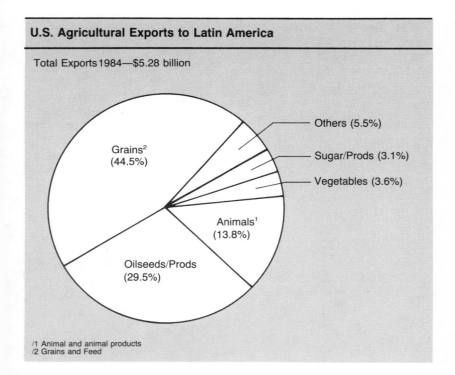

U.S. Agricultural Exports to Latin America

Total Exports 1984—$5.28 billion

- Grains[2] (44.5%)
- Others (5.5%)
- Sugar/Prods (3.1%)
- Vegetables (3.6%)
- Animals[1] (13.8%)
- Oilseeds/Prods (29.5%)

/1 Animal and animal products
/2 Grains and Feed

Agriculture in Africa and the Middle East

By Cheryl Christensen,
Michael E. Kurtzig, *and*
Arthur J. Dommen,
agricultural economists,
International Economics Division,
Economics Research Service

The Africa and Middle East region contains some of the world's richest developing countries (Middle East oil exporters) and some of its poorest (in sub-Saharan Africa).

Expanded oil revenues, and their stimulus to trade and employment within the region, made the 1970's and early 1980's a period of rapid economic growth in North Africa and the Middle East. Increased income fueled rapid increases in food imports, which led to major improvements in diets. The region's agriculture, however, hampered by lack of water, land shortages, and low productivity, declined in economic importance despite various government efforts.

For most of the poor countries in sub-Saharan Africa, the past decade was a period of economic decline and crisis. Poor agricultural performance stimulated more food imports, but diets deteriorated because countries lacked the income to import enough to offset production declines. Real per capita income fell, as the global recession, combined with inappropriate national policies, created economic crises in many countries.

North Africa and the Middle East

North Africa and the Middle East includes 21 countries with a population nearing 260 million in 1984. The region includes wealthy oil-exporting countries such as Saudi Arabia, and large agricultural producers such as Turkey. The region has been both an agricultural exporter and an importer. In recent years, driven by vast petroleum export earnings, continued high population growth and the inability of agricultural production to keep pace with increasing demand, the region's agricultural imports have risen to an estimated $31 billion, triple the level of a decade ago.

The major problem facing all these countries is the low productivity of their agricultural sectors, especially when compared with the size of the labor force engaged in farming. Despite recent injections of capital, the agricultural sector's contribution to the gross domestic product declined in the 1970's, ranging in 1981 from

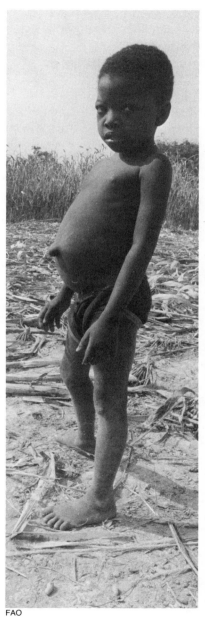

Sub-Saharan Africa continues to have serious agricultural production problems resulting from drought, war, and political instability. (A child from Ghana suffering from malnutrition stands in a grain field ruined by drought.)

FAO

Africa & the Middle East

21 percent in Egypt and Turkey to about 1 percent in Saudi Arabia.

Agriculture Limited by Water. In most countries of this region, agricultural production is dominated by traditional, small-scale farmers, who face a combination of physical, economic, and policy constraints. Rainfall is erratic and inadequate, except in Egypt where all cultivated areas are irrigated. In Saudi Arabia, Libya, Iran, and Iraq, 30–40 percent of the arable land is irrigated. In Morocco, Tunisia, Syria, and Algeria, irrigation covers less than 10 percent of the arable land.

In all these countries, the possibility of expanding the cultivated area is at best limited because the land is either exhausted or being lost to urban uses. The major production increase must come from technological innovation and varietal improvement. The region's dependence on water is paramount and most of its agriculture is rainfed. As a result, droughts are common and despite improved technology and inputs, wide production fluctuations are not unusual. Some breakthroughs have occurred over the years, such as the use of high-yielding wheat varieties

in Turkey, increased irrigated agriculture in Saudi Arabia, and intensive use of drip irrigation in Israel.

Grain Dominates. The region is a large producer of grain totaling 45 million metric tons in 1984. Wheat is by far the dominant crop at 26 million tons, with barley second at 10 million tons. Other major crops include cotton, tobacco, citrus, and many types of horticultural products such as dates, and an assortment of nuts. The region is a mutton-and lamb-eating area and possesses vast flocks of sheep and goats. Grains dominate the diet. More recently, however, efforts at increasing proteins have led to increased poultry, dairy and livestock production, with commensurate increases in feed grain and animal imports. In addition, consumption of fruits and vegetables has been encouraged.

Huge Oil Revenues Lead to Rising Expectations. Over the last decade, beginning with the 1973/74 oil price hike, export earnings from oil and other commodities soared, and the region's foreign exchange earnings rose dramatically. Higher incomes raised living standards and expectations of further improvements. The rapid increase

Africa and the Mideast

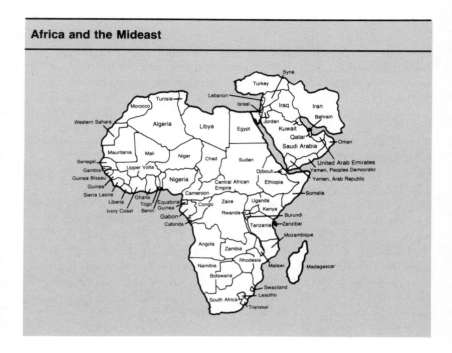

in food imports was an effective way of demonstrating economic prosperity and meeting the population's rising expectations. Furthermore, to prevent possible political unrest, import levels were even higher than required and became institutionalized in a complex subsidy system which sought to keep a price lid on basic food products, particularly in urban areas.

At the beginning of the 1980's, with the world oil glut and a commensurate decline in oil prices, the region's foreign exchange earnings plummeted from an estimated $200 billion in 1981 to $120 billion in 1984. At the same time, food imports continued to increase, although at a diminishing rate. In some countries, government efforts to reduce the budgetary burdens by reducing consumer subsidies led to food riots such as in Morocco and Tunisia in 1984.

Increasingly Dependent on Imports. Most countries of the region are net importers of food and agricultural products. Major agricultural importers include oil rich Saudi Arabia ($6 billion a year); Egypt, (approximately $4 billion, a substantial portion of which is financed under concessional terms); Iran, ($4 billion annually), and Iraq ($3 billion, a sharp increase in the U.S. share because of credit).

Imports encompass a vast variety of products. They are led by wheat and wheat flour, an estimated 27 million tons in 1984, feedgrains at 14 million tons, and rice at nearly 3 million tons. Other items include livestock and products, poultry and dairy products, fruits and vegetables, vegetable oils, pulses, and specialty items such as tobacco, tea and coffee. Within the last decade, imports of processed and semiprocessed products have become important, as incomes have risen and new products have been introduced.

In addition, a diversification of the region's suppliers has occurred. A decade ago, the United States and the European Economic Community held 45 percent of the market, but that share dropped to one-third recently. The new suppliers include recognized world exporters such as Australia and

Canada, as well as newer exporters such as Thailand, Turkey, and Argentina. In addition, a multitude of arrangements, including bilateral agreements and countertrade, have become common.

The region also has a number of agricultural exporters whose market shares have expanded in recent years. For example, Turkey's exports rose from $1.6 billion in 1978 to $2.3 billion in 1983, with a shift from raw to processed or semiprocessed commodities. While in the past cotton and tobacco led the export list, more recently, livestock has dominated. Egypt has been a substantial exporter of horticultural products, and citrus and cotton are major foreign exchange earners for Israel.

Governments Determining Agriculture Policies. The countries' governments have been active in determining agricultural policies, as well as intervening in the marketing and trading of agricultural commodities. With few exceptions, these interventions have not been successful enough to substantially improve agriculture's performance. With efforts to provide adequate food and remove the uncertainty facing farmers, governments have become involved in policy activities such as providing consumer and producer subsidies, setting commodity prices, purchasing commodities, distributing inputs at subsidized prices, and offering subsidized credit.

At the same time, intractable political problems reduce the likelihood of dramatic shifts in food production and consumption policies, so that food imports are forecast to continue to rise. To date, these countries have not experienced serious food import declines like other developing nations with serious financial problems. Since the dramatic decline in oil export revenues, however, pressures are increasing to reduce spending on development projects or to discourage new ones. As a result, foreign workers have left, and economic development has slowed. The reduced oil revenues also are having ramifications in neighboring countries whose development has been tied to foreign worker remittances or aid from the oil exporters.

With expectations already established and commitment to a system of food subsidy continuing, significant budgetary reductions are not practical and may even lead to internal backlashes, further destabilizing

some economies already in difficulty. Governments are likely to maintain per capita consumption, at least at recent levels.

For the United States, this vast region offers opportunities and challenges. The U.S. share of the $30 billion food import market was just under 12 percent in 1984, half the share of a decade ago. The region's emergence as a major food importer, its changing trade flows, and its increasing price sensitivity and responsiveness, have led to keen competition among suppliers. In the future, this will be a difficult and changing market, with market share determined by nonprice considerations such as trade arrangements, exchange rates, and credit facilities, as much as price.

Sub-Saharan Africa

Agriculture is critical to most countries in sub-Saharan Africa. Despite increasing urbanization, agriculture still employs more than 80 percent of the population in most countries and accounts for more than half of gross national product. Most employment is on small farms, using family labor to produce a variety of staple food crops, including grains such as sorghum, millet, corn, and rice, as well as root crops and pulses. Africa has large herds of cattle, especially in drier areas where pastoralism is an important livelihood. In addition, agricultural exports, such as coffee, cocoa, tea, sisal, rubber, peanuts, tobacco, and cotton, are the major source of foreign exchange for all but a handful of countries.

Disruptions to agricultural production—including not only adverse weather, but also political instability and warfare—have been frequent, reducing national income and foreign exchange. Furthermore, inappropriate policies and low investment have hampered agricultural development in much of the region, while population continues to grow unchecked.

Food-Deficit Countries. Per
capita food production in sub-Saharan Africa has declined over the past two decades. Imports quadrupled between 1966 and 1984, but were still not enough to fully offset decreased production. Many countries have less food available per person than they did a decade ago. And even under "normal" conditions, diets are inadequate.

Production shortfalls, common in many countries, now quickly translate into major food emergencies. Within the last few years, drought has struck in all the major regions of Africa (the Sahel in 1972–74, 1980, 1983–84; East Africa in 1976, 1980, 1984; Southern Africa in 1980, 1983–84) further reducing agricultural production, and in countries like Ethiopia, Mozambique, Sudan, Niger and Mali, triggering starvation despite dramatically increased food aid.

Agricultural Production Diverse. High population growth
has put pressure on traditional agricultural systems, while government policies have in many instances short-changed farmers. The continent includes three major rainfall zones, each with different agricultural systems.

The *semiarid tropical zone* includes the inland portions of West and East Africa around the Horn to Southern Africa. Production is almost entirely rainfed. The main crops are millet, sorghum, corn, peanuts, and cotton. Rainy seasons are short, and farmers cannot plant before the rains begin. Rainfall is highly variable, and poor rains not only depress yields of rainfed crops but also affect flood recession cropping (in the Sahel) and irrigated agriculture

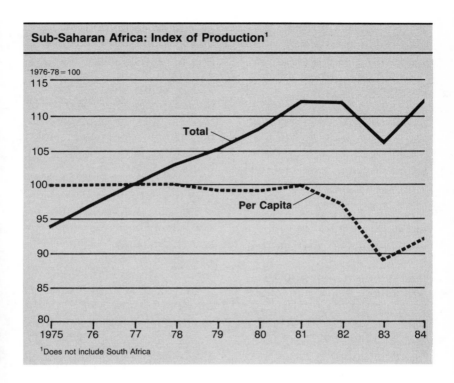

Sub-Saharan Africa: Index of Production¹

¹Does not include South Africa

(in Sudan, Mali, Zimbabwe).
Livestock production also is
subject to rainfall variability,
since pastures depend on rainfall. Soils are light, porous, and
shallow, creating moisture retention problems, leaching, and
erosion.

The *humid tropical rain forest zone* extends from Gambia
on the west through Central
Africa, to the mountains on
Zaire's borders with Uganda,
Rwanda, and Burundi on the
east. Major crops include rice,

cocoa, coffee, oil palm, rubber,
and root crops like cassava,
yams, and cocoyams. Soils are
extremely fragile once the forest cover has been removed,
and this limits potential for expanding food production.

The *highland regions* of East
and Southern Africa constitute
a zone of their own. The high-
lands of Kenya and Ethiopia
have sandy loam soils with
high organic matter content,
stable structure, and high
moisture retention capacity.

These regions are among the most productive on the continent.

Traditional Systems Under Pressure. Small farms of 7–12 acres account for most African food production, using family labor and hand tools. Zimbabwe and South Africa, however, have well-developed modern agricultural subsectors. Labor shortages often occur during critical periods such as planting, weeding, and harvesting. Rural labor shortages have been aggravated by urbanization and, in some countries, emigration. Women are often responsible for food production, while men concentrate on cash crop production or work in other countries.

Because agricultural production often occurs in physically difficult environments, with little irrigation and few modern inputs, crop yields are among the lowest in the world. Fertilizer use is low, except in South Africa and Zimbabwe's commercial subsector, Sudan's large irrigation schemes (Gezira), and to some extent in Kenya. Complex traditional cropping patterns, based on intercropping and long fallow periods, are the major means for managing soil fertility. Crops grown are, by and large, the traditional varieties cultivated in Africa for centuries. These varieties are extremely hardy, yielding a minimal harvest even under the worst conditions. On the other hand, their yields in good growing conditions are low. Few successful varieties of improved seed have been developed, with the exception of hybrid corn and a recent hybrid sorghum variety.

The degree to which these subsistence farming systems satisfy the household's basic food, fuel, and shelter needs makes conversion to another system of production extremely difficult. The traditional African systems are not monocultures, as are most modern agricultural systems, and the alternative systems may not yet be sufficiently researched to justify risking the destruction of the traditional. Nevertheless, increasing population density poses a real threat to the viability of existing systems.

Policies Unfavorable for Agriculture. Although agriculture is the main source of employment and foreign exchange in many African countries, governments have not been concerned with agriculture as part of the development process, except to extract resources from farmers when they can. They

FAO

typically intervene heavily in agriculture, setting producer prices, requiring that products be marketed through government agencies, distributing agricultural inputs, and handling the import and export of agricultural commodities. Prices paid to producers of food and cash crops have been held below market value, often in an attempt to subsidize urban consumers. As a result, black markets and unofficial trade at much higher prices are common. Inputs like fertilizer have not found their way to farmers, extension services have been inadequate, research efforts have not been focused on increasing staple food production,

A small family farm in Swaziland with little or no irrigation and few modern conveniences produces corn yields which are among the lowest in the world.

and taxation of export crops has been heavy, both directly and through overvalued currencies.

African governments are trying some policy reforms which, if implemented, should benefit agricultural production. These include raising producer prices, restructuring inefficient marketing institutions, and encouraging agricultural exports by devaluing overvalued currencies. Some governments have begun drafting and implementing national food strate-

Total Cereals Yield Comparison, 1965-83

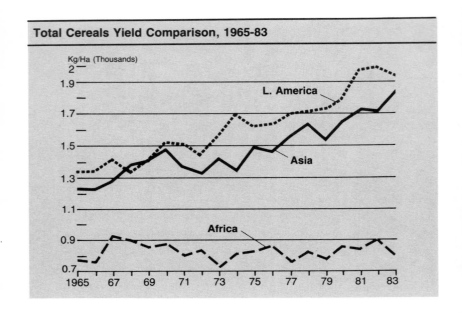

Roots and Tubers Yield Comparison, 1965-83

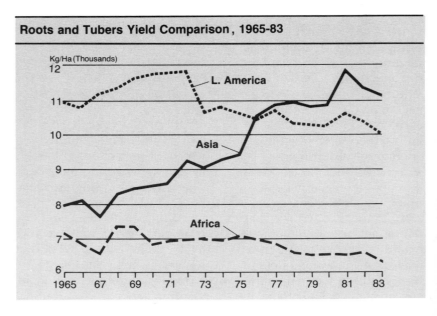

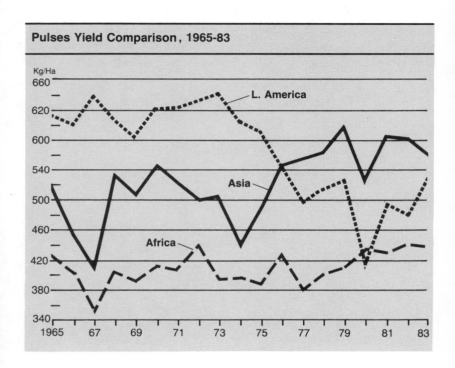

Pulses Yield Comparison, 1965-83

gies in cooperation with donor countries and international agencies. Policy reforms and improved planning for agricultural production and nutrition are important components of these programs.

More Food Imports Likely.
Despite severe foreign exchange shortages in recent years, grain imports by sub-Saharan African countries have had to increase, meaning that less money is available for investment elsewhere in the economy. Sub-Saharan Africa (excluding South Africa) imported a record 10.7 million tons of grain in 1984, 3.3 million tons, or 30 percent, as food aid. Without changes in production patterns, total grain imports by 1990 would need to rise 40 percent simply to maintain 1980–84 consumption levels. Without major improvements in foreign exchange earnings and trade prospects, food aid will continue to be crucial.

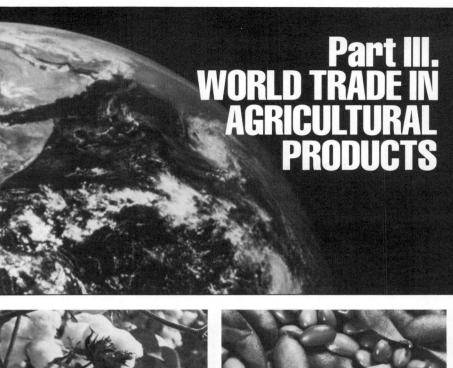

Part III.
WORLD TRADE IN AGRICULTURAL PRODUCTS

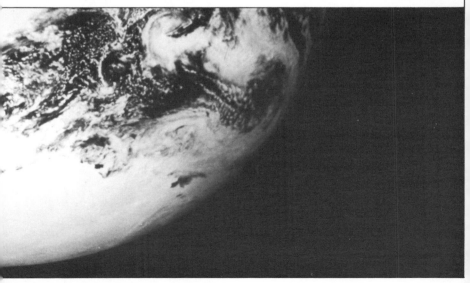

The Importers and the Exporters

By Eileen Marsar Manfredi,
grains analyst, World Agricultural Outlook Board

Global trade in agricultural products was $228 billion in 1983. Virtually all countries participated in the international exchange of grains, feedstuffs, meats, fruits, vegetables, beverages, sugar, spices and nonfood items like fiber, tobacco and rubber. World trade in food has grown in the past decade even with a steady increase in total food production. From 1975 to 1984, the rate of growth in world food production was 2.1 percent. This rate of increase in output exceeded population growth so that world food production per person also has grown. The distribution of output, however, has not been even across countries and that, plus a desire for different types of food, has spurred rapid gains in world food trade.

World Food Trade

World trade in food products expanded about 60 percent between the mid-1970's and 1983. Trade accelerated during the 1970's as a combination of income growth, policy changes encouraging consumption, and weather-related harvest declines stimulated imports in a number of countries and regions. Since 1980 the growth of world trade has slumped, and the volume of trade in some foods has actually declined.

Grains, primarily wheat, rice and corn, are a major component of food trade, accounting for roughly one-fifth of the value of total world food imports in recent years. Total grain trade rose from 110 million tons in 1970/71 to 216 million in 1980/81. Trade accounted for over one-third of the increase in global grain consumption in that period. The share of total grain consumption traded rose from 10 to 15 percent during that decade. Thus, 1 out of every 7 tons of grain used by people or animals originated in a different country from where it was consumed.

Many of the food commodities being traded are interrelated. For instance, many grains like corn, barley, sorghum, and oats are imported by countries as animal feeds. Some of the resulting meat products, beef, veal, pork, poultry, butter, cheese and milk, are then often exported to other countries. For some commodities, trade is a major share of total world production as output is concentrated in only a few countries. In contrast, for basic foods like rice and meats,

trade represents a small share of global consumption. Less than 5 percent of the world's annual rice crop leaves the country where it was grown.

Food is exchanged among most countries of the world, even by those for whom self-sufficiency is an important policy goal. Most trade in food products is carried on by the developed countries. Other groupings have emerged, however, as food imports by centrally planned economies and by the middle income developing countries have grown rapidly, especially in the last 10 years.

Food Trade Growth

International trade is the exchange of one type of good or service for another, generally through the use of currencies as payment. Trade benefits all parties by allowing each participant to specialize in producing those items for which it has a comparative advantage in exchange for other commodities that cannot be produced as efficiently domestically. Some foods cannot be grown in some countries because of soil and climate. In many countries, food is imported whenever there is an imbalance between domestic production and the level of domestic consumer demand. This imbalance may be a constant level, a growing level, or an erratic level from year to year. Weather-related fluctuations in crop production can turn an exporter into an importer, as was the case with the Republic of South Africa for corn in recent years.

Even in areas where food output is expanding, food imports may also increase for a variety of reasons, such as rapid population growth, low levels of food consumption, income growth, and a desire to vary diets. Looking at these factors a little more closely will yield some insight into changes in world trade in foods over the last decade.

Rapid Population Growth.

For the poorest countries, population growth rate may be the major factor determining food imports. If domestic production fails to grow at or above the population growth rate, proportionate food imports will be needed, even if scarce foreign exchange earnings must be diverted from other planned uses. Food production in developing African countries as a group grew by an average of 1.9 percent per year in the last decade. Population growth however, averaged 3 percent

annually. Without growing food imports, consumption per person would fall. Because of the low income levels of developing African countries, food imports tend to be concentrated into basic foods, especially grains. Over the past decade, wheat and rice imports by these countries have more than doubled.

Low Food Consumption Levels.

Continuing high growth rates in food trade in developing countries is accounted for by the generally low levels of food intake per person. For instance, to increase consumption Egypt has become a major importer of foods and is currently the third major wheat importing country in the world. Two-thirds of all daily caloric intake comes from basic grains there. Egyptian grain consumption on average now exceeds the minimum daily caloric intake recommended by the United Nation's Food and Agricultural Organization (FAO). In many countries average consumption levels fall below FAO minimums. If financing permits or international food aid is available, these countries rely on increasing food imports to raise food consumption. Tremendous pressure exists on governments in poor countries to ensure politi-

cal stability and to further social equity by increasing food imports.

Income Growth. As incomes grow in lower income countries, spending on food rises. Thus, a strong, positive relationship exists between income growth and food consumption in countries where food consumption is low. Global income growth rates, adjusted for inflation, grew by 3.5 percent a year in the 1960's and accelerated to an average annual rate of 3.7 percent in the 1970's. In the early 1980's the economic growth rate slowed. In keeping with the income growth, the value of food products traded rose sharply from 1970 to 1980.

The major areas where income growth was highest were neither the developed countries nor the poorest developing

In countries such as Taiwan, Mexico, Brazil, and South Korea, growing incomes for an expanding middle class have triggered higher food consumption levels and higher imports.

countries, but a group of middle-income newly industrializing countries. In countries such as South Korea, Taiwan, Mexico, and Brazil, growing incomes for an expanding middle class are translated directly into higher consumption levels and higher imports. Consumers in less developed countries generally tend to spend a larger share of their income on food than consumers in developed countries. As incomes rise, spending on food in middle income countries also rises, although the types of foods consumed will likely expand and the relative shares of various foods in total intake will change.

Varied Diets. A direct result of higher incomes is the ability of consumers to vary their diet and improve the range of foods consumed. The variety can include different cereals, such as wheat-based noodles in a predominantly rice-eating area, and processed products like confectionaries and preserved fruits. As policies in many countries over the past few decades have stressed industrialization and production for export, urbanization has grown. Many Third World cities have grown sharply with several such as Cairo and Mexico City becoming huge metropolitan areas. This change and higher incomes for many residents go hand in hand with dietary changes. While meat consumption per person has barely changed in the United States over the last 10 years, it has tripled in Saudi Arabia, doubled in South Korea, and risen by 50 percent in Egypt. And there is room for further growth since people in all of these countries are currently consuming less than two-fifths as much meat as the average American.

Importing Countries
Poorest Countries. While the needs of the poorest coun-

tries are large relative to available supplies, these countries as a group are not the major food importers. Large populations and large-scale malnutrition may motivate a country to increase food imports, but ability to pay is a determining factor governing the level of such imports. Hunger is related to food aid shipments, but commercial imports are constrained in the poorest countries by financial problems.

Food aid shipments in 1984/85 are estimated at 11.7 million tons or about 20 percent of total food imports in low-income, food-deficit countries. Some 69 developing countries fall into the category of countries needing food aid. If all people in these countries were eating at minimal nutritional standards this year, an additional 8 million tons would be needed as imports over and above expected food aid shipments and likely commercial imports. Most of the countries in direst need are in sub-Saharan Africa and South Asia.

Newly Industrialized Countries. In contrast to the poorest countries, the newly industrializing countries are major food import markets. A combination of factors—such as trade orientation, access to foreign exchange resources, middle income levels, and increased urbanization—have expanded imports of basic foods, feeds for the domestic livestock economies, and processed products. For example, a handful of these dynamic economies account for over 25 percent of world trade in feed grains. The demand for greater consumption of meats in middle income countries spurs increased levels of imported feeds, both grains and oilmeals, to fuel their expanding livestock numbers. As many of these countries move from backyard hog and chicken operations to commercialized feeding industries, their need for high-quality feeds increases.

In addition to expanding their output of meat domestically, many middle income countries have become important importers of meat and other processed and semiprocessed products. As internal demand, backed by economic growth, expands, imports are needed because domestic capacity is inadequate or unavailable. Saudi Arabia, for instance, is now a leading poultry importer and several other oil exporting countries are major markets for milk, butter, cheese, and fruits.

Centrally Planned Economies.

Perhaps the most important markets in the last decade and a half have been the centrally planned economies— U.S.S.R., Eastern Europe, and China. These countries have become key players in food trade because of the large volume and annual volatility of their purchases of grains, meals, meat, and dairy products. Various factors determine import levels, and conditions have differed substantially among these countries which, nevertheless, share an approach to trade based on centralized control and decision-making in contrast to more market-oriented economies. Weather, domestic production and trade policies, and income and credit problems have affected their food imports.

The **U.S.S.R.** became a major world grain buyer in the early 1970's when poor production and a policy decision to attempt to maintain domestic meat consumption with imported feeds led to large grain imports. Annual levels of imports since then have varied widely with weather. The U.S.S.R. is an important buyer accounting for about one-quarter of world grain trade in 1984/85. The Soviets have long-term grain agreements with a number of exporting countries in which they pledge to buy a minimum volume of grain each year at prevailing market prices. The U.S.S.R. is also a leading import market for butter and beef and could become a significant user of soybean meal if animal rations were to become more efficient.

Eastern European Countries as a group are important importers of food products, especially feeds. Meat consumption per person in these countries is quite high—about 70 percent of that of Americans. Both meat consumption and feed imports for their livestock however, have dropped in recent years because of financial constraints. Some East European countries, especially Poland, had to cut imports when access to borrowing and trade credits was curtailed. Debt levels are quite high, with some countries having had to attempt to reschedule debts with their creditors and set up a new time table of payments. Debt repayment is directly linked to food import levels because it reduces the hard currencies these countries have left to pay for imports after meeting some of their debt obligations. In addition, official

trade credits, which some exporting countries offer to promote sales, have been suspended. This removes the easy credit which aided rapid import growth by East European countries in the late 1970's.

China is an example of rapid change in domestic production and trade because of domestic policy changes. Favorable weather and movement towards more market-oriented agriculture have sharply raised their food and agricultural production during the 1980's. This occurred along with a few years of large food imports as official policies allowed domestic consumption of wheat and meat to surge. China is the world's largest pork producer. Yet with the world's largest population, their total meat consumption per capita is quite small. Rising income levels for peasants and urban workers alike are translated into a desire for more and different foods. Imports were needed to supplement domestic output of wheat, and in the future as meat consumption grows, the need for imported feeds is likely to rise. The immediate hurdle to be faced by a large, developing country like China is to improve internal transportation and to build more facili-

TASS

ties to provide concentrated animal feeds and efficient feeding operations to meet the latent food demand.

Developed Countries. Although developing countries will be the growth markets of the future for food imports, the major buyers today are developed countries. These countries have the income and trade infrastructure to handle a large volume of foods. In addition to their dominance in volume of food trade, developed countries import a wide variety of food products, including high-value products. Developed countries are major producers of several food products, but climatic constraints or cost efficiencies imply a large volume of imports of some commodities.

For instance, Japan imports

The centrally planned economies of the U.S.S.R., Eastern Europe, and China have been some of the most important import markets in the last decade and a half because of their volume of purchases. (Czechoslovakia, feeding breeder cattle.)

a large volume of wheat, feed grains and soybeans for consumption by its people and livestock, but the country is more than self-sufficient in rice production. Although Western European countries are exporters of wheat and barley, they import large quantities of soybeans for crushing into meal for high-protein animal feed. With soybean production more limited geographically than production of grains, trade is extremely important. For developed countries, livestock products and meat consumption play a major role in the diet, and access to meat and animal feeds is vitally important. From 1970 to the early 1980's, the volume of soybeans crushed into meal doubled, but the volume of trade in soybeans and meal almost tripled.

In addition to significant imports of bulk food commodities like grains and meals, the developed countries are the major importers of expensive and exotic foods. Western European countries and the United States import over half of the value of all high-value products, even though these countries have only one-tenth of global population. Some of these commodities are tropical, and not produced in temperate zone developed countries, some are imported seasonally, and others are specialty products which differ from those produced locally, such as French cheeses and Italian wines imported by Americans.

A direct link exists between affluence, diversifying diets, and trade. Although high-income people do not necessarily increase their level of food consumption as incomes rise, they do shift to more expensive foods. The United States is a major food importer, annually spending over $18 billion for food product imports.

Exporting Countries

The major food exporting countries are basically a handful of developed countries, with the United States the leading exporter of a number of food categories. Developing countries like Argentina, Brazil, and Thailand are major exporters of commodities like grains, feeds, tropical products, and meat, and several developing countries are leading exporters of specific commodities like tea. Exports are strongly concentrated among a few countries: five countries account for over 90 percent of total wheat exports; seven for over 90 percent of feed grains; four over 95 percent of soybeans and products; six over 80 percent of beef; and only two regions account for over 85 percent of all pork exports.

The reasons for the large volume of food exports originating in several developed countries are a combination of factors—agronomic, economic, scientific, and political. The agronomic factors include large land bases, good soils, and climatic conditions. Added to that is the large-scale use of modern technology adapted to individual farm conditions. Yields tend to be high in developed

USDA

countries because of intensive farming of the land with timely applications of fertilizers and herbicides, and controlled irrigation, as well as the use of specialized equipment for planting and harvesting. In addition, modern storage techniques and facilities minimize post-harvest losses and quality deterioration. Relative affluence among consumers in many developed countries stimulates demand for a variety of products and large trade flows of both food and nonfood items. The economic incentive to produce surpluses of food in developed countries for export to

The major food-exporting countries are a handful of developed countries with the United States being the leading exporter of a number of food categories.

meet demand in other markets is enhanced by a relatively free trade environment in most major food exporting countries. Domestic agricultural policies to provide some income safeguards for farmers in many exporting countries and market stimulation lead to large-scale production. Trade is a vital link in the health of the farm sector in those countries which use their surpluses to meet global needs.

Importers & Exporters

Major Importers of Basic Commodities Traded in the World

Wheat	Feed Grains	Soybeans & Products	Beef	Pork
U.S.S.R.	Japan	European Community	United States	United States
China	U.S.S.R.	Japan	U.S.S.R.	Japan
Japan	European Community	Spain	Japan	U.S.S.R.
Egypt	Mexico	Taiwan	European Community	European Community
Eastern Europe	Taiwan	Mexico	Egypt	Hong Kong
European Community	South Korea	Eastern Europe	Canada	
Brazil	Eastern Europe	U.S.S.R.	Saudi Arabia	
	Saudi Arabia	India		

Major Exporters of Basic Commodities Traded in the World

Wheat	Feed Grains	Soybeans & Products	Beef	Pork
United States	United States	United States	European Community	European Community
Canada	Argentina	Brazil	Australia	Eastern Europe
Australia	Canada	Argentina	Argentina	
France	South Africa	European Community	New Zealand	
Argentina	Thailand		Brazil	
	Australia		Canada	
	France			

Food Grains Around the World

By Frank R. Gomme, *agricultural marketing specialist, Grain and Feed Division, Foreign Agricultural Service*

Much of the world's population continues to depend on two major food grains, wheat and rice, for a significant portion of its daily food intake. In sharp contrast to food habits in the United States, where rice is most often a side dish, in many areas of the world a bowl of rice may be the total meal. In other areas, wheat products are the most important part of each meal. Many countries of the developed world are consuming less wheat and rice per capita today than 25 years ago. Because of production shortfalls and subsistence agriculture, however, unfulfilled world demand for food grains is still large.

World food grain production more than doubled in the past 25 years reaching well over 800 million metric tons this past year. Despite this spectacular increase, many areas still suffer annual shortages. Food grain consumption has risen an average of more than 3.5 percent annually since the early 1960's, with some of the sharpest increases in consumption in the less developed and OPEC countries. Although world trade in food grains has increased steadily over this period, much of the increase in consumption has been dependent upon domestic production.

Wheat Production Doubled

Since 1960, the area devoted to wheat in the world has risen about 15 percent while production has more than doubled. In many areas, wheat yields have shown a dramatic increase, in some cases doubling. In 1984/85, world wheat production exceeded 500 million tons for the first time.

The top five wheat producers in the world—China, the U.S.S.R., the United States, India, and the European Community (EC)—usually account for over two-thirds of world production. China, the U.S.S.R., the EC, and India also import significant quantities of wheat. If major wheat exporters—Canada, Australia, and Argentina—are included in the grouping, nearly 80 percent of the world's wheat crop is accounted for.

The world wheat market has frequently been oversupplied. While wheat-producing countries, particularly the United States, have tried to reduce stocks from time to time, stocks have continued to increase, despite the fact that in 12 of the last 20 years, the United States has limited wheat acreage.

Much of the Western and developed world relies on wheat as a principal food grain. World wheat utilization has more than doubled since the early 1960's, totaling over 500 million tons in 1984/85. Much of this growth has taken place in the developing world where consumption has nearly tripled to 150 million tons in 1984/85. China, the U.S.S.R., and India account for about 45 percent of world wheat consumption. The major exporters—Australia, Argentina, Canada, the EC, and the United States—collectively account for about only 14 percent of world wheat use. Wheat going into livestock feed has grown steadily with the sharpest gains in Eastern Europe, the EC, and the United States. Feed use in 1984/85 at 98 million tons accounts for about 20 percent of wheat utilization.

Wheat Trade Expanding

Since the early 1960's, world wheat trade more than doubled, increasing from an average of 47 million tons in 1960–64 to an average of 101 million tons for 1980–84. A number of factors have contributed to this sharp increase. Wheat import-

FAO

ers, particularly developing countries, experienced strong population growth. In addition, some nations benefited from rapid income growth. Income growth was most dramatic in oil-exporting and other middle-income developing nations. This growth, accompanied by the continued migration of population from rural areas to cities, caused a shift in demand away from some traditional foods to wheat foods such as bread. With demand increasing more quickly than domestic

Wheat production has increased in developing countries. India, for example, has expanded its supplies and has even entered the wheat export market. (India, grinding wheat into flour.)

production, imports increased. Some nations, such as those in central Africa, increased grain imports because per capita production actually declined. In others, such as Pakistan, Brazil, and Egypt, government policies of subsidizing wheat for consumption encouraged demand and imports. In the U.S.S.R. and China, policies of

Food Grains

meeting production shortfalls and rising demand with imports have resulted in a significant level of imports.

Major Wheat Traders

Over the past two decades, the United States, Canada, and Australia have generally accounted for about three-fourths of the wheat moving in world commerce. These relative shares of world trade, although fluctuating from one year to the next, have not changed significantly. In sharp contrast, the market shares for the EC and Argentina have increased. The most striking gain is in the EC, which has shifted from an importer to a position as the world's third largest wheat exporter.

U.S.A. The United States has been the world's largest wheat exporter for much of the twentieth century. In many years, it has supplied roughly half of the world import market. The United States is unique among the major wheat exporters, producing in exportable quantities five major types of wheat. It has numerous port facilities open all year. Large supplies make it a reliable shipper at any time during the year. The United States also is unique among the major exporters in

that private trade handles virtually all of the grain export sales.

U.S. wheat policies have determined its role as an exporter. When the U.S. price support loan rate and acreage reduction program provide a price floor under the world market, other exporters increase sales to the world market at U.S. expense while importers buy less; U.S. exports fall and the United States finds itself in the role of a residual supplier to world wheat markets. With its wheat-stocking program, the United States absorbs much of the changes in stocks resulting from changing world market conditions.

Grain price variability also has been associated with changes in the world monetary system. The 1972 devaluation of the dollar and the shift from a fixed to a floating exchange rate have led to variations in the value of the dollar in relation to other currencies. The boom in U.S. wheat exports in the 1970's was probably due, in part, to the dollar's depreciation against foreign currencies. In turn, the dollar's appreciation against foreign currencies in the early 1980's, together with escalated floor price levels, has tended to raise the price of

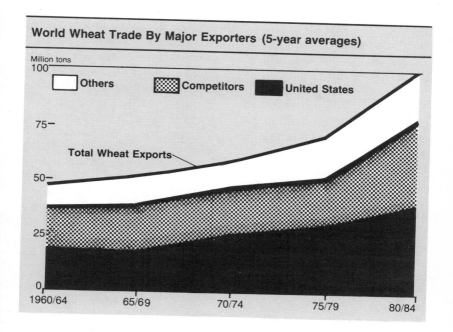

World Wheat Trade By Major Exporters (5-year averages)

Million tons

Others Competitors United States

Total Wheat Exports

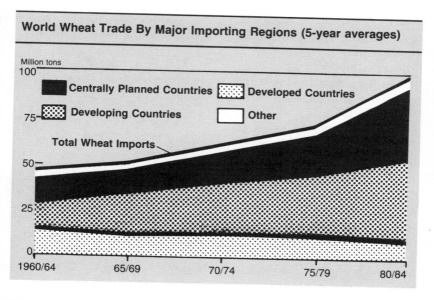

World Wheat Trade By Major Importing Regions (5-year averages)

Million tons

Centrally Planned Countries Developed Countries

Developing Countries Other

Total Wheat Imports

Food Grains

U.S. wheat and reduce U.S. competitiveness.

Canada. Canada accounts for about 20 percent of world wheat trade. Canadian wheat exports have generally increased over the past 25 years peaking at 22 million tons in 1983/84. In recent years, the U.S.S.R. has been its major customer followed by China, the EC, and Japan. In the late 1970's, Canada was not able to capture its share of world wheat trade because transportation bottlenecks at ports and railroad facilities limited annual export growth. It subsequently launched an expansion program in it grain transporting and handling industry. The Canadian Wheat Board is the sole legal exporter of wheat. To assure markets for its annual wheat production, Canada has signed trade agreements with a number of countries, accounting for 12 to 15 million tons or two-thirds of its total exports.

Australia. Australia's share of the world wheat market has averaged about 12 percent with the year-to-year share highly dependent on Australia's fluctuating crop output. Over the past 20 years, Australia has been the world's third largest wheat exporter. In 1981/82, however, it lost that position

to the EC. A significant share of Australia's wheat exports has moved to its Asian neighbors, with China and Japan the most important customers. As sales to China have declined in recent years, reflecting smaller imports and a loss in market share to other suppliers, Australia has countered successfully by stepping up sales efforts in the Middle East. Sales to this region in 1983/84 accounted for nearly 40 percent of total shipments, compared with about 20 percent a decade earlier. In contrast, sales to Asian countries accounted for about 37 percent of exports in 1983/84, compared with nearly two-thirds a decade ago. Another major change has been a significant expansion in sales to the U.S.S.R.

The Australian Wheat Board is the major marketing authority for domestic and export sales. Because of limited storage capacity, Australia has restricted the amount of wheat carried from one year to the next. It has a number of wheat sale agreements covering about 3 million tons of annual trade.

Argentina. Argentina's share of the world wheat market has varied sharply over the years, but recently has taken a big jump. Argentina's policy of holding only minimum stocks usually means that each year's production in excess of modest domestic requirements is immediately available to the export market. This policy has resulted in annual export levels ranging from a low of less than 1 million tons in 1970–71 to a high of 9.9 million in 1982/83.

Latin America has traditionally been the principal buyer of Argentine wheat. This trend changed sharply in 1980, when Argentina increased sales to the U.S.S.R. In the 1982/83 marketing year, sales to Latin American countries totaled less than a half million tons while shipments to the U.S.S.R. soared to more than 4 million. The past two marketing seasons have witnessed another shift in Argentina wheat exports as large exportable supplies permitted them to not only continue large sales to the U.S.S.R. but to resume sales efforts to their Latin American neighbors. Wheat export sales are transacted by the National Grain Board and private companies, with the private sector increasing its role in recent years. Argentina also has sought grain agreements, with more than a million tons of each year's sales now covered by them.

The EC. The EC has probably had the most dramatic impact on world wheat trade evolving from a significant importer of wheat to a formidable export competitor. This change reflects price support and trade policies that encourage production in excess of domestic needs and that subsidize exports. In the mid-1970's, EC imports from and exports to third countries both totaled about 5 million tons. By 1984/85, EC wheat imports fell to 2.5 million tons while exports soared to an estimated 17.5 million.

Other major exporters have suffered a substantial reduction in sales to the EC and sharply increased competition from EC wheat in the world market. Over the past 3 years, the U.S.S.R. has become the major market for EC wheat, taking roughly a third of the EC's 1984/85 shipments. The Middle East also has been an important market for EC soft wheat and durum. France, the EC's major wheat exporter has dramatically increased its share of the world export market by using its EC export subsidies and by using export credit guarantees from the French Export Guarantee Agency (COFACE).

Growth in Wheat Imports

Over the past two decades, wheat imports of developing and centrally planned countries have grown rapidly while those of developed countries have declined—from about 30 percent in 1960–64 to about 15 percent of world trade in 1980–84. Most of the decline occurred in the EC. The wheat market share of developing nations peaked during 1975–1979. The recession and the rise in interest rates in the early 1980's caused debt-servicing problems for many of these nations and a decline in imports. Further, the cost of subsidizing consumers proved burdensome, causing some nations to shift towards self-sufficiency.

In recent years, with world wheat trade roughly 100 million tons, centrally planned countries have accounted for about a third of total world imports. Over the past 6 years, the U.S.S.R. has been, by far, the major importer of wheat, accounting for about 20 percent of world trade. Their current wheat buying practices can be traced back to 1972/73, when they decided to import grain rather than absorb crop shortfalls internally. Although erratic, Soviet wheat imports have generally been large since then. China emerged as the second largest wheat importer in the late 1970's. Import potential seemed almost unlimited given a huge population and improving economic conditions. Some slowdown in economic growth and a series of record crops, however, have sharply reduced China's requirements for the near term.

The Japanese share of the world wheat market increased during the early 1970's with income growth and a change in food habits favoring bread or noodles. Since the mid-to-late 1970's, the growth in wheat demand has slowed.

Although wheat production has risen sharply in the developing world since the early 1960's, imports also have soared. In 1984/85, these countries accounted for over half the world wheat trade. Much of this increase in imports has occurred since 1980. In the early 1960's, production, importation, and consumption of wheat were modest in the OPEC countries. Since the 1970's, improved incomes have prompted a surge in wheat consumption, much of it based on imports. Wheat consumption on the African continent also has risen sharply, nearly tripling in the past 20 years. With limited production potential, much of this gain has been from higher imports.

Growing Reliance On LTA's

The growing importance of centrally planned and developing countries in world wheat trade in the past decade has led to an increasing reliance on long-term agreements (LTA's). The state trading agencies, which control grain trade for many of these countries, frequently prefer arrangements that assure long-term supplies. In addition, the growing debt problems experienced by many developing and Eastern European countries in the past 3 years has exacerbated shortages of foreign exchange and triggered interest in barter arrangements, once almost exclusively confined to trade among centrally planned countries.

Wheat Stocks Piling Up

Wheat stocks have risen sharply in recent years as production in the major exporting countries has outstripped their ability to find markets. Not all the growth in stocks has been in the major exporting coun-

tries, however. The EC has seen a rapid increase in stockpiles as sharply expanding production has outstripped increases in domestic use and export demand. India, with a series of good crops, has added sharply to wheat stocks and moved into the export market.

Although stocks are at record or near record when compared to the current high levels of utilization, they are not as high as they were in the mid-1960's when they were equivalent to one-third of a year's utilization. The United States still absorbs a significant portion of the cost of storing wheat from one year to the next.

Rice Production Doubled

World rice production has doubled since 1960. Most of the increase has been due to growth in average yields. Since 1960, harvested area has increased 20 percent, but yields have risen by 65 percent. In 1984/85, global rice production is estimated at a record 470 million tons.

Asia produces approximately 90 percent of the world's rice. China alone harvests 40 percent of the global crop. Since only half of the Asian crop is irrigated, 40 percent of the world rice harvest depends on the

FAO

critical timing of the Asian monsoon.

Rice accounts for about one-fifth of the world's grain consumption, including wheat and coarse grains, and is the primary staple in developing countries. Nearly 2 billion people depend on rice for over 80 percent of their diet. China, India, and Indonesia together claim almost two-thirds of global rice consumed annually, with China alone consuming nearly 40 percent.

Rice accounts for one-fifth of the world's grain consumption, and China alone consumes nearly 40 percent of the total. (China, rice field fertilization.)

Kinds of Rice

Four types of rice are consumed in the world—glutinous, aromatic, japonica, and indica. These types are distinguished by length of grain, starch content, and cooking qualities. Countries have specific tastes and preferences for particular types of rice. Consequently, there is not always perfect substitution among the four types. Indica (long grain) rice is grown principally in China, South and Southeast Asia, and the Southern United States and makes up the bulk of world trade. Of the total rice traded, perhaps only one-sixth is the shorter, scented rice grains.

Rice Trade Volatile

Despite the importance of rice as a food staple to a third of the world's population, the volume traded annually is small. Out of a world rice crop of 300 million tons, only about 12 million—or less than 5 percent—is traded in the world market. From 65 to 70 percent of world exports are supplied by five countries: Thailand, the United States, Burma, Pakistan, and China. The United States and Thailand normally account for half the rice exported in the world. Because of the unpredictability of weather, the importance of rice in diets of the developing world, and the concentration of trade among a few key countries, the world rice market has earned the description of being thin and volatile. These same factors have led many governments to try to manage rice supplies. Over the years, trade

patterns changed frequently and drastically, as growing conditions shifted a country from an importing position to temporary self-sufficiency or, in the extreme, to an exporter.

The world rice market is inherently unstable with respect to price and sources of demand and supply. With a limited number of traders, an unexpected or new buyer can have dramatic consequences on trade, and hence on prices. A sudden downturn in demand of a key importer, or a seller caught with a large exportable surplus and inadequate storage, will cause equally sharp price swings.

No single world market price exists. There is a lack of commonly used grades and standards, despite understood definitions of rice quality. The price depends on specific quality characteristics. Because consumer preferences can exert a powerful influence over demand, prices for different types or qualities move somewhat independently of each other based on the supply-demand factors for that market.

Rice Imports

Governments are increasing their role in the world rice trade. In developing countries

USDA

The world rice market is unstable, subject to sudden and sharp price changes. (Hong Kong, rice auction.)

primarily, governments attempt to assure adequate supplies, especially in urban areas, and to provide for the welfare of the rice farmers who often account for a significant share of the population. These two objectives often imply tight control of both domestic trade and government imports. Only a handful of countries trade rice privately: the United States, Australia, Italy, Argentina, Uruguay, and Spain. Even the world's current leading ex-

porter—Thailand—sold nearly 40 percent of its rice through a government agency.

Developed Countries. Developed countries account for a relatively small, stable portion of world imports. Within this group, developments in Japan have been the most critical. Japan has long maintained a policy of high price supports for-producers. Japanese rice consumption peaked in the early 1960's at 12 million tons—and has been falling since then with a resulting stock buildup. Japanese production increased through the late 1960's, and stabilized thereafter at 11–12 million tons. Japan, an importer of rice from 1960 to 1967, became an exporter in most years after 1968.

Centrally Planned Countries. Rice imports by centrally planned nations have increased slightly as a share of world imports since the early 1960's. This increase is largely due to more purchases by the U.S.S.R. in the late 1970's and early 1980's.

Developing Countries. Developing nations account for about 70 percent of world imports. While this group's total share of world rice trade has remained relatively constant, individual countries have experienced major changes in market shares. Since the early 1960's, African and Middle Eastern nations have increased their share of world imports while the shares of Asian nations have fallen. Several factors are responsible for these changes.

In the 1970's, rapid rates of income growth and expanding urban populations pushed up the demand for rice in many African and Middle Eastern nations.

Increased urbanization shifted consumption patterns from staple diets of cassava toward rice and wheat. From 1962 to 1971, rice imports by the Middle East averaged 352,000 tons annually. But in the next 10 years, total rice imports tripled, to an annual average of 1.2 million tons. In 1983, the Middle East imported a record 2 million tons. African rice imports followed a similar pattern, averaging almost 700,000 tons from 1963 to 1971, then doubling to nearly 1.5 million tons annually in the following decade, reaching a record 3 million tons in 1983.

In general, Asian nations have reduced their shares of world trade. Income growth, increased urbanization, and oil exports by Indonesia, expanded demand in the 1970's. Two differences, however, caused Asian nations to reduce their share of world trade while that for African nations increased. Unlike African nations, Asian countries did not tax producers, with the exception of Thailand. Nominal rates of protection for rice producers in East Asia have been rising. India pursued policies designed to encourage production and stocks. Whereas yields in Africa stagnated or declined, yields in Asia rose considerably because of the adoption of high-yielding varieties of rice. Asian nations have been better able to expand production to meet consumption growth than African nations, which have relied on area expansion.

Rice Exports Dominated by Few

In the early 1960's, the volume of world rice exports was between 6 and 7 million tons, compared with current levels of 12 million tons. About 70 percent of the world's rice exports were supplied by four countries—Thailand and Burma (more than 3 million tons, or about 50 percent), the United States (about 1 million tons or 15 percent), and China (between 7 and 9 percent). By 1972, three countries were supplying 63 percent of the 8.4 million tons traded in the world rice market: Thailand (2.1 million tons), the United States (1.8 million), and China (1.4 million). By 1981, the leaders changed position again. Total rice exports grew to a record

13.2 million tons. The leading exporter was still Thailand, at 3.05 million tons, followed by the United States with 3 million, and Pakistan with almost 1.2 million tons.

During the late 1970's, Thailand imposed export taxes and domestic sales quotas for exporters. In the early 1980's, Thailand adopted a more export-oriented policy and expanded its market share. The United States is currently the second largest rice exporter. During the 1970's, U.S. rice exports expanded rapidly while world prices were more than the U.S. loan rate. The United States also provided aid to several Asian markets—South Vietnam, South Korea, Kampuchea, and Indonesia—and targeted market development activities to Iran. By the 1980's, global recession, policy developments in Indonesia and South Korea, government changes in South Vietnam, Kampuchea, and Iran, and reduced food aid activities all reduced demand, and U.S. prices fell to loan levels. The loan rate acts as a price floor and allows other exporters to undercut the U.S. price, as Thailand has done with its policy changes, so the U.S market share has been falling.

Feed Grains Around the World

By Donald J. Novotny, *director,*
and
Philip A. Shull, *agricultural economist, Grain and Feed Division, Foreign Agricultural Service*

Feed grains are among the most important agricultural commodities the world produces, comprising almost 50 percent of total grain production and consumption. Feed grains—corn, barley, sorghum, oats, and millet—are planted on close to one half of all land planted to grain. Production and consumption have increased almost every year since 1960, with global production projected to reach 816 million metric tons in 1985/86.

Consumption

Feed grains are consumed throughout the world as food for people and as feed for animals. In the developing countries of Latin America and Africa, corn and millet are staples in human diets, whereas in the more developed countries of Asia, Europe, and North America corn is principally used as feed. Most nations which import these grains use them for livestock feed or for industrial purposes such as making cornstarch or alcohol. Generally, as nations grow richer, the consumption of meat, and therefore feed grains, rises. For example, Saudi Arabia, a Middle Eastern country which has grown quite wealthy over the last decade from its large oil

Gene Alexander

exports, fed almost no grain to animals before 1973. Since that time, feed grain consumption and imports have increased to the point where Saudi Arabia is now the single largest importer of barley in the world, over 90 percent of which is fed to animals.

Of all the feed grains, corn is by far the most important in both production and trade. It is attractive to buyers because of its comparatively high nutritional value and to sellers mainly because of its larger yields. Corn comprises almost 57 percent of all feed grain production, and about 70 percent of the world feed grain trade.

Barley has been increasing its share of the feed grain market in recent years, jumping from 14 percent in 1981/82 to an estimated 18 percent in 1984/85. This increase is primarily due to increased exports by the European Community (EC). Sorghum comprises the lion's share of the remaining feed grain trade.

Corn is a vital commodity that comprises almost 57 percent of all feed grain produced and over 72 percent of total world feed grain trade. (South Dakota, corn harvest.)

World Feed Grain Trade, by Commodity[1]

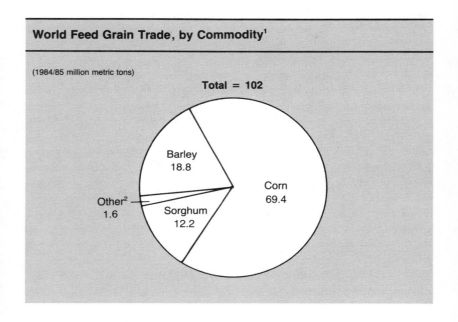

(1984/85 million metric tons)

Total = 102

Barley
18.8

Other[2]
1.6

Sorghum
12.2

Corn
69.4

World Feed Grain Trade 1960/61-1985/86[1]

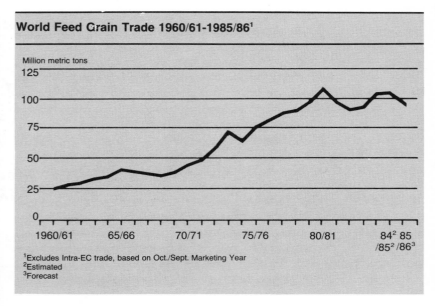

Million metric tons

[1]Excludes Intra-EC trade, based on Oct./Sept. Marketing Year
[2]Estimated
[3]Forecast

Feed Grains   **199**

Major Trends

The world feed grain situation has undergone a number of fundamental changes over the past quarter century, with modifications in agricultural trade policies, domestic production programs, marketing strategies, and economic development being the driving forces. Rapid economic development in several key countries and the founding of the EC have resulted in the emergence of new major feed grain exporters and importers. For example, Taiwan and South Korea collectively imported about 200,000 metric tons of feed grains a year in the early and middle 1960's. By 1983/84 this figure had exceeded 8 million tons. In contrast, the EC, which was the largest feed grain importer in 1967, is a major net exporter today.

One of the most striking characteristics of the global feed grain trade over the past 25 years has been its spectacular growth. World trade in feed grains has nearly quadrupled over this period and has gone through three definite phases. The 1960's were a time of slow, stable growth at relatively low levels, while the 1970's were marked by tremendous increases and fluctuations. The 1980's have, so far, been a time of general stagnation with less dramatic changes in trade from year to year, and world production far outpacing demand.

1960's and 1970's Development of Livestock Production.

The slow, stable growth of the 1960's was due to the steady development of livestock production in Japan and Western Europe. The tremendous growth in import demand throughout the 1970's was fueled by several events. Most important was the decision of the U.S.S.R. to increase its production of red meat despite chronic domestic crop shortfalls. Previously, it had absorbed frequent crop shortfalls through reduced consumption and the slaughter of livestock. Their new policy necessitated the import of large quantities of feed grains. As a result, the U.S.S.R. remains the world's leading importer of feed grains.

Secondly, the rapid economic growth over the 1960's and 1970's of countries such as Brazil, Mexico, Taiwan, and South Korea, and the overnight riches accrued by many of the Arab members of the Organization of Petroleum Exporting Countries (OPEC) in the wake of the 1973 oil crisis allowed countries which had been na-

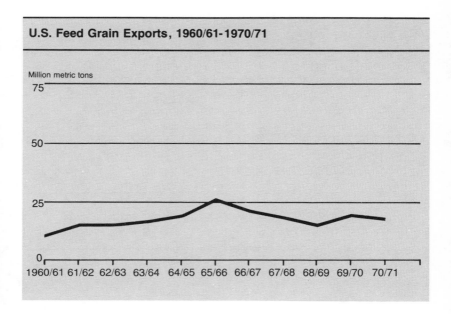

U.S. Feed Grain Exports, 1960/61-1970/71

Million metric tons

tions of nomadic herdsmen, or almost exclusively cereal consumers, to begin developing livestock industries. These developments were further accelerated by the wide availability of cheap and easy credit from Western banks, the relatively low cost of feed grains, and the weakening of the dollar in relation to other major world currencies. All these factors culminated in a tremendous increase in demand for feed grains.

1980's Stagnation. The 1980's have seen a stagnation of growth with the world feed grain trade falling in 1981/82 by almost 12 million tons. This precipitous drop and subsequent stagnation is due to several factors: 1) the EC becoming a net feed grain exporter because of its system of import levies and price supports; 2) the increasing displacement of feed grains by nongrain feed ingredients such as tapioca, (also known as manioc, cassava) and citrus pulp; 3) the general economic downturn in the 1980's; 4) tighter credit and mounting hard currency problems in places like Eastern Europe causing some countries to cut back on imports; 5) the

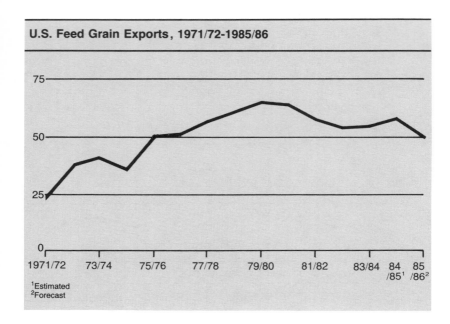

U.S. Feed Grain Exports, 1971/72-1985/86

¹Estimated
²Forecast

rapid appreciation of the U.S. dollar accentuating debtor nations' problems and making U.S. feed grains more expensive for other countries to import; and 6) importing countries such as Indonesia and China increasing domestic production and significantly reducing their imports.

Production of feed grains in the major exporting countries has risen faster than total world demand. The resulting surplus has driven down prices for feed grains and brought political and economic pressures on exporting countries to for-mulate policies for dealing with the domestic and international grain glut.

Major Exporters

The major exporters (United States, Canada, Australia, the EC, Argentina, South Africa, and Thailand) typically account for over 90 percent of total feed grain exports. This list has remained fairly constant over the past quarter century with the major exception of the EC.

South Africa, normally a major exporter, has been forced to import feed grains temporarily because of a devastating

U.S. Feed Grain Exports, by Commodity, 1984/85[1]

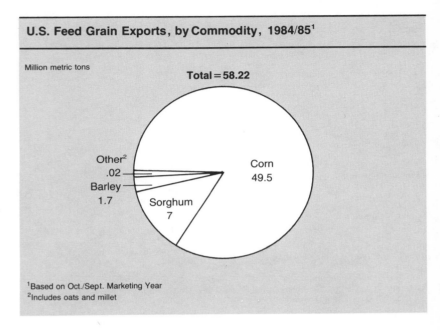

Million metric tons

Total = 58.22

Other[2]
.02
Barley
1.7
Sorghum
7
Corn
49.5

[1]Based on Oct./Sept. Marketing Year
[2]Includes oats and millet

drought over the last 3 years. Most recently, China has become a temporary major net exporter of feed grains because of its policy changes and lack of a distribution system to use the grain internally.

United States. The United States has traditionally been the world's largest exporter of feed grains. Its share of the world feed grain trade has fluctuated between 40 and 72 percent since 1960. Corn is by far the largest U.S. feed grain export. In 1984/85 the United States exported about 50 million metric tons or 80 percent of world corn exports, or 50 percent of total world feed grain exports. The United States also is the largest corn producer in the world, accounting for 43 percent of world production, followed by China with 16 percent. The United States consumes about one-third of the world's corn. Since the 1950's, the United States has, in most years, controlled production and provided further support for farm gate prices through government purchasing and storage programs.

Because of the dominance of

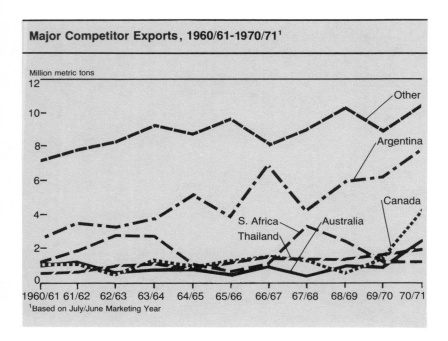

Major Competitor Exports, 1960/61-1970/71[1]

Million metric tons

[1]Based on July/June Marketing Year

the United States in the world feed grain market, its feed grain prices also have tended to be the international prices. As world production has increased in the wake of stagnant demand, other countries have lowered their prices below the U.S. price, forcing the United States into a position of residual supplier.

Canada. Barley is Canada's largest feed grain crop, second only to wheat in production and exports. Canada has been the world's largest barley exporter with 40 percent of the

market share, exporting two to three times more than does the United States. But it now appears certain that the EC will force Canada into the No. 2 position in 1984/85.

Other than a credit program, the Canadian Government markets its feed grains without special incentives to foreign buyers. Canada also competes against third-country feed grains through the occasional export of feed quality wheat. Canada has taken steps to expand its export capacity, including making major port and rail investments. The Canadians currently have long-term agreements for feed grains with the U.S.S.R., East Germany, Japan, and Israel.

Approximately 50 percent of the barley crop is consumed domestically. Canadian farmers can sell barley privately, or they can deliver it to the Canadian Wheat Board (CWB), the sole agency for exporting barley in Western Canada. If they choose the latter, farmers receive an initial payment from the CWB and can receive an additional payment at the end of the marketing year, depending on export sales and world prices. The area planted to barley has fluctuated over the years depending on the prices of other commodities, especially rapeseed. Farmers can plant as much grain as they like, but can deliver to the CWB only a specified quantity per quota-acre. The CWB can alter quotas in response to market demand, thereby exerting a strong influence on production.

Australia. Barley and sorghum are Australia's primary feed grain exports. Like Canada, however, Australia occasionally exports a significant amount of feed grade wheat which competes directly with coarse grain exports from third countries. Domestic consumption of coarse grains has remained fairly constant over the last decade, with most of the surplus being exported. Australia maintains minimal stocks. Barley is Australia's largest feed grain crop in volume and value. Domestic and export sales of barley, as with all feed grains, are controlled by state marketing boards. Domestic barley use is relatively small, but it increases during drought years when grain supplements forage. With highly variable production, barley exports have ranged from 600,000 in 1982/83 to 3.7 million tons the following year. Southeast Asia and the Middle East are Australia's largest barley customers. Japan is the only country with which Australia has a long-term agreement for feed grain sales.

EC. Barley is by far the dominant feed grain exported by the EC and is expected to comprise 40 percent of world barley trade in 1984/85 as compared to 25 percent in 1981/82. Feed grain production and trade are strongly influenced by the Common Agricultural Policy (CAP) for grains, an intricate system of target prices, intervention (support) prices, and threshold (minimum import) prices designed to stabilize internal agricultural prices and to encourage free grain movement among member countries. This system effectively protects domestic producers and consumers from price changes in the world market. For example, variable levies charged on barley imports insulate EC farmers from lower priced world supplies. Export subsidies are paid to bridge the gap between the normally higher domestic EC prices and world prices.

As a result of the intervention price support program which rewards the quantity produced without regard to quality, EC barley production rose from 26.6 million tons in 1967, the first year of full implementation of the CAP, to over 44 million tons in 1984/85. CAP's massive subsidies on production and exports have enabled the EC to move from a major net importer to a major net exporter of feed grains. In more recent years, however, EC barley area has declined as improved wheat varieties, particularly higher yielding feed wheat varieties, have provided farmers greater returns than barley.

Argentina. Argentine feed grain exports, mainly corn and sorghum, have increased over the past few years and now comprise over 12 percent of the world market. Total Argentine coarse grain exports increased from an average of 10 million tons in 1977–79 to 12.7 million tons in 1983/84.

There are several reasons for Argentina's growing share of the feed grain market. First, the Government temporarily eliminated export taxes in 1977 and set floor prices for corn based on the world price. Before 1977, export taxes on wheat, corn, and sorghum were as high as 50 percent. In 1982, export taxes again rose to 25 percent and are currently close to that level. Secondly, Argentina sought to reduce the degree of overvaluation of its currency by allowing the peso to depreciate against the U.S. dollar, resulting in a cheapr price for Argentine grain on the world market. Finally, Argentina benefited greatly from the 1980 U.S. grain embargo of the U.S.S.R. Following this action, Argentina negotiated a new agreement with the Soviets for large quantities of corn and sorghum at a premium price. In addition, Argentina has agreements with China, Mexico, Algeria, Cuba, and a few other countries.

Since 1976, Argentina's grain marketing system has been market oriented. Exporters must register foreign sales with the National Grain Board (NGB) by month of shipment, although not by destination. Argentina currently offers no significant producer support prices for feed grains to its farmers.

South Africa. Corn, the primary grain export of South Africa, is marketed through the Maize Board. This parastatal organization protects producers and consumers from fluctuations in the world market through a stabilization fund, and by setting minimum selling prices below producer prices. Although South Africa is normally a major corn exporter, a severe drought, which has ravaged the country since 1982, has turned it into a temporary net corn importer. South Africa is the largest producer and exporter of white corn used primarily for human consumption in Africa and parts of Latin America.

Thailand. Corn is Thailand's main feed grain export. It has been increasing its share of the market and now accounts for 5 percent of world corn exports. One of the main reasons for this gain is the more competi-

tive price for Thai corn because of the relaxation of export taxes to generate customs revenue and control domestic market supplies. Even so, the Government still controls corn exports through minimum export prices and quota allocations.

Thailand has an open corn market with relatively few restrictions or incentives for corn production or exports. The Government, however, has had a long-term bilateral supply accord with Taiwan and actively negotiates annual bilateral agreements for corn exports. The recent expansion in Thai corn production resulted from an increase in acreage planted. Because of space restrictions, further increases will depend on the allocation of foreign exchange to purchase fertilizer from abroad or to produce it domestically, and on the availability of improved hybrids to boost yields.

China. Recent changes in feed grain production policy which caused burgeoning supplies (increases of 40 million tons over 3 years), combined with a lack of internal transportation facilities have transformed China from an importer of 3 million tons (mostly from the United States) in 1981/82 to a 5-million-ton exporter in

1984/85. Although more feed grains could easily be consumed domestically, facilities are inadequate to transport grain from surplus to deficit areas. The main reason for this production boom is the implementation of the New Responsibility System first adopted as a national policy in 1981. Under this system farmers have more freedom to decide which crops to plant, can sell all above-quota production on the local market, and can keep what they earn.

The Chinese Government also has sought to decentralize grain exporting by allowing individual provinces with surplus grain to authorize grain exports. It remains unclear whether these changes will make China's position as a large corn exporter permanent. As internal transportation systems improve and the livestock industry becomes more developed, more of the feed grains may be used internally.

Major Importers

The most important shifts among major importing countries over the last 25 years have been the moves of the EC from major importer to net exporter, and the emergence of the U.S.S.R. as the single largest

importer. Eastern Europe grew at a rapid rate throughout the 1970's, but hard currency and credit problems have forced cutbacks in the 1980's. Japan has been a growing, stable market for years, as have Korea and Taiwan. Saudi Arabia has recently emerged as the world's largest barley market. Non-EC Western Europe has become a smaller market as more countries have joined the EC and as consumption has leveled off. The imminent accession of Spain and Portugal to the EC over the next few years will contribute to the deterioration of the non-EC Western Europe market for third-country exporters.

Centrally Planned Economies. Eastern Europe's and the U.S.S.R.'s import share of the world feed grains trade increased from 7 to 25 percent between the early 1960's and late 1970's. Between 1978/79 and 1982/83 the U.S. export share of the world feed grain market declined by 6 percent, in part because of the U.S.-imposed embargo of the U.S.S.R. in January 1980. During this time major countries that competed with the United States in the world grain market expanded their grain production and exports. For example, the

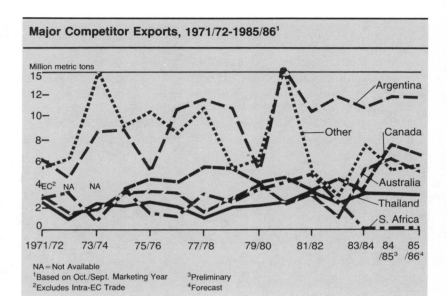

Major Competitor Exports, 1971/72-1985/86[1]

Million metric tons

NA = Not Available
[1]Based on Oct./Sept. Marketing Year   [3]Preliminary
[2]Excludes Intra-EC Trade   [4]Forecast

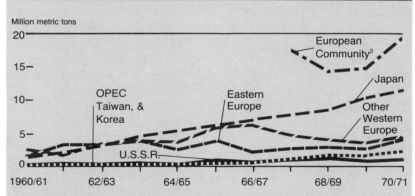

Major Importers, 1960/61-70/71[1]

Million metric tons

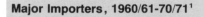

[1]Over this period these countries accounted for an average of 60%– of world feed grain imports.
[2]The Common Agricultural Policy of the European Community did not become fully integrated until 1967.
  The values exclude Intra-EC trade and are based on the EC-10.

TASS

Once a net feed grains exporter, the U.S.S.R. now imports to maintain domestic meat consumption. (U.S.S.R., corn harvest.)

Canadian share of the world wheat and coarse grains market rose from 11 to 15 percent, while the Argentine share increased from 6 to 10 percent. After the embargo, the U.S.S.R., the EC, Japan, Eastern Europe, and China all increased their imports from major U.S. competing sources. Meanwhile, the U.S.S.R. cut its purchases of U.S. wheat, feed grains, and soybeans. In 1982/83, the U.S.S.R. imported only 20 percent of its wheat and coarse grains from the United States, down from the 72 percent in 1978/79. The U.S. share of Soviet feed grain imports, however, now is rising

to about one half as a result, in part, of a new long-term agreement that began in 1983/84.

Eastern Europe expanded its feed grain imports, mostly corn, during the 1975–79 period by obtaining credit guarantees from the U.S. Government and borrowing from Western banks. These sources of credit dwindled in the 1980's as Eastern Europe experienced debt-servicing difficulties. Corn imports have consequently fallen by almost two-thirds, from 11.5

million tons in 1979/80 to an expected 3.4 million tons in 1984/85.

The U.S.S.R. until 1971/72 had been a net exporter of feed grains. In that year the Soviets changed their standard policy of absorbing production shortfalls internally and bought 4 million tons of feed grains on the world market, almost three-fourths from the United States from which it had never before bought feed grains. This policy change reflected the desire of Soviet leaders to maintain domestic levels of meat consump-

tion rather than drastically reduce herd sizes as it had done in past times of shortfall production. That policy has continued with imports being totally dependent on domestic production. Since 1971/72, Soviet imports of feed grains have ranged widely between 2.7 million and 28 million metric tons, causing considerable fluctuations in the world market.

EC. The EC has reduced its corn imports over the past two decades. In 1960–64, the countries which eventually made up the EC accounted for an aver-

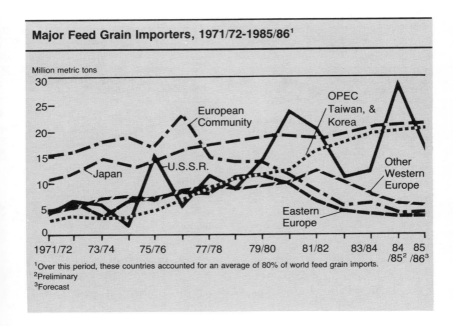

Major Feed Grain Importers, 1971/72-1985/86[1]

Million metric tons

European Community

OPEC Taiwan, & Korea

Japan   U.S.S.R.

Other Western Europe

Eastern Europe

1971/72 73/74 75/76 77/78 79/80 81/82 83/84 84 /85[2] 85 /86[3]

[1]Over this period, these countries accounted for an average of 80% of world feed grain imports.
[2]Preliminary
[3]Forecast

USDA

age of 55.5 percent of world corn imports. That share fell to 17.5 percent by 1981/82. U.S. corn exports to the EC declined steadily from almost 20 million tons in 1976/77 to 3.7 million tons in 1983/84.

Much of the reason for this decline is the EC's increased imports of cereal substitutes known as nongrain feed ingredients (NGFI), excluding oilseed meal, and the increased

Japan is almost totally dependent on imports for its feed grain requirements. (Japan, grain silo.)

production of feed grains, mainly barley, and soft feed wheat. This production increase stems from the EC's high support price systems and import protection policies. Moreover, high corn prices have resulted in displacing corn as feed by manioc, citrus pulp,

World Trade in Agricultural Products

and other cereal byproducts not subject to such restrictive import barriers. In fact, since EC policy encourages using domestically produced feed grains for livestock feeding, U.S. corn exports to the EC are now primarily used for industrial products, not for feed. EC imports of nongrain feeds surged from about 4.2 million tons in 1972 to 16.2 million tons in 1982, helping make the EC a net feed grain exporter.

Japan. Japan's share of the world feed grains market has been growing slowly and steadily since the early 1960's, from 13 to almost 25 percent projected for 1984/85. The primary cause for this increase has been higher incomes and the growing demand for meat. During the 1970's Japan shifted its feed operation from forage to grain, and is almost totally dependent on imports for its feed grains.

Non-EC Western Europe.

The total market share of coarse grains for non-EC Western Europe initially increased with the rising demand for meat. But large increases in feed grain production over the past two decades combined with a leveling off of consumption beginning in 1979/80 have resulted in falling demand.

Spain and Portugal, two of the largest feed grain importers and important U.S. markets in this region, are about to join the EC. This event will have a dampening effect on world demand for feed grains. In fact, Thailand is already trying to market tapioca in Spain in anticipation of the higher prices Spanish livestock producers will have to pay for feed grains after accession.

Rapidly Developing Countries.

OPEC and rapidly developing countries such as Taiwan, South Korea, and Mexico have shown the biggest jump in imports over the last 20 years. In the early 1960's these countries combined were importing less than 1 million tons. The estimate for 1984/85 is over 25 million tons, almost 13 million tons by OPEC countries. This tremendous increase has resulted from the accumulation of wealth by these countries and, in turn, demand for more meat. Saudi Arabia has become the world's largest barley importer, estimated to take 7 million tons in 1984/85, or over 40 percent of total barley world trade. Steady growth in demand for feed grains should continue in these countries as long as their economies continue to prosper.

Fruits and Vegetables Around the World

By Gilbert E. Sindelar, *director, Horticultural and Tropical Products Division, Foreign Agricultural Service*

Like most sectors of the world agricultural community, the growing of fruits and vegetables has undergone major changes during this century. Advances in production technology and innovations in marketing know-how have been many and rapid. These have done much to shape and re-shape world competition and markets. The pace at which international trade has responded to such changes, however, has been tempered by the economics and politics of market access.

U.S. Role

In the first few decades of this century, when world trade and competition in horticultural products were still at modest levels, the United States was a leading exporter of horticultural products such as fresh apples, pears, grapes, and citrus. It was also a prominent supplier of dried fruits as well as canned fruits and vegetables and juices. Other than Canada, our markets were mostly in Europe.

Then came World War II which triggered an almost complete break with the past and left international trade in shambles. The economies of many of our former market countries were crippled. Import barriers came up almost without warning, limiting imports strictly to essential "hardware" items, with horticultural imports automatically a victim. As a gesture toward stimulating recovery, the U.S. Government temporarily suspended its trading rights with many of its former markets. Under the veil of protectionism against imports from the outside world, the agricultural communities, especially in Western Europe, saw an excellent opportunity to capitalize on the situation.

The economies of many of these countries, stricken by poverty and internal strife, were desperately in need of a new sense of direction, particularly in the agricultural sector. A highly rural population, extremely low wage rates, and vast unemployment were common. To many national planners, horticultural products became a far more attractive candidate for exploitation than did the more basic agricultural commodities so frequently plagued by worldwide surplus. This new interest was enthusiastically supported at the highest levels in government. American know-how in plant breeding, disease and insect control, and other cultural techniques spread to other countries at a rapid pace. Soon, varieties of American parentage were common to most parts of the world.

New Era in Competition
An almost reckless expansion in post-World War II productive capacity generated a near explosive situation, particularly in Western Europe. In a number of our former markets on the Continent, local supplies had mushroomed far in excess of domestic needs. With storage facilities bulging, the export market became a natural and immediate target. Toward the mid-1960's signs were beginning to appear that our once dominant supplier position was being subjected to forces of competition and the reemergence of protectionistic policies by many foreign governments.

Trade Barriers
The growth in world production and trade has not been without its painful moments. Many former U.S. markets abroad are themselves today strong competitors in third countries. At the same time, however, the respective governments of these new suppliers have done much to protect the home market from the forces of import competition.

Dana Downie

The EC.

One of the more notable examples of protection for the home market has been the European Community (EC). In the early 1960's, the formation of the EC was heralded as a fulfillment of an American dream. Not only would its existence act as a buffer to the spread of communism, but at the same time many U.S. political leaders saw it as a great trading partner. The passing of each year, however, witnessed one bitter disappointment after another. The trading wall around the EC has grown higher and higher, more and more protective.

Norwegian children reconstitute concentrated Florida apple juice which the European Community imports from the United States.

EC's common agriculture policy (CAP), as it relates to horticulture, evolved in three parts. First, on the production front, it soon became apparent that the EC's aim was to produce as much of its needs as possible at prices of its own choosing. This inevitably prompted the employment of a network of subsidies.

Second, on the import front, the CAP sought to admit imports of its residual needs, again at prices of its own choosing. A series of reference prices or minimum import prices for most fresh fruits and vegetables were adopted. In the processed area, the CAP developed a system of processor subsidies, which could be used for either the domestic or export markets, for eight individual canned items including peaches and pears as well as tomato products. These subsidies were generous and available to processors on the condition that the processor respect a minimum price to growers.

The third and final dimension of the CAP was designed to export surplus supplies, again subsidizing to lower the EC chosen prices to world price levels. In recent years this subsidy prompted the California raisin industry as well as the canning industry, on behalf of canned peaches, pears and fruit cocktail, to challenge the EC in the General Agreement on Tariffs and Trade forum.

In its early stages, the EC adopted a number of auxiliary measures to insulate its drive toward achievement of these three goals. The early 1960's witnessed the adoption of a highly ideological set of quality standards. A sugar-added levy was imposed on imports of canned fruits in 1968. Then, in 1969 the EC launched a system of tariff rate preferences on fresh citrus which eventually embraced every citrus-producing country in the Mediterranean Basin. These preferences are still in place today.

Japan. Japan, now a tremendous force in the trading world for industrial goods, also has maintained a protective home front. It was well recognized that a great market potential existed in Japan for many fruits and vegetables. The United States led the way in attempting to remove the trade barriers that existed, a tremendous undertaking. Despite repeated efforts by the U.S. Government and industry over many years, the Japanese resisted liberalization of citrus fruits to protect their own producers. Since liberalization of lemons in 1964, and grapefruit in 1971, the Japanese market has responded well. Some progress also has been made in the enlargement of the Japanese import quota for oranges.

South Korea. Other than Japan, many countries in the Far East still are far from fully liberalized. Among the more important ones are South Korea and Taiwan. Although the United States has made many attempts to open the South Korean market more fully, the results have been exceedingly slow. Raisins were one of the first commodities to be liberalized in that country a few years ago. Although the response has not been overwhelming, considerable work remains to be done by the U.S. raisin industry to acquaint consumers and others with the many uses of the product.

A significant breakthrough was made recently in South Korea. The Government agreed to transfer 26 agricultural items from the import restricted list to an automatic approval licensing status effective July 1, 1985. Among the more important horticultural products included were fresh grapefruit, fresh cherries, almonds, tomato catsup, and canned corn.

Taiwan. To the extent that Taiwan has liberalized its imports, U.S. trade with Taiwan has improved. For example, in 1979 the Taiwanese Government liberalized the imports of fresh apples. In 1979/80, Taiwan became the No. 1 market for U.S. apples, absorbing 3.4 million cartons, as opposed to about 150,000 cartons in preceding years. The following season, 1980/81, U.S. exports

to Taiwan totaled 3.9 million cartons, quite an accomplishment because the basic import duty into Taiwan for apples was 75 percent ad valorem plus many other charges. Import duties for other products also have been high and a serious impediment to furthering trade with Taiwan.

In 1984 Taiwan enjoyed a trade surplus of more than $11 billion with the United States. The Taiwanese are beginning to realize that continuing large trade surpluses could harm high-level trade relations and, most notably, would jeopardize Taiwan's GSP status. Negotiations are continuing.

Other countries in the Far East bloc with good potential for U.S. fresh produce are Malaysia, the Philippines, Thailand, and Indonesia.

Pesticides and Fumigants

The pesticide issue has flared up in a number of countries, all of which are important markets for the United States. Unless this issue, which has been gaining momentum since the beginning of this decade, can be arrested or minimized, it could have a serious impact upon the direction of U.S. exports over the next few years. The sensitivity of this issue is

Dana Downie

acute, not only in the United States but also in Canada, Western Europe, and the Far East, especially in Japan. In some instances the charges against a given pesticide are fully substantiated by responsible research findings. In other cases, however, the benefits of using a certain pesticide far outweighs the risks.

The use of fumigants too has come under heavy scrutiny and attack, a particular concern to citrus growers and growers in

Many countries in the Far East are adopting modern marketing methods. (A shopper purchases imported fruit in a Philippines supermarket.)

tropical-producing areas where plant pests are most abundant. Crops affected include tropical fruits such as mangoes, avocados, and papayas and a host of tropical vegetables. Uncertainty exists as to suitable substitutes for fly fumigants, making the international trade situation unstable.

Fruits & Vegetables

Competition in Processed Fruits

Not too long ago, the United States was the unchallenged world supplier of many processed fruits. Because of advanced production and marketing know-how, as well as efficiencies of large-scale operations, it was in the enviable position of capitalizing on the expanding world market beginning in about the early 1960's. American ingenuity in producing and marketing a quality product was well recognized. As such, the U.S. label often commanded a premium in offshore markets. Today the quality gap has narrowed appreciably and, in some instances, is nonexistent.

The rapid pace at which

American know-how has been transplanted to other producing areas has contributed much to the improvement in marketing processed fruits. Many countries successfully encouraged U.S. investments with the accompanying managerial and engineering skills. The training of foreign personnel in the United States, too, provided an important expansionary influence.

With assurances of protection against outside competition and active encouragement from their own governments through various support meas-

Until recently Florida's orange industry ranked No. 1 in processed orange juice but has lost some export markets because of weather-related crop damage. (Florida, sorting citrus.)

USDA

ures, growers in many competing areas have not only placed their home country in or near a self-sufficient status, but have turned to the export market with enthusiasm.

Canned Fruit. Western Europe was initially a key market for U.S. canned goods. Today, however, chances of U.S. survival in this market are dimming rapidly. After a few years of supremacy in the European market during the early 1960's, the United States first faced competition from Australia and South Africa which had lost commonwealth preferences when the United Kingdom became a member of the EC. The next thrust of competition came from Italy and Greece, today the leading suppliers to the EC market. When Spain becomes a new member of the EC on January 1, 1986, the doors to imports of canned peaches and other canned fruits will be virtually closed to the outside world, with the possible exception of canned pineapple.

Hawaii's supremacy in producing and marketing canned pineapple of consistently high quality had been one of many years' standing. Its reputation was well established throughout the lucrative Western European markets. High wage rates and land values, however, began to plague the Hawaiian industry in the late 1960's and into the 1970's. As a result, Hawaii's role in the international market has dwindled to an almost token supplier. Competition from lower cost producing areas has sprung up rapidly from distant points in Asia as well as Africa. According to the Food and Agriculture Organization of the United Nations, the Far East accounted for 70 percent of the 1983 world traffic in canned pineapple. The Philippines, Thailand, and Malaysia are the major suppliers to markets in the United States and Western Europe. In Africa, four countries dominate the export scene— Kenya, South Africa, the Ivory Coast, and Swaziland.

Dried Fruits. Raisins and dried prunes are by far the leading U.S. dried fruits exports. In the case of raisins, the ability of the United States to remain in the international scene has been challenged by policies adopted by the EC since the full accession of Greece in 1981. Protected by a system of minimum grower prices, processing subsidies and storage aids, and later minimum import prices, Greece has been in the unique position of capitalizing upon the two prize EC markets, West Germany and the United Kingdom. Turkey also has provided heavy supplies of sultanas at low prices. The traditional suppliers from Australia and South Africa, too, are experiencing potential displacement in the market on the Continent.

Despite EC policies designed for the protection of the French prune industry as well as the strong position of the U.S. dollar, U.S. exports of dried prunes have held up well in the European market. Japan, too, has developed into a reasonably good market for the California product.

Competition in Fresh Fruits

Today, we find the traffic in international trade of fresh fruit crowded with players—many new and many old. What has been most striking in this increased trade is the vast improvement in the market presentation of such fruits.

Whether it be an apple from New Zealand, a clementine from Morocco, or a papaya from Brazil, they are coming to market at their very best, well packaged and of high and more uniform quality.

Fresh Citrus. World trade in fresh citrus has increased tremendously over the past several decades. Trade in fresh oranges, the largest dollar earner of the citrus family, increased from a level of 2.6 million metric tons in the early 1960's to a peak of almost 4 million tons in the mid-1970's. Since then, orange output has more or less stabilized at a level of about 3.7 million tons.

The growth in global trade of tangerine-type fruit (tangerines, mandarins, etc.) also has been quite dramatic, rising from an average level of 239,000 tons in the early 1960's to about 1.1 million tons in the early 1980's. World exports of fresh lemons and grapefruit have experienced growth too, but at a slower pace. Lemons increased from 473,000 tons to 952,000 tons during the same period, with grapefruit exports rising from a mere 189,000 tons to a high of 769,000 tons at the beginning of this decade.

The largest exporters of fresh citrus are in the Mediterranean Basin. Countries in this region have accounted for nearly three-fourths of the world total in recent years. Spain is by far the largest Mediterranean exporter followed by Israel, Morocco, and seven other countries.

The United States is also a prominent world exporter of fresh citrus, but its share of the world total in recent seasons has only been between 12 to 15 percent. Other world suppliers of some significance include South Africa and Cuba. Although Brazil is already the world's largest citrus producer, its production is confined mostly to oranges used largely for frozen concentrated orange juice for the export market, primarily to the United States and Western Europe.

A large portion of the exports of fresh citrus originating in the Mediterranean Basin move to markets within the EC. Beginning in 1969, the EC began extending tariff rate preferences to the Mediterranean region. Today, virtually every citrus-producing country in this region is a beneficiary of such preferences.

Largely because of the EC preferences, U.S. exports of fresh oranges and lemons to the Community have declined significantly, but exports of fresh grapefruit have continued at a favorable pace due to the relatively low EC duty, limited competition, and superior product quality.

Since the liberalization of fresh lemons in 1964 and fresh grapefruit in 1971, Japan has become the No.1 U.S. export market for these items. Japan and Hong Kong also are important markets for U.S. oranges, although imports are still subject to a quota system.

Fresh Noncitrus. Perhaps one of the most notable examples of forces that have contributed to the reshaping of international trade lies in the area of deciduous fruits, particularly apples. France's fantastic rise in apple production within a short span of time and its almost simultaneous emergence as a major world exporter represents an outstanding horticultural achievement.

During the latter half of the 1950's, the French dessert apple crop averaged about 20 million bushels. By 1969 the French output reached 79 million bushels, an almost fourfold gain. Production continued to rise and finally reached its peak in 1975 with a crop of almost 105 million bushels.

Before the explosion of French production, the United States, Canada, and other distant suppliers looked to Western Europe as their prime offshore market. But by the late 1960's, with Western Europe's productive capacity rapidly approaching self-sufficiency, the United States and other distant suppliers were forced to look elsewhere.

The liberalization of Taiwan's apple market in 1979 was a turning point in U.S. export activity. In that season the U.S. apple did well not only in Taiwan, but also in a number of Far East markets; e.g., Hong Kong, Malaysia, Singapore, and the Arabian Peninsula. In the Middle East, particularly in Saudi Arabia, the United States was exposed to subsidized competition from the French, but, fortunately, consumers in that area showed a marked preference for the American red varieties. Since then the Arabian Peninsula has become one of the leading markets for U.S. apples. Although competition within the markets of the Far East and Arabian Peninsula was minimal at first, this relative freedom from competitive forces is now over.

According to FAO, the top three noncitrus fruits moving into international trade are bananas, apples, and grapes. The FAO tally indicates that exports of bananas in 1983 totaled 6.2 million tons, 1.5 million tons, or 32 percent above the base year, 1960. Of the top three, apples showed the greatest growth in both absolute and relative terms. Apple exports in 1983 totaled 3.6 million tons, 1.6 million tons or 83 percent above the base year.

Market observations indicate an apparent but substantial growth in a number of the more exotic fruits in the marketplace. These include nectarines, kiwi fruit, mangoes, papayas, avocados, and a number of more tropical items. North America and Western Europe appear to be the primary targets for the movement of such fruits.

Longer Term Outlook

Competition is likely to intensify in the years ahead. Assistance measures granted by the world powers to the developing countries will do much to intensify this competition. Many areas in Asia, Africa, and Latin America desperately need export earnings. Unable to turn to some of the more basic crops in international commerce, they may turn to horticultural pursuits, a repeat of the situation following World War II. Many U.S. horticultural industries also recognize the critical need for the export market. To keep it will require even more innovative thinking to stay one step ahead of the competition.

Cotton Around the World

By Henry O. Wagley, Jr.,
*agricultural economist, Tobacco,
Cotton and Seeds Division, Foreign
Agricultural Service*

For more than five thousand years cotton has played an important role in the economies of many countries. History tells of cotton grown and traded by ancient Egyptians. Bits of cotton fabric and string dating from 3000 B.C. were found in Pakistan. In Greece, historians reported cotton growing during the second century A.D. European explorers reaching the Western Hemisphere found the Indians using native cotton for cloth, cordage, fishing nets, and other items.

Despite the inroads made by synthetic products, world cotton consumption is at a record level and expanding modestly. Cultivation extends to all continents. World production reached a record level of 1984/85, over three times the 1946 benchmark.

Production

Cotton is a tropical plant which needs a growing period of about 200 days between killing frosts and a minimum summer average temperature of 77 °F. These conditions can be met in areas as far north as Central Asia in the U.S.S.R. and as far south as Argentina and Australia.

Although cotton is native to

USDA

many regions of the world, only a few species are generally grown on a commercial basis. Upland is the most important cotton grown and accounts for most of the world's production. Extra-long staple Egyptian and American Pima are produced in smaller amounts.

Cotton is grown commercially in more than 75 countries, but only a few provide the bulk of the world's production. Fifty years ago the world's major producers were the United States, the U.S.S.R., China, India, Brazil, and Egypt. Today, three countries— China, the United States, and the U.S.S.R.—account for 62 percent of world production.

China. China is the largest producer with 27.9 million bales during 1984/85. Cotton is mainly grown in the Northern China Plain and Central China.

Even though China has been a leading producer for many years, it is only now emerging as an important supplier in the international market. Before the 1983/84 season, China produced essentially for the do-

Cotton is a tropical plant that needs a growing period of about 200 days at an average temperature of 77°F. These conditions exist as far north as Central Asia and as far south as Argentina and Australia. (Arizona, cotton field.)

USDA

mestic market, and as late as 1980 was a major cotton importer. Chinese production averaged 9 million bales a year during 1960–79, but increased rapidly following production incentives established in 1978. These incentives included higher prices, the household production responsibility system where the household became the basic production unit,

China is emerging as an important world cotton supplier even though being a leading producer for years. In the past China has produced for the domestic market. (China, cotton harvest.)

improved varieties, more chemical fertilizer, and pesticides. Incentives were reduced in October 1984 to alleviate burdensome stocks resulting from the phenomenal production increase. China, however, is expected to remain the world's largest cotton-producing country.

The United States. Cotton has been grown in the United States since colonial times. Production and trade grew rapidly in the early days of the republic. By 1810, production had climbed to 178,000 bales and exports to 124,000 bales. For many decades, the United States was the world's largest producer. Today, it is the world's second largest producer, harvesting 13 million bales during 1984/85.

U.S. cotton farmers can participate in a voluntary acreage set-aside program under legislation covering production through the 1985/86 season. The program is designed to enable farmers to produce for the marketplace and still protect

The U.S.S.R. is the second largest cotton-consuming nation in the world. It also is the third largest producer, harvesting 11.7 million bales in 1984/85. (U.S.S.R., cotton harvest.)

USDA

income should prices drop drastically. U.S. cotton is produced in 18 States, generally divided into the southern, delta, southwestern, and western areas. Upland cotton accounted for 99 percent of U.S. production in 1984/85 and the extra-long staple Pima cotton for 1 percent.

U.S.S.R. The U.S.S.R. is the third leading producer harvesting an estimated 11.7 million bales in 1984/85. Soviet production reached self-sufficient levels in the early 1930's, and a small export market was developed at that time. U.S.S.R. production expanded steadily following World War II reaching an average 9.9 million bales from 1960 to 1979. Production has slipped in the past three seasons compelling the U.S.S.R. to make substantial cotton imports to obtain sufficient cotton for domestic and East European markets. Cotton is produced in six republics mainly in Soviet Central Asia, with Uzbekistan accounting for almost 60 percent of total area in the U.S.S.R. Approximately 10 percent of the cotton area is in extra long staple varieties.

Other Countries. India, Brazil, and Egypt harvested 7 million, 3.9 million, and 1.8 million bales respectively in 1984/

85. Pakistan, which was included with India before the independence of both countries, accounted for 4.6 million bales. Together, this group represents 20 percent of the world's 84.9 million bales produced in 1984/85. Other countries producing a million or more bales in recent years are Turkey, Mexico, Australia, and Sudan.

Growing and Harvesting

Cotton growing and harvesting is highly mechanized in the United States and many major cotton-producing countries. Cultural and harvest practices vary among countries and production areas within countries based on climate, soils, plant diseases, insect and weed control problems, and labor cost and availability.

Irrigation is an important factor in many cotton-producing countries and areas. In the United States, rain-grown cotton is produced in the Southeastern and Midsouth Delta States. Irrigation is used for part of the Texas crop and all cotton grown in the Western States. Water application ranges from less than 1 acre foot to as much as 6 acre feet annually depending on area. In the U.S.S.R., water from melt-

USDA

Cotton growing and harvesting is highly mechanized in the United States and many other cotton-producing countries. (Texas, cotton-picking machine.)

ing snow in the mountains of Central Asia is used for irrigation. Cotton also is irrigated in China, Egypt, Pakistan, and parts of India.

Harvesting may be mechanical or by hand. All U.S. cotton is machine harvested. Among the other leading producing countries, cotton is picked by hand in China, India, Pakistan and Egypt, and is mainly machine picked in the U.S.S.R.

Consumption

World cotton consumption reached a record 69.8 million bales in 1984/85. Trends have shown a slow but gradual increase in its use although they vary widely among countries.

Since the end of World War II, cotton has faced increasing competition from synthetic fibers. Synthetic fibers' share of the textile fiber market increased from 12 percent in 1946 to 47 percent in 1983. Much of this increase has come at the expense of cotton with its share of the market dropping from 73 percent to 48 percent in the same period. The largest synthetic fiber gains came in the 1950's and 1960's. In recent years, the market shares of both cotton and synthetic fibers have been relatively stable.

The U.S. textile industry was the world's largest consumer until the late 1960's. Reaching a peak of 11.2 million bales in 1941, U.S. consumption remained above 9 million as late as 1967. Consumption has generally declined in recent years as textile imports increased, dropping to 5.3 million bales in 1984/85.

China became the world's largest cotton consumer in 1969/70. Chinese consumption has grown dramatically over the last 10 years although the increasing popularity of synthetic fiber items has tapered gains during the last three seasons.

The U.S.S.R. is the second largest consumer at 9.5 million bales in 1984/85. Soviet trends indicate a slow but general increase in cotton consumption. U.S.S.R. consumption increased from 8.2 million bales in 1970/71 to 9.2 million in 1980/82 and 9.5 million in 1984/85.

Western Europe, the third largest consumer, has seen consumption fall slightly over the last 15 years as imported textiles have replaced domestic production. Its consumption totaled 6 million bales in 1970/71 but only 5.8 million in 1984/85.

In Asia, development of tex-tile industries for the export market has sharply increased consumption in Burma, Taiwan, Indonesia, South Korea, and Thailand. General long-term trends show cotton utilization shifting toward low-wage developing areas.

Textile Industry

The textile industry was the principal market for the 69.8 million bales of cotton consumed in 1984/85. The textile production process has four steps: (1) preparation, (2) spinning, (3) weaving, and (4) finishing. When the cotton arrives at the textile plant, the bales are opened and blended to ensure uniformity of fiber. Machines remove impurities and form lint into rolls called laps. The laps are fed into cording machines which straighten the fibers.

The spinning process involves a spinning frame which twists the fiber strands to form yarn. During this process cotton and synthetic fibers can be twisted together to produce a blended yarn.

The next process produces fabric through weaving, tufting, or bonding. Weaving is the oldest fabric process. Warp yarn and weft yarn are woven together on a loom to produce grey cloth. Tufting is used to make carpets. The bonding process chemically or mechanically bonds yarns together to produce nonwoven fabrics. Disposable diapers and some dishcloths are made by this process.

The finishing or final step includes bleaching, dyeing, and sanforizing to prevent shrinking.

World Trade

The international cotton trade has shifted dramatically toward Asia, as Asian nations have developed cotton textile industries.

Importers. In 1950/51, Europe accounted for 64 percent of world imports and Asia, 29 percent. Imports into Japan and Hong Kong increased rapidly in the 1950's and 1960's. By 1971/72, Asia's imports had increased to 47 percent, and Europe's declined to 46 percent. Current reports indicate that Asia will represent 50 percent and Europe 42 percent of 1984/85 world imports.

Countries reporting the largest import increases since 1971/72 are South Korea, Taiwan, and Thailand, their consumption growing along with the development of their textile industries. Chinese imports increased meteorically during

1977–80, but fell just as fast when Chinese production exceeded utilization.

In Europe, the United Kingdom, France, Netherlands, and Belgium have reported the largest declines in imports since 1971/72, while Portugal and Italy have reported gains. In Africa, Nigeria and Algeria reported increased imports during the period.

Exporters. Leading exporters of cotton are the United States, the U.S.S.R., China, Pakistan, and Sudan, providing 62 percent of 1984/85 world exports. The United States, the U.S.S.R., and Pakistan have been major exporters since the late 1940's and 1950's. Sudan emerged as a major exporter with the expansion of the Gezira Scheme in the late 1950's. The Gezira Scheme is an irrigated agricultural area of about 2.1 million acres developed between 1911 and 1972. Sudanese exports faltered with smaller crops in the last half of the 1970's but have been staging a comeback in the 1980's. China was an important supplier to Japan before World War II, but it is only now reappearing as an important cotton exporter. Egypt has been the major exporter of extra-long staple cotton for many years.

World Cotton Production, Consumption and Trade —1984/85

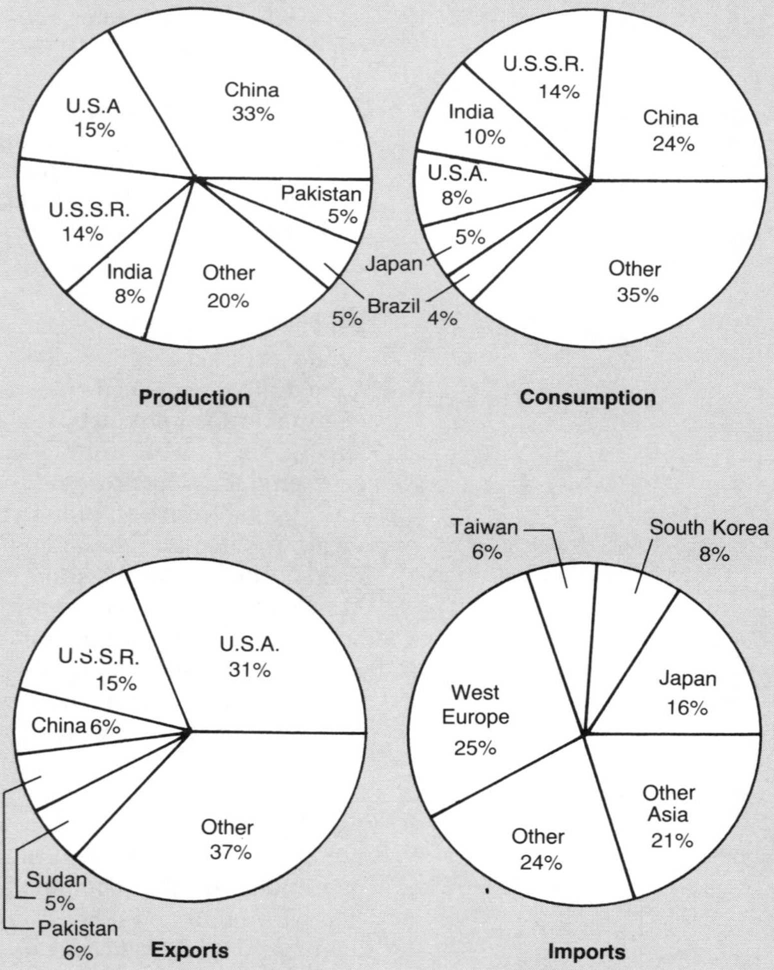

Production

China 33%
U.S.A 15%
U.S.S.R. 14%
India 8%
Other 20%
Brazil 5%
Pakistan 5%

Consumption

China 24%
Other 35%
U.S.S.R. 14%
India 10%
U.S.A. 8%
Japan 5%
Brazil 4%

Exports

U.S.A. 31%
Other 37%
U.S.S.R. 15%
China 6%
Pakistan 6%
Sudan 5%

Imports

West Europe 25%
Other 24%
Other Asia 21%
Japan 16%
South Korea 8%
Taiwan 6%

Cotton

Oilseeds Around the World

By Philip L. Mackie, *director,*
Oilseeds and Products Division,
Foreign Agricultural Service

World demand for oilseeds and oilseed products increased dramatically during the 1960's and 1970's, but has stagnated during the 1980's. The United States is still the world's leading producer and exporter of oilseeds, but U.S. exports have declined in the 1980's as markets have been limited by economic recession, shortages of foreign exchange, the strength of the U.S. dollar, and by increased competitive production.

Uses

While some oilseeds are consumed directly as food such as peanuts or food products such as tofu, the bulk of world oilseed production is processed into vegetable oil and protein meal. The demand for oil and meal is separate and distinct. Most vegetable oil is consumed as liquid salad or cooking oil or in margarine, shortening, vanaspati, or other hardened fat products. Vegetable oils have many industrial uses, however, and a significant portion of world production is used for nonfood purposes. Protein meal is primarily used in combination with grain and other ingredients as a feed for livestock and poultry.

Although all the oilseed products serve the same or similar end uses, all also are unique. They vary, particularly, in their relative yields of oil and meal, in the fatty acid composition of the oil, and in the protein content and amino acid composition of the meal. Each product is relatively better suited to some particular uses than others, although all are, to some degree, substitutes. This uniqueness makes for a highly complex demand structure.

The United States is the world's leading producer of oilseeds, most of which are processed into vegetable oil and protein meal for animal feed. Soybean is the dominant oilseed product. (U.S., soybeans.)

USDA

Major Oilseeds and Related Products

	Oil Yield	Meal Yield	Protein Content of Meal
	Percent		
Soybeans	17.7	79.5	44.0
Cottonseed	16.0	46.5	41.0
Peanuts (shelled basis)	45.0	54.0	50.0
Sunflowerseed	35.0	45.0	42.0
Rapeseed	35.0	60.0	36.0
Flaxseed	34.0	63.0	35.0
Palm Kernel	47.0	51.0	18.0
Coconut	64.0	35.0	22.0
Fish Products	10.0	22.0	65.0

Production

The major world oilseeds in tonnage produced are soybeans, cottonseed, peanuts, sunflowerseed, rapeseed, and flaxseed. Production of these oilseeds in 1984/85 totaled 181 million metric tons. In analyzing world supply and demand factors for oilseeds, the U.S. Department of Agriculture also considers several major commodities closely related in terms of product use. These are the tree crops—palm oil, palm kernel oil and meal, coconut oil and meal, and olive oil—and fish meal and oil. In addition, many other oilseeds or related products are important in particular countries or for specialized uses such as sameseed, safflowerseed, castorseed, and jojoba, but they have a limited impact on the overall market.

In 1984/85, 80 percent—145 million tons—of the six major oilseeds were crushed to produce 33 million tons of vegetable oil and 94 million tons of protein meal. In addition, tree crop oil and meal production totaled 12 and 2 million tons, and fish oil and meal production 1 and 5 million tons respectively.

World Production of Oilseeds and Related Products, 1984/85

	Seed	Oil	Protein Meal
	Million metric tons		
Soybeans	90.7	13.4	59.2
Cottonseed	34.3	4.2	12.6
Peanuts	[1]19.7	3.3	4.6
Sunflowerseed	17.7	6.3	7.0
Rapeseed	16.5	5.6	9.2
Flaxseed	2.2	.6	1.2
Palm Kernel	2.2	.9	1.1
Palm Oil	—	7.0	—
Coconut	[2] 4.4	2.7	1.4
Olive Oil	—	1.7	—
Fish Products	—	1.4	5.5
Total	187.7	47.1	[3]100.4

[1]In-shell basis. [2]Copra basis. [3]Total does not add up because of rounding.

Trade

Unlike most other agricultural commodities, a relatively large share of world oilseeds and products enters world trade. In 1984/85, nearly 20 percent of world oilseed production and more than 30 percent of world production of oils and protein meals were traded internationally.

Soybeans dominate world trade in oilseeds and protein meals, accounting for 78 percent of world oilseed and 71 percent of world protein meal trade in 1984/85. World trade in oils is more diffused among the various commodities. Palm oil is the leading oil traded internationally with 29 percent of the world market, followed by soybean oil with 25 percent.

Oilseeds. The major world markets for oilseeds are the countries of Western Europe and Japan. In addition, several newly industrializing nations such as Taiwan, Korea, and Mexico are rapidly increasing imports. All these countries have a demand base for both

Soybeans account for 78 percent of the world oilseed trade and 71 percent of the world protein meal trade. (Iowa, soybean harvest.)

Tim McCabe

World Exports of Oilseeds and Related Products, 1984/85

	Seed	Oil	Protein Meal
	Million metric tons		
Soybeans	25.7	3.6	21.8
Cottonseed	.3	.4	1.0
Peanuts	.9	.3	.5
Sunflowerseed	2.0	1.8	1.8
Rapeseed	2.9	1.0	1.2
Flaxseed	.5	.2	.5
Palm Kernel	.2	.6	.7
Palm Oil	—	4.2	—
Coconut	.3	1.1	.7
Olive Oil	—	.4	—
Fish Products	—	.8	2.6
Total	32.8	14.4	30.8

USDA

oils and protein meals enabling them to support a crushing industry based on imported oilseeds. The United States is the dominant world exporter of oilseeds, followed by Argentina, Brazil, Canada, and China.

Protein Meals. The major world markets for protein meals are the countries of Western Europe and Eastern Europe. These countries generally have high levels of livestock product consumption and sophisticated animal feed industries. The demand for protein feeds for these industries requires them to import protein meals in excess of production from domestic and imported oilseeds, and it exceeds their demand for oils. In addition, the demand for imported protein meals is increasing in several countries of the Middle East, North Africa, and the Caribbean Basin where livestock industries are expanding. The major world exporters of protein meals are Brazil, the United States, Argentina, Chile, Peru (fish meal), India, and China.

The major markets for U.S. oilseeds are Japan and Western Europe while the major markets for protein meal are Western and Eastern Europe. (A U.S. animal nutritionist calculates soybean meal feed rations for a Japanese dairy farmer.)

Vegetable Oils. The major world import markets for vegetable oils are generally developing countries which have rapidly growing populations and low levels of per capita oil consumption, but do not have a demand base to support a sophisticated livestock industry. Oil imports are widely dispersed among a number of these countries—much more widely than are imports of oilseeds or protein meals. Ten major world importing countries—India, Pakistan, Egypt, Iran, Algeria, Turkey, Venezuela, Nigeria, Morocco, and Iraq—account for 30 percent of world oil imports. The U.S.S.R. also is a major world vegetable oil importer. Several major industrialized countries such as West Germany, the Netherlands, and the United States both import and export oils to balance the requirements of their more sophisticated oil using industries, or as transshipment trade centers. The major world oil exporters are Malaysia, Argentina, the United States, Brazil, the Philippines, Spain, and Indonesia.

Government Policy

World trade in oilseeds and oilseed products is more market oriented than trade in many other agricultural commodities. Imports into most of the major industrialized markets are unrestricted or subject to relatively low duties. Imports into these traditional markets—which account for two-thirds of world imports of oilseeds and more than one-half of world imports of protein meals—are generally determined by commercial market factors.

Policy factors, however, are becoming a more important determinant of world oilseed imports. Growth in consumption of oilseed products has stabilized in many traditional markets as their livestock and food industries have reached maturity. Each year, a larger share of world oilseed and product trade is accounted for by the newly industrializing and developing countries in response to their rapid population growth and developing livestock industries. Imports into the majority of these countries are generally subject to government controls—either in the form of licensing to protect domestic producers, foreign exchange allocations, or direct state trading. For example, India, the largest world importer of vegetable oils, prohibits oilseed imports and maintains internal vegetable oil prices which are substantially above world market levels. The State Trading Corporation of India contracts for all imports of vegetable oils. India also controls the types and quantity of imported oils used in the manufacture of vanaspati—the most important fat product consumed in India.

Government policies also are becoming a significant factor in determining oilseed and product imports in many traditional markets, although usually not in the form of direct import restrictions. As the European Community (EC) has become a surplus producer of grain, it has increasingly turned to stimulating production of oilseeds with high producer support prices. Production of sunflowerseed and rapeseed in the EC has increased from an average of 2.2 million tons in 1978–82 to 4.6 million tons in 1984. The EC also has considered imposing a consumption tax on fats and oils to raise money to support the Common Agricultural Policy. The oilseed sector is the only agricultural sector in the EC not rigidly controlled by that policy.

The accession of Spain to the EC will increase policy tension in the oilseed sector. Spain is a major importer of soybeans, but restricts consumption of soybean oil with a quota on sales in the domestic market. This policy is designed to protect Spanish producers of olive oil and sunflowerseed, but is inconsistent with the market rules of the EC. In addition, support prices for olive oil are much higher in the EC than in Spain. Adoption of EC prices in Spain would stimulate production of Spanish olive oil, which is already in surplus.

Major Commodities

Soybeans. Soybeans are by far the leading world oilseed in production and trade, and soybean meal is the leading protein meal produced and traded. Soybean oil is the leading vegetable oil in world production, but palm oil exceeds it in world trade. The phenomenal increase in world production and trade of soybeans in the 1960's and 1970's was stimulated by economic growth and sharp increases in world demand for livestock products. Soybeans have the highest relative yield of protein meal of any of the oilseeds, and the protein is of high quality.

The United States is the leading world producer of soybeans, with 56 percent of world production in 1984/85, followed by Brazil, China, and Argentina. The United States also is the leading world exporter of soybeans shipping 70 percent of the world total in 1984/85, followed by Brazil and Argentina. The leading world importers of soybeans are the EC, Japan, Spain, Mexico, Taiwan, and Portugal.

The United States also is the leading world producer of soybean meal, but Brazil exported twice as much soybean meal as did the United States in 1984/85. Argentina is the third leading exporter of soybean meal, and has been the most rapidly increasing producer and exporter of soybeans and soybean products during the 1980's. The leading importers of soybean meal are the EC and Eastern Europe. The U.S.S.R. increased imports of soybean meal rapidly in the early 1980's, but imports dropped sharply in 1983/84 and 1984/85. The U.S.S.R. has a major and chronic deficit of protein feeds for livestock.

Brazil is the leading exporter of soybean oil followed by the United States, Argentina, the EC, and Spain. The leading importers are India, Iran, and Pakistan.

In 1984/85, the United States accounted for 45 percent

of total world exports of soybeans and soybean products, while Brazil and Argentina together accounted for 35 percent. While exports from the United States are primarily soybeans, exports from Brazil and Argentina are primarily meal and oil. The Governments of Brazil and Argentina have provided large subsidies for processing oilseeds into products for export, primarily through applying differential tax rates on the export of oilseed products and the raw material. Oilseed production in Brazil and Argentina is not directly subsidized, although financial incentives for the agricultural sector are available. Lower tax rates on the export of products than on the oilseeds provides a powerful incentive for developing the domestic oilseed processing industry and exporting the product rather than seed.

Cottonseed. Cottonseed is a byproduct of cotton. The demand for cotton rather than for protein meal and vegetable oil determines world production.

Cottonseed is the second leading world oilseed in terms of production. Little cottonseed is traded internationally because cottonseed is a bulky commodity which make transportation relatively expensive.

Most cottonseed meal and oil also is used in the country in which the cottonseed is produced with less than 10 percent entering world trade.

China is by far the world's leading producer of cottonseed, accounting for 35 percent of world production in 1984/85, followed by the U.S.S.R., the United States, India, Pakistan, and Brazil.

Peanuts. World peanut production totals about 20 million metric tons per year, with India, China, and the United States the world's leading producers. About 60 percent of world production is crushed for the production of oil and meal, and about 30 percent is consumed directly in edible form. Only about 5 percent of world peanut production is traded. In the past 10 years, fewer peanuts are being traded for crushing, and an increasing number are being shipped as edibles. The leading exporters of edible peanuts are the United States, which accounts for more than 40 percent of the world total, China, and Argentina. The leading importers are

U.S. exports of oilseeds account for about one-third of the total world trade of oilseeds and products. (U.S., oilseed storage.)

USDA

the EC, Canada, and Japan. World trade in peanut oil and peanut meal is relatively minor.

Rapeseed and Sunflowerseed.
Rapeseed and sunflowerseed together account for less than 20 percent of world oilseed production, but world output is increasing rapidly. The leading world producers of rapeseed are China, the EC, Canada, India, and Eastern Europe, and the leading exporter is Canada. The leading producers of sunflowerseed are the U.S.S.R., Argentina, Eastern Europe, the United States, China, the EC, and Spain, and the leading exporter is the United States.

Palm Oil. World palm oil production totals nearly 7 million tons annually, and nearly 60 percent of production enters world trade. Malaysia is the most important producer and exporter, accounting for 56 percent of world production and about 85 percent of world exports in 1984/85. The leading world importers are India, Pakistan, the U.S.S.R., the EC, and the United States. Imports are increasing rapidly in the Middle East and Africa.

Palm oil is a tree crop that can be produced effectively and economically under tropical conditions. Palm oil production in Malaysia has increased ninefold since 1970, stimulated by large investments of private and public funds in plantation-type operations. The trees bear for about 25 years, which, along with new plantings, assures continued large world supplies of palm oil for the future.

Malaysia has stimulated the development of a domestic refining and processing industry with a complicated differential export tax system, and is exporting an increasing proportion of refined palm oil products.

U.S. Oilseed Exports

U.S. oilseed production totaled 59.2 million tons in 1984/85 and about 42 percent—19.4 million tons of oilseeds and 5.6 million tons of oilseed products—was exported. Exports were valued at $6.7 billion—20 percent of the total value of U.S. agricultural exports, accounting for nearly one-third of total world trade of oilseeds and products.

Livestock, Poultry, and Dairy Around the World

By John E. Riesz, *director, Dairy, Livestock and Poultry Division, Foreign Agricultural Service*

Livestock and poultry production, international trade, and consumption affect the social, economic, and nutritional standards of the world's population. Generally, as the purchasing power of the world's population increases, so does the per capita consumption of livestock and poultry meat products. The consumption level for each type of meat is affected by the traditional supply and demand situation, particularly in countries where a free market system operates, such as the United States. In addition, government policies often result in artificially high prices through domestic price supports or import barriers, or both, such as those in Japan and the European Community (EC) as well as in periodic shortages because of price controls or subsidized prices, or both, as in most of the centrally controlled economies. Cultural and social customs, where because of tradition, one type of meat product has a higher level of consumer preference, and religious customs that discourage or forbid eating certain meat products (e.g. Moslems and Hebrews do not consume pork, and Hindus restrict bovine slaughter) also may be factors in determining consumption levels.

Consumption

Worldwide per capita consumption of beef and veal, pork, and poultry—has gone up, on the whole, at a relatively modest rate since 1979, despite a downward trend in beef and veal.

Beef and Veal. Countries with the highest per capita beef and veal consumption are Argentina, Uruguay, New Zealand, the United States, and Australia. The range in 1984

was from a high of about 169 pounds to a low of 88 pounds. Countries with the lowest consumption rate include India, less than 1.1 pounds, followed by Taiwan, the Philippines, South Korea, Hong Kong, and Japan, where consumption is in the 3.3- to 13.2-pound range.

Pork. Per capita pork consumption is highest in selected European countries—Hungary, German Democratic Republic, Czechoslovakia, Belgium, Denmark, and West Germany— ranging from a high of 207

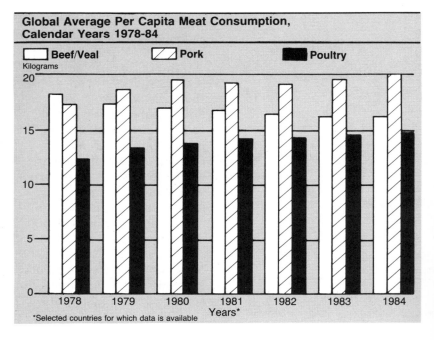

Global Average Per Capita Meat Consumption, Calendar Years 1978-84

☐ Beef/Veal   ▨ Pork   ■ Poultry

*Selected countries for which data is available
Years*

TASS

pounds down to 103 pounds in 1984. South American countries averaged 15 pounds or less.

Poultry. Poultry meat per capita consumption had a much narrower range. In 1984, Israel had the highest rate, more than 88 pounds, followed by Saudi Arabia and the United States, at 77 and 66 pounds, respectively. South Korea appeared to have the lowest level, less than 9 pounds.

Cattle and Hog Population

Cattle. Based on data from 50 countries, cattle numbers have been fairly stable in recent years. During 1981–84,

The U.S.S.R. has the largest cattle population (excluding India because of religious policies) followed by the United States in second place. (U.S.S.R. cattle-breeding complex.)

they ranged from 943 to 947 million head and are expected to remain near the midpoint of that range in 1985.

India continues to account for about one-fourth of the total. Because of religious policies that restrict cattle slaughter, however, India contributes less than 1 percent to the world's beef supply. Of the remaining 49 countries, the U.S.S.R., beginning in 1981, had the largest number of animals, followed by the United States, Brazil, the EC, Argentina, Mexico, Colombia, Australia, Turkey, and South Africa.

Excluding India, the top 10 countries account for 60 percent of total cattle population and over 80 percent of total beef and veal production. Production volume of beef and veal, however, does not always correlate with the size of the cattle population, even when there are no religious barriers. For example, in 1984, the United States produced 54 percent more beef and veal from fewer than 114 million head than the U.S.S.R. produced from 120 million cattle. Productivity varied substantially, ranging from a high of 96 metric tons per million head in the United States to a low of 13 tons in Turkey. The others included the EC at 93 tons per million head, followed by the U.S.S.R., 59; Australia, 57; Argentina, 44; Mexico, 39; Colombia, 26; Brazil, 24; and South Africa, 23.

The reasons for the variations in productivity include breed type, climate, age at slaughter, type of feed, management practices such as range vs. confinement, and pest and disease control. Factors contributing to the lack of growth in the size of cattle herds are related to: 1) climatic conditions in the major producing countries; 2) poor economic conditions resulting in low returns or negative returns to producers; 3) a general decline in per capita consumption of beef in developed countries; 4) economic stagnation in the developing countries; and 5) governmental policies.

Hogs. From a recent low of 693 million in 1982, the world's total hog population has shown a slight but steady increase in the 35 countries for which data are available. This trend is projected to continue during 1985 and is expected to reach nearly 708 million. China has, by far, the highest number ranging from 294 million to 300 million head, nearly 43 percent of the recorded total. The EC is second, ranging from 73 to 79 million head, followed by the U.S.S.R., 68–79 million; the United States, 54–64 million; and Brazil, 33–37 million head. In 1984, these five hog-producing countries accounted for nearly 78 percent of the more than 703 million hogs.

Like beef, the productivity rate for pork also varied greatly. China, with the largest hog population, had the lowest productivity rate at 47 tons per

FAO

million head, followed by the U.S.S.R. at 75 and Poland at 80. The highest productivity rates were in Japan, the EC, the United States, and Hungary, which averaged two and one-half to three times China's productivity rate. Some of the same factors that affect beef productivity also apply to pork productivity, e.g., breed types, type of feed, management practices, and pest and disease control.

Production

Beef and Veal. From an average of 41.7 million metric tons in 50 countries during 1976–80, production declined

China has by far the highest number of hogs ranging annually from 294 to 300 million head. (China, communal hog farm.)

to 40.7 million tons in 1981, then reached a recent peak of over 41.8 million tons in 1984. It is expected to decline slightly in 1985 to 41.7 million tons. In 1984, eight of the top producing countries accounted for nearly 80 percent of the world beef and veal production. The United States was the leading producer with 26 percent, followed by the EC and the U.S.S.R. at 18 and 17 percent, respectively. The others in the top eight with their percentage of production were: Ar-

Global Meat Production, 1976-80 and 1981-85

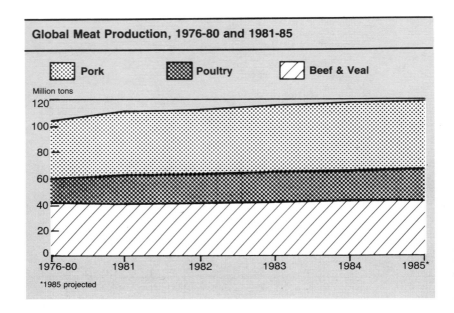

Global Beef and Veal Production— CY 1984

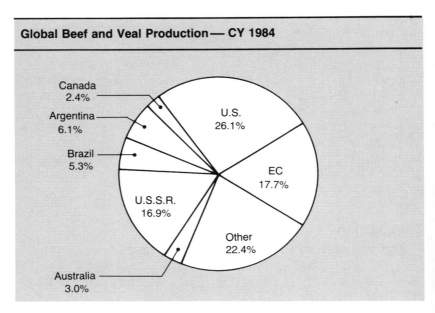

Global Pork Production — CY 1984

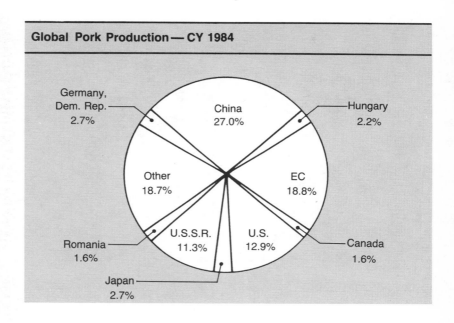

Global Poultry Meat Production — CY 1984

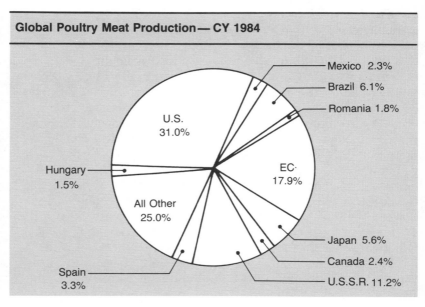

Murray Lemmon

gentina (6.1); Brazil (5.3); Australia (3.0); Canada (2.4), and New Zealand (1.1).

Pork. The trend has been gradually upward from an annual average of 42.6 million tons during 1976–80 to 52.7 million tons projected for 1985. In 1984, four of the major producing countries accounted for over 70 percent of the world's pork production, which totaled more than 52 million tons. China was the leading producer with 27 percent, followed by the EC, United States, and Soviet Union at 18.8, 12.9, and 11.3 percent, respectively. Other countries that accounted for 2 percent or more were Japan, the German Democratic Republic, Poland, and Hungary.

Five major producing countries account for 72 percent of the world's poultry meat production. The United States is the leading producer with 31 percent. (Indiana, poultry processing.)

Poultry. Poultry meat production in the 44 countries for which data are available has shown considerable growth. From an average of 18.7 million tons during 1976–80, it has grown 33 percent to a projected 24.9 million tons for 1985. In 1984, five of the major producing countries accounted for nearly 72 percent of the world's poultry meat. The United States was the leading producer with 31 percent followed by the EC, the U.S.S.R., Brazil, and Japan at

World Trade in Agricultural Products

17.9, 11.2, 6.1, and 5.6 percent, respectively. Other countries that accounted for 2 percent or more were Spain, Canada, and Mexico.

Imports

Beef and Veal. These imports have been declining since the recent high of 2.6 million tons in 1982. Annual imports declined 1 percent in 1983 and 4 percent in 1984 from the previous year with the downward trend continuing in 1985. In 1984, five of the major markets accounted for nearly 80 percent of the imports. The United States was the leading importer, taking one-third of the total, followed by the U.S.S.R., EC, Japan, and Canada with a market share of 20.0, 11.3, 8.4, and 4.7 percent, respectively. The U.S.S.R. showed the largest gains from an annual average of less than 250,000 tons in 1976–80 to the current rate of 500,000 tons. Japan also showed measurable gains. Performance by EC countries showed just the reverse—imports declined from an annual average of nearly 400,000 tons in 1976–80 to less than 300,000 tons currently. Canada and the United States also showed a slight decline.

Pork. Total import trade in pork has shown a cyclical pattern. The most recent peak occurred in 1984 and was slightly over 1.1 million tons, more than 22 percent above the 1976–80 annual average. Four of the major markets accounted for over 80 percent of the import trade. The United States was the leading importer, taking over 38 percent, followed by Japan, the EC, and the U.S.S.R. with a market share of 25, 11 and 8 percent, respectively. The United States showed the largest gain, nearly 100 percent, from the 1976–80 period followed by Japan with a 69-percent gain, while the market share by the EC declined nearly 50 percent. The forecast for 1985 projects import trade under 1 million tons.

Poultry Meat. Total import trade in poultry meat has remained fairly stable in the 1.1-million-ton range, after a 73-percent rise in 1981 from the 1976–80 annual average of 670,000 tons. In 1984, four of the major markets accounted for nearly 60 percent of the import trade. The U.S.S.R. and Saudi Arabia were the top two markets with nearly a 19-percent market share each, followed by Egypt and Japan at 11.4 and 10.2 percent, respectively. Kuwait, Iraq, and Hong Kong each with about a 7-percent market share also were important markets. All of the major markets showed substantial import gains in 1984 from the 1976–80 annual average (Egypt more than 400 percent followed by Iraq, the U.S.S.R., Japan, and Saudi Arabia with 133, 90, 86, and 63 percent gains, respectively).

Dairy Products. Many countries import dairy products but only a few are major factors in the international dairy product market. In 1983 about 4.2 million metric tons of manufactured dairy products were imported worldwide (excluding EC intra-trade). Food aid from the United States, EC, Australia and a few other nations accounted for 0.4 million tons with more than half the remaining 3.8 million tons bought by Algeria, the U.S.S.R., the EC, United States, Japan, Saudi Arabia, Iran, Mexico, Nigeria, and Venezuela.

In 1983, U.S. imports of manufactured dairy products— mostly cheese and casein— amounted to 205,000 tons with nearly 60 percent of the total under quota. Quota and nonquota, at 130,000 tons, represented 6 percent of U.S. cheese production. Casein, a nonquota milk protein, has not been manufactured in the

Dairy Products and Their Importers, 1983

Product	Million Metric Tons	Leading Importers
Cheese and Curd	0.9	U.S., EC, Japan, and Iran
Butter and Anhydrous Milkfat[1]	0.8	U.S.S.R., EC, Algeria, and Iran
Dry Milk Powders	1.7	Mexico, Japan, Venezuela, and Algeria
Condensed and Evaporated Milk	0.7	Algeria, Nigeria, Libya, and Saudi Arabia
Casein	0.1	U.S. and Japan
Total	4.2	Worldwide

[1]Anhydrous milkfat: butter oil and ghee

United States since 1968. With the establishment of the dairy price support program in 1949, it became more economical to import it. Over the years, casein imports have grown rapidly, reaching 72,000 tons in 1983.

Exports

Beef and Veal. These exports have shown a slightly cyclical pattern with an upward trend. The most recent peak, in 1982, was slightly over 4.5 million tons, more than 8 percent over the 1976–80 annual average. In 1983 and 1984, exports de-

clined 3 and 4 percent, respectively, from the previous year's level. The 1985 forecast projects an 8-percent increase.

In 1984, six of the major exporters accounted for three-fourths of the exports. Brazil more than tripled and the EC more than doubled their respective percentages of market share in 1984 over the 1976–80 annual average. The United States also more than doubled its market share but at a much lower volume. Most of the gains occurred at the expense of Australia and Argentina.

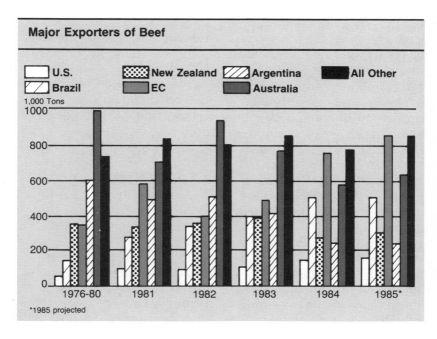

Major Exporters of Beef

U.S. New Zealand Argentina All Other
Brazil EC Australia

1,000 Tons

*1985 projected

Their shares declined from 30.6 percent and 18.5 percent, respectively, in 1976–80 to 17.5 percent and 7.5 percent in 1984.

As a result of these shifts, the EC became the No. 1 exporter in 1984 with a market share of 23 percent, a rapid rise from fourth position, at 11 percent, during 1976–80 followed by Australia with a market share of 17.5 percent; Brazil at 15.2 percent; New Zealand at 8.8 percent; Argentina at 7.5 percent; and the United States at 4.6 percent. For 1985, the projections indicate continued expansion for the EC, Australia, New Zealand, and the United States— while Argentina and Brazil are expected to remain near their 1984 performance levels.

The EC's rise to the No. 1 exporter in 1984 was a phenomenal achievement considering that only a decade earlier it was a net importer of beef and veal. It achieved that position in such a short period because of an overly generous Common Agricultural Policy (CAP) which resulted in: 1) a 22-percent rise in beef and veal production between 1973 and 1984; 2) a near-stagnant consumer demand due to high retail prices; 3) a growing stock-pile that reached 813,000 tons by the end of 1984, up nearly 120 percent from the 374,000 tons on hand in 1976; and 4) a highly subsidized export policy. EC-subsidized prices undercut world export beef prices by 30 percent.

Pork. Total export trade in pork increased every year since 1980 except 1982. During 1984, six of the major markets accounted for nearly two-thirds of the export trade. The EC was the leading exporter, with 24 percent, followed by the German Democratic Republic, Canada, Hungary, Romania, and the United States with 12.8, 10.4, 9.2, 4.6, and 4.5 percent, respectively. The German Democratic Republic, Hungary, and Canada showed increases in export volume between the annual 1976–80 percentage and 1984, ranging from 180 to 150 percent, while U.S. exports declined nearly 50 percent.

Poultry Meat. Total export trade in poultry meat has declined since the peak in 1981 of nearly 1.5 million tons, which was almost double the 1976–80 annual average of 765,000 tons. One reason for the decline is that several importing countries expanded their domestic production, re-

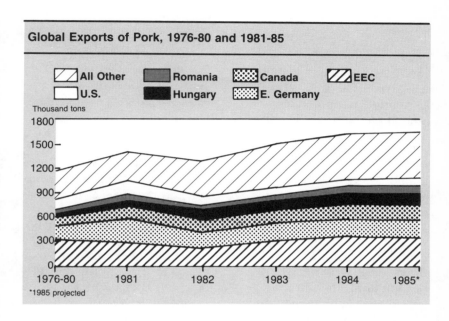

Global Exports of Pork, 1976-80 and 1981-85

Legend: All Other, U.S., Romania, Hungary, Canada, E. Germany, EEC

Thousand tons

*1985 projected

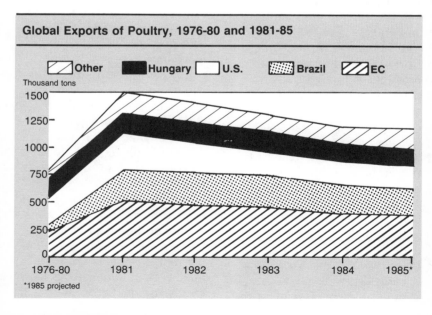

Global Exports of Poultry, 1976-80 and 1981-85

Legend: Other, Hungary, U.S., Brazil, EC

Thousand tons

*1985 projected

ducing reliance on imports. Another factor may have been the downturn in the importing countries' economies and abilities to buy. The EC, as the No. 1 exporter, accounted for around one-third of the export trade each year in the 1980's. Four producers accounted for over 86 percent of the export trade in 1984. Following the EC, which had a market share of one-third, were Brazil, the United States, and Hungary with 21.4, 18.1, and 13.4 percent, respectively. EC-subsidized prices were nearly 20 percent lower than Brazil's subsidized poultry export prices.

Dairy Products. In 1983 exports of milk, cream, butter, and cheese were valued at $11.5 billion—5½ percent of world trade for all agricultural products. Although trade in dairy products is relatively small compared to grains and certain other products, dairy sales are important sources of income for several Western European nations and New Zealand.

The EC is the world's largest dairy product manufacturer and exporter, accounting for about 40 percent of the major dairy products exported. This excludes trade between EC member nations. Oceania sup-

plies another 25 percent (17 percent for New Zealand and 8 percent for Australia); the United States about 10 percent, and Austria, Finland, Sweden, and Switzerland about 9 percent of the world total.

The dairy policies of the EC have a major impact on world trade. The EC's dairy industry supplies its 270 million inhabitants and produces a substantial surplus. Excess milk is processed into exportable products (primarily butter and nonfat dry milk) which are then purchased by the governments of member nations. The EC also provides export refunds (subsidies) to allow its exporters to successfully compete for international dairy markets. This costly process helps the EC remove its surplus milk output.

In April 1984, the EC adopted a 5-year program to reduce surplus milk production. Quotas in milk deliveries were established at 99.6 million tons or about 1 percent more than 1981 deliveries for most EC members. Milk production declined about 2 percent in 1984 from 1983 levels, and another 2 percent drop is projected for 1985. Even with the reduction, the milk surplus is about 15 million tons. Large stocks of butter and nonfat dry milk will

Dairy Products: Value and Percentage of World Farm Trade, 1983

Country	All Products	Dairy	Dairy as a Percentage of Farm Trade
	Million dollars		Percent
New Zealand	3,452	866	25
Switzerland	991	283	29
Finland	659	169	26
European Community	66,427	8,531	13
Australia	6,949	302	4
United States	37,537	328	1
World	207,537	11,483	5½

SOURCE: Food and Agricultural Organization of the U.N. Values include EC intra-trade and donations.

remain, and the EC will be forced to continue to move these stocks by subsidizing exports.

The EC also controls imports to help protect its dairy industry. Variable levies are imposed on dairy products to offset differences between domestic EC prices and the lower world market prices. A license is required to import milk or milk products from third countries.

These restrictions have effectively closed the EC import market for dairy products except for special arrangements with certain third countries. New Zealand butter is imported by the United Kingdom at a reduced levy under a special quota (89,000 tons in 1985) which is gradually being phased out. There also are several bilateral agreements—

mostly for certain categories of cheeses—with Finland, Norway, Switzerland, Austria, Canada, Australia, New Zealand, and Spain. Total 1983 EC imports of manufactured dairy products from third countries amounted to somewhat over 0.2 million tons or 6 percent of the commercial world trade.

New Zealand is one of the few countries that produces milk to sell on the international market. About 80 percent of its 7.6 million tons of milk produced in 1984 was manufactured into dairy products and exported. New Zealand can compete on world dairy markets because of lower production costs. With a climate that encourages year-round grass growth, feed costs are minimal. Capital investment also is low because cattle are kept outside year-round. Only a milking shed is needed on a typical New Zealand dairy farm.

The New Zealand Government does not provide export subsidies, and only limited assistance to the industry. The New Zealand Dairy Board, a cooperative owned by dairy farmers, is the single centralized buyer of products for export. The Board sells directly to world markets through its international network of agents. Since domestic prices are close to export levels, dairy product exports into New Zealand are limited.

Australia produces a milk surplus and exports about 25 percent of its milk as dairy products. Prices in international markets are much lower than the fixed domestic levels. Australia has an intricate equalization scheme to average returns from domestic and export sales to ensure that all dairy farmers share equally in sales of milk for manufacturing.

Separate pools operate for butter, certain cheese, casein, skim milk powder, and whole milk powder. The Government underwrites minimum gross pool returns for each product but has not had to finance the pools since 1979/80. Levies are assessed on products sold do-

mestically (the difference between domestic wholesale prices and assessed export prices) and go into the pools to be distributed to producers. Like New Zealand dairy producers, Australians also benefit from a relatively low cost of producing milk because of the moderate climate.

Although general tariffs, ad valorem duties, and strict sanitary controls are imposed on dairy product imports, there are no quantity restrictions. Australia imports about 20,000 tons of cheese annually, about 20 percent of its cheese consumption, and limited quantities of other dairy products.

U.S. exports are largely government donations of nonfat dry milk and a few special government-to-government sales of surplus dairy products. The United States does not compete on the world commercial dairy market because domestic prices are two to three times higher than world levels and exports would require considerable government subsidization. To protect its price support programs from cheaper foreign imports, the United States has import quotas on many dairy products including cow's milk cheeses, nonfat dry milk, and butter.

Sugar Around the World

By John L. Nuttall, *chief, Sugar Group, Foreign Agricultural Service*

Since the late 1970's, the world sugar market has been characterized by persistent oversupplies, resulting from stagnant consumption coupled with sustained production increases. The world sugar situation is not expected to change significantly over the next few years. In general, as the ratio of stocks to consumption rises, the world price of sugar declines. Today, world supplies are a record high of almost 45 million metric tons, with a record ratio of stocks to consumption approaching 50 percent. The world price of sugar begins to strengthen as the ratio of stocks to consumption declines to 30 percent or less. The current level has pushed world prices to their lowest point since 1968—under 3 cents a pound. Moreover, since the sugar supply is so large, it will be some time before prices begin to strengthen.

A major reason for the stock buildup lies in the policies of the European Community (EC), which subsidizes sugar exports. Until 1977, the EC was a net importer of sugar. Since then, EC net exports have exceeded 20 million tons, without any increase in stocks. The rest of the world had to bear the cost of the stock buildup resulting partly from EC sugar policies.

Another reason for the increased world supply is that depressed world prices are not influencing production trends. Normally, such low prices would trigger a decline in sugar production and planted area. In the current situation, however, little of the sugar produced worldwide is traded—only 10 percent or less of world production. The rest is subsidized in the country where it is produced or is traded under

preferential arrangements at much higher prices than the world market price. As a result, market signals reflected by the world price do not fully impact on producers in individual countries.

In addition, sugar consumption in many developed countries is stagnating or declining. For example, in the United States high fructose corn syrup has evolved over the past 10 years as an effective substitute for sugar in beverages.

World Sugar Production, Consumption, and Stocks

Crop Years	Production	Consumption	Stocks
	Million metric tons, raw value		
1972/73	75.1	77.7	17.2
1973/74	80.0	80.0	17.3
1974/75	78.5	77.1	18.9
1975/76	81.7	79.2	21.0
1976/77	86.3	81.9	24.8
1977/78	92.7	86.2	30.0
1978/79	91.3	89.6	30.6
1979/80	84.6	89.5	23.6
1980/81	88.5	88.5	22.2
1981/82	100.3	90.5	32.1
1982/83	.101.2	93.8	39.5
1983/84	96.2	95.7	40.0
1984/85	99.4	95.9	43.5

Beet and Cane Sugar Production Up Again

World sugar production is forecast at 99.4 million tons (raw value) in 1984/85, 3 percent more than the year earlier. Despite the production gain, world output is still 1.1 million to 1.6 million tons less than the peak recorded in 1981/82 and 1982/83.

Global production from cane is forecast at 61.8 million tons, or 62 percent of the world sugar output, while sugar from beets is pegged at 37.6 million,

or 38 percent of the total. The expected sugar increase this year stems primarily from improved growing conditions for cane in South Africa and increased beet area and higher yields in the EC.

Latin America's two largest sugar-producing countries, Brazil and Cuba, are expected to account for two-thirds of that region's output. Brazil will likely keep its position as the largest single country producer of centrifugal sugar, with an output of 8.9 million tons from

Sugar Production by Region

Region	1983/84 Beet	1983/84 Cane	1984/85 Beet	1984/85 Cane
	1,000 metric tons			
North America	2,697	5,944	2,763	6,036
South America	261	14,132	390	13,873
Central America	0	1,760	0	1,792
Caribbean	0	9,981	0	9,809
European Community	11,647	0	13,248	0
Other West Europe	2,297	10	2,245	12
East Europe	5,632	0	5,772	0
U.S.S.R.	8,700	0	8,800	0
North Africa	498	1,028	516	1,095
Other Africa	0	5,054	0	6,137
Middle East	2,300	100	2,281	200
Asia	1,551	18,961	1,586	18,878
Oceania	0	3,689	0	3,942
World total	35,583	60,659	37,601	61,774

USDA

98 million tons of cane. Cuba's sugar production is forecast at 8.2 million tons, unchanged from the previous season.

Sugar production in the EC is projected at 13.2 million tons, a gain of 14 percent from

Although world consumption of sugar is stagnating, sugar production in the European Community was high. (Austria, sugar factory.)

the year earlier. France, the largest EC producer, is expected to produce 4.3 million tons of sugar and harvest an additional 107,500 acres of beets. Low world prices have had little impact on EC production. The EC support price, although unchanged from the previous year in terms of European Currency Units, actually translates into a higher support price for some members such as France resulting from changes among EC country currencies. This support price provides a moderate stimulus to EC beet area and sugar production.

Elsewhere in Europe, Spain's sugar production is expected to fall 14 percent following a decline in planted cane area. Poland's output is placed at 10 percent less than last year's near-record crop.

Sugar production in the U.S.S.R. is forecast at 8.8 million tons, slightly more than last year's. Transportation and storage of beets continue to be serious problems despite some improvements in recent years in expediting shipments to mills. The Soviet sugarbeet area of 8.75 million acres is slightly less than last year.

South Africa is expecting a record sugar crop of 2.5 million tons in 1984/85 after a drought-induced production drop of 35 percent the previous

season, and its exports should recover.

In four of the six largest producing countries in Asia—China, Indonesia, Thailand, and Pakistan—sugar output is likely to increase this season. The Philippine sugar output, however, may fall more than 35 percent because of a growing gap between low producer prices and high production costs.

Australia's sugar production is forecast at 3.5 million tons following good weather during the growing season and through the early harvesting. As in South Africa, the production increase should enlarge Australia's share of the world sugar market.

Slight Increase in Consumption

World consumption is generally stagnating, with annual growth being less than the population growth. Increases in the developing countries tend to be offset by substitution of alternative sweeteners in developed countries despite a general recovery of the world economy.

World consumption of sugar in 1984/85 is expected to increase only slightly over year-earlier levels. Last year's consumption figures were revised

Sugar Consumption by Region

Region	1982/83	1983/84	1984/85
	Million metric tons		
North America	12.3	12.0	11.8
Caribbean	1.3	1.4	1.4
Central America	0.8	0.9	0.9
South America	10.7	10.8	10.9
European Community	10.2	10.0	10.1
Other Western Europe	2.8	2.8	2.8
Eastern Europe	6.0	6.0	6.4
U.S.S.R.	13.0	13.2	13.3
North Africa	3.7	3.7	3.7
Other Africa	4.2	4.3	4.2
Middle East	4.5	4.8	5.1
Asia	23.4	24.7	24.2
Oceania	1.0	1.0	1.0
World total	93.8	95.7	95.9

Totals may not add up because of rounding.

upward because of consumption gains in India, where more sugar was released by the Government for domestic use as purchasing power increased in the rural areas following the rise in agricultural production. Elsewhere, sugar consumption is projected to increase in the Caribbean, South America, the U.S.S.R., the EC, and the Middle East, but will decline in Asia, Africa and North America. The outlook for other regions is unchanged from last year.

Sugar Imports and Exports To Decline

World sugar imports are projected to decline in 1984/85 for the third straight year. North America's imports will decrease primarily because of reduced consumption in the United States where the use of sugar substitutes has the greatest momentum. The EC is expected to import less because of the production recovery. The U.S.S.R. continues to lower sugar import levels as part of its long-range goal of increasing self-sufficiency. Imports also are expected to decline in South America, Eastern Europe, southern Africa, and Oceania. Asia is the only area likely to increase imports.

Global sugar exports during 1984/85 also are forecast to decline from last season's levels. Smaller export levels are expected from South America, the EC, and the Far East. These declines may be offset by larger exports from Africa (especially South Africa) and Oceania.

Overall, rising production in importing and exporting countries combined with stagnating world consumption patterns translates into reduced trade.

Stocks and Prices Up and Down

Depressed world market prices continue, reflecting the record world carryover stocks. Stocks are projected to hit 43.5 million tons in 1984/85, representing a record 45 percent of consumption. During the first half of 1985 the world price reached a crop-year low of 2.61 cents a pound, its lowest level since 1968.

Prices dropped below 5 cents a pound on May 2, 1984—the first market day after the collapse of negotiations for a new

International Sugar Agreement with economic provisions. The market reacted bearishly, most likely in anticipation that stocks held under the current agreement would eventually flood the market. The current agreement expired at the end of 1984, and was replaced by an agreement with administrative provisions only.

Free Market

The International Sugar Organization (ISO), composed of the world's major exporting/importing countries, estimates world free market demand at less than 16 million tons. If the sugar traded under long-term agreements and other arrangements at prices other than those reflected by the world price is subtracted from the free market as defined by the ISO, the world free market would be much smaller—perhaps 10 million tons or less.

The surplus of world production can have an even more depressing effect on prices. For example, if the projected 1984/85 increase in stocks of 3.5 million tons attempted to find its way into a free market of 10 million tons, it would constitute an enormous excess supply in percentage terms.

As a result, it comes as no

Sugar Imports by Region

Region	1981/82	1982/83	1983/84	1984/85
	1,000 metric tons			
North America	4,893	4,428	4,179	3,114
Caribbean	385	136	195	160
Central America	20	23	—	—
South America	823	988	706	386
European Community	2,402	2,111	2,734	2,726
Other Western Europe	1,009	1,015	871	883
Eastern Europe	1,115	1,038	1,365	938
U.S.S.R.	6,883	5,926	5,600	5,400
North Africa	2,095	2,194	2,150	2,200
Other Africa	1,032	984	1,253	1,975
Middle East	2,593	2,715	2,825	2,845
Far East	5,826	6,369	5,520	6,060
Oceania	157	299	220	214
World total	29,233	28,226	27,618	25,901

Totals may not add up because of rounding.

Sugar Exports by Region

Region	1981/82	1982/83	1983/84	1984/85
	1,000 metric tons			
North America	327	254	375	309
Caribbean	8,919	8,004	8,265	8,370
Central America	679	1,084	828	771
South America	4,335	4,284	4,070	3,745
European Community	6,855	6,776	5,988	5,475
Other Western Europe	240	316	194	207
Eastern Europe	479	838	751	760
U.S.S.R.	268	165	250	300
Africa	2,567	2,635	2,211	2,578
Middle East	150	195	525	550
Far East	5,106	3,912	3,649	3,337
Oceania	3,052	3,127	2,890	3,136
World total	32,977	31,590	29,996	29,538

surprise that current world prices have settled around 3 cents a pound. It remains to be seen if exporting and importing countries will respond to the low prices by reducing planted area and production, or by increasing consumption. Recent experience indicates that production can be below trend and consumption above trend and there can still be a buildup of stocks, which, in turn, depresses prices further. The questions remain: why haven't exporting countries responded by substantially reducing area and production, and why haven't importing nations reacted by dramatically increasing imports and consumption?

Part of the answer lies in the difficulty in adjusting production subsequent to large-scale labor and capital investments, a social question in many countries, involving national well-being and unemployment. Another part of the answer is that only a small portion of production—perhaps as little as 10 million tons—is traded at the current depressed prices. For example, if one-third of 1984/85 exports of 30 million tons moves at 5 cents a pound on the free market and the remainder is traded at 15–20

cents a pound under long-term agreements and other arrangements, then the effective average price is in the vicinity of 12 to 15 cents a pound, a price not low enough to cause dramatic responses from producers and exporters.

Finally, the marginal cost of imported production inputs for a pound of sugar may still be less than the 5 cents a pound which can be obtained on world sugar markets. If developing countries can earn more foreign exchange from the export of a product than the import cost required to make it, then they may have an incentive to continue to produce for export—despite the fact that world sugar prices of under 5 cents a pound are less than production costs.

On the consumption side, it may be that a general saturation point has been reached for traditional uses for sugar. Promotion of alternative sugar uses, such as for fuel and alcohol production, could spur consumption and bring demand more in balance with supply.

Barring major production adjustments or new uses of sugar, it could take a long time to restore balance to the international sugar market.

Tobacco Around the World

By Daniel J. Stevens, *agricultural economist, Tobacco, Cotton, and Seeds Division, Foreign Agricultural Service*

Tobacco was America's first export. More than 150 years before the Declaration of Independence—in 1613—colonists shipped 2,500 pounds of tobacco from Jamestown, Virginia, to England. That was the beginning of an agricultural export trade that today includes virtually all commodities.

Tobacco presently accounts for 3.7 percent of U.S. agricultural exports and 4.7 percent of the value of domestic crop production. The tobacco area, however, accounts for less than three-tenths of 1 percent of total crop area. In the five largest tobacco-producing countries other than the United States— China, India, Brazil, Turkey, and Italy—tobacco occupies less than 1 percent of the acreage in agricultural production.

Tobacco is produced in more than 90 countries around the world. Because of its high value per unit of land area, tobacco is an important cash crop for many developing countries, particularly those with limited land and excess labor.

The tobacco plant grows in climates from the equator to the temperate zones. It is grouped into seven categories which reflect the method of curing and genetic characteristics. (North Carolina, tobacco field.)

USDA

Tobacco   **271**

The return from an acre of tobacco is several times the return from an acre of many other crops, even though more labor is required to produce tobacco. It generates substantial export earnings without taking a large percentage of the land area. For example, in 1983, tobacco accounted for 57 percent of Zimbabwe's agricultural export earnings but required only three-tenths of 1 percent of the crop area. In Greece and South Korea, tobacco earnings accounted for 15 and 19 percent, respectively, of the total agricultural export income while requiring only four-tenths of 1 percent of the cropland in Greece and 2 percent in South Korea.

Types of Tobacco

The tobacco plant, *Nicotiana tabacum*, thrives in climates that range from the equator to temperate zones such as Ontario, Canada, and New Zealand's South Island. The types of tobacco, often grouped by curing methods and genetic characteristics, are as varied as the areas in which they are produced.

Flue-cured. Flue-cured tobacco is cured with heat and used primarily in cigarettes. The temperature is varied during the 4- to 6-day curing period to set the characteristic yellow color in the leaf and to dry the leaves to a uniform moisture content. While flue-cured tobacco output in 1965 totaled only 1.6 million metric tons with the U.S. share at 30 percent, world production in 1984 totaled 3.1 million tons, with China producing almost 50 percent of this amount, an estimated 1.4 million tons. The United States ranked a distant second with 392,191 tons or 13 percent of world output; other major producers were Brazil (265,000 tons), India (135,200 tons), Zimbabwe (119,636 tons), Japan (79,978 tons) and South Korea (63,097 tons).

Light Air-cured. Burley and other light air-cured tobaccos are cured with natural, unheated air in enclosed barns and used primarily in cigarette manufacture. World output of burley and other light air-cured tobacco in 1965 totaled 758,489 tons, with the U.S. share of world output at 37 percent. In 1984, the United States produced 31 percent of the 1.1 million tons harvested. Other major producers were Italy (61,830 tons), Japan (55,499 tons), Brazil (44,000 tons), Mexico (40,740 tons), South Korea (31,075 tons), and Greece (29,900 tons).

Oriental. Oriental tobacco is cured in direct sunlight. This small-leafed, aromatic tobacco used mostly in cigarettes is not grown in the United States. World output in 1984 totaled 952,974 tons, a 34-percent gain over 1965 production, with Turkey, Bulgaria, Greece, Italy, and Yugoslavia accounting for more than one-half of its production.

Dark Air-cured. World production of dark air-cured tobacco (other than cigar types) and sun-cured tobacco increased from 1 million tons in 1965 to 1.1 million tons in 1984. These tobaccos are used for a variety of products including cigarettes, smoking tobacco, chewing tobacco, and snuff. Asia accounted for almost three-fourths of the world output during 1984. India was the major producing country (358,600 tons) followed by China (178,748 tons) and Poland (54,857 tons).

Dark air-cured cigar tobacco is cured with natural, unheated air. These varieties are used primarily in cigars, but some of the tobacco is used in cigarettes and other products. World output in 1984 was 215,907 tons, about 40 percent more than the 151,412 tons produced in 1965. China, Cuba, and Brazil, with crops of 60,747 tons, 40,000 tons, and 33,000 tons, respectively, accounted for 62 percent of the 1984 production. U.S. production fell from 54,432 tons in 1965 to 16,413 tons in 1984.

Fire-cured. Fire-cured tobacco is cured over an open fire at a moderate temperature in enclosed barns to obtain a maximum amount of smoke. The cured leaf is dark, heavy bodied, and has a distinctive smoky aroma. The United States is the largest producer of this tobacco, used primarily in snuff, smoking tobacco, and cigars. In 1965, the U.S. harvest was 20,947 tons or about 35 percent of the world crop, rising in 1984 to 25,683 tons— about the same percentage of the world crop. Malawi, Poland, and Italy were the other major producing countries in 1984 with 16,500 tons, 13,435 tons, and 9,893 tons, respectively.

World Production

The total world tobacco harvest in 1984 was 6.3 million metric tons—5 percent more than that of 1983 and 47 percent more than the 1965 output of 4.4 million tons. The 1985 world tobacco crop is forecast at 6.26 million tons, 1 percent below

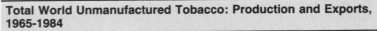

Total World Unmanufactured Tobacco: Production and Exports, 1965-1984

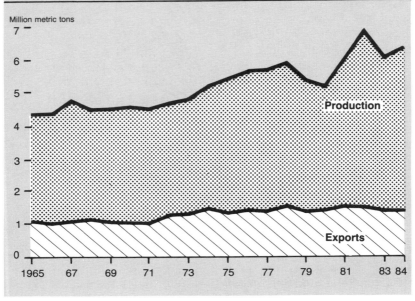

World Tobacco Production By Type, Selected Years

Leaf Type	1965	1970	1975	1980	1984	Est. 1985
	1,000 metric tons					
Flue-cured	1,576.5	1,768.2	2,308.2	2,353.1	3,107.0	3,103
Burley	369.3	404.8	563.6	560.5	751.5	688
Oriental	710.0	740.3	918.0	881.6	953.0	957
Dark air/sun-cured	1,083.7	976.3	1,095.6	928.2	1,116.0	1,108
Light air-cured	389.2	347.0	339.2	232.6	130.3	123
Dark air-cured, cigar	151.4	180.8	126.0	162.9	215.9	212
Dark fire-cured	59.4	50.9	51.9	48.6	72.4	67
Total	4,339.5	4,468.3	5,402.5	5,167.5	6,346.1	6,258

1984's crop and 9 percent below the record 6.9 million-ton crop in 1982.

The 1985 tobacco crop in China, the world's largest producer, is estimated at 1.8 million tons, 7 percent more than the 1984 crop but 19 percent below the record 1982 level of 2.2 million tons. Other countries with expected sizable crop increases during 1985 include Indonesia, Colombia, Pakistan, South Africa, Bulgaria, Yugoslavia, and Mexico. Smaller crops are expected in the Philippines, Argentina, Japan, Canada, South Korea, Zimbabwe, Brazil, the U.S.S.R., and Greece. In the United States, production is projected to fall because of large carryover stocks and lower domestic use.

Trade

Over one-fourth of world tobacco is sold internationally. World exports during 1984 totaled 1.4 million tons. The value of this leaf is estimated to be more than $3.6 billion.

Exporters. Tobacco ranks high as an earner of foreign exchange for many countries. It is the No. 1 agricultural export for Zimbabwe, Greece, South Korea, Bulgaria, and Malawi. Tobacco ranks high among agricultural exports in many

other countries including the United States where it was the fifth highest valued agricultural export in 1984 following soybeans, corn, wheat, and cotton.

The United States is the leading exporter of tobacco in the world—a distinction it has held for more than 370 years. The U.S. share of world tobacco exports, however, has steadily declined during the past 20 years. The U.S. world market share was 17 percent in 1984, down from 22 percent in 1965 and well below the 39 percent held in 1955.

Brazil, among others, has emerged as a major competitor, with exports increasing from 55,299 tons in 1965 to 189,000 tons in 1984. Flue-cured tobacco exports and, to a lesser extent, burley have been responsible for much of this growth.

Zimbabwe was the leading U.S. flue-cured tobacco competitor in world trade during the early 1960's. In 1965, however, United Nations imposed trade sanctions following Zimbabwe's Unilateral Declaration of Independence. These sanctions hampered tobacco exports until 1979 when they were lifted. Zimbabwe exported 84,887 tons of tobacco in 1984—triple the amount

USDA

shipped in 1966 but 29 percent below the record 1965 shipments of 120,898 tons.

India's 1984 exports totaled 80,687 tons, up from 62,000 tons in 1965. The U.S.S.R. and the United Kingdom were India's major markets.

Tobacco shipments from Greece and Italy, the two major European Community exporters in 1984, were 98,325 and 96,796 tons, respectively. They primarily export burley and oriental tobacco.

Turkey shipped 69,674 tons of tobacco, almost all oriental-type leaf, overseas in 1984,

The United States is the leading exporter of leaf tobacco in the world. Brazil has emerged as a major competitor. (North Carolina, tobacco auction.)

with the United States the leading destination.

More than 625,000 tons of flue-cured tobacco moved in export channels during 1984. The United States supplied about one-fourth of the total flue-cured leaf that moved worldwide during 1984, compared to over one-half the flue-cured trade in 1965. Most of the U.S. market share in this type leaf has been lost to the Brazilians. Brazil's exports of

Total Unmanufactured Tobacco

Year	World Production	U.S. Production	U.S. Exports	World Exports	U.S. Share of Exports
	— Metric tons—				Percent
1965	4,384,970	848,569	213,936	988,107	21.7
1966	4,370,003	860,326	251,651	924,328	27.2
1967	4,711,325	897,537	260,636	987,978	26.4
1968	4,472,762	779,273	274,127	1,068,029	25.7
1969	4,469,915	820,733	264,978	999,643	26.5
1970	4,517,258	866,794	234,192	991,570	23.6
1971	4,472,404	777,625	217,334	1,024,652	21.2
1972	4,678,825	795,541	278,077	1,235,549	22.5
1973	4,795,253	793,167	283,667	1,253,877	22.6
1974	5,145,299	904,317	300,315	1,411,116	21.3
1975	5,392,566	991,618	259,091	1,263,977	20.5
1976	5,650,925	970,979	266,310	1,365,058	19.5
1977	5,661,155	869,959	290,130	1,331,163	21.8
1978	5,910,571	919,799	320,861	1,469,406	18.9
1979	5,451,547	693,320	259,380	1,372,108	20.1
1980	5,213,837	810,883	273,477	1,358,520	17.9
1981	5,978,384	936,302	266,104	1,484,374	17.8
1982	6,878,341	904,824	260,700	1,464,066	17.8
1983	6,036,827	648,280	239,390	1,365,531	17.5
1984	6,303,823	746,000	246,156	1,394,768	17.6

these types increased from negligible amounts in 1965 to an estimated 155,000 tons in 1984. The quality of the Brazilian leaf also has improved dramatically, making it more substitutable for the U.S. leaf. Brazil's share of world flue-cured exports has increased from less than 1 percent in 1965 to an estimated 23 percent in 1984. Other major exporters in 1984 were Brazil (145,000 tons), Zimbabwe (84,887 tons), India (62,000 tons), Canada (24,806 tons), China (23,000 tons), Thailand (20,141 tons), Argentina (19,098 tons), Malawi (19,000 tons), and the Philippines (10,747 tons).

World burley exports in 1984 were an estimated 170,000 tons. The U.S. share was about 20 percent, down from about 50 percent in 1965. Other major exporting countries were Malawi, Brazil, Italy, Greece, Mexico, Thailand, and South Korea.

Both Exporters and Importers. A paradox of tobacco trade is that many of the major exporting countries also are significant importers. The United States was both the world's largest exporter and importer of leaf tobacco during recent years. About 40 percent of the 192,954 tons imported by the United States in 1984 was oriental tobacco. Another 13 percent was cigar tobacco that supplemented declining domestic output. More than 45 percent or about 90,000 tons of the imported tobacco, however, consisted of competing types—primarily flue-cured and burley leaf. Italy, Thailand, the Philippines, Bulgaria, Greece, South Korea, Indonesia, Colombia, and France also have significant two-way tobacco trade. These countries import tobacco to obtain different types or qualities of leaf for blending.

Prices. International tobacco prices vary widely among and within countries. For example, the average export values for a kilogram of tobacco shipped from the United States, Brazil, India, Argentina, and Zimbabwe during 1983 were $6.14,

$2.95, $2.00, $1.70 and $3.44, respectively.

Although tobacco has certain measurable characteristics such as tar, nicotine, and sugar content—and visible characteristics such as color and percent leaf damage—these characteristics have never been classified or organized into formal internationally accepted reference grades. Each tobacco manufacturer and exporter usually maintains a unique grading system, and tobacco is bought and sold in the international market based on specifications and samples. This absence of internationally recognized grades has led to a complex price structure. The prices vary widely because of quality differences, domestic support programs, reliability of supplies, and shipping cost differentials.

Cigarettes

Cigarettes are estimated to account for more than 90 percent of the tobacco used in the world. The most popular cigarette blends are oriental or aromatic, dark, English, and American

The oriental blend, found primarily in Eastern Europe, the Mediterranean countries, and the Middle East, is made entirely of oriental tobaccos. The dark tobacco blend is made from the dark air-cured and dark sun-cured tobacco, and is found in a wide variety of locations. The English blend contains only flue-cured tobacco, and is associated with the British and former British Commonwealth countries. The American blend consists of a blend of flue-cured, burley, oriental, and Maryland tobaccos. The American blend has been gaining popularity in recent years and is found worldwide.

World cigarette output in 1984 was 4,695 billion cigarettes, up slightly from the 4,541 billion produced in 1983, but little changed from the 1981 level of 4,560 billion. The world cigarette output grew steadily during the 1970's but leveled off during the early 1980's, and declined marginally in 1983 before the 1984 recovery. If China's production is excluded, world cigarette output shows no growth during the past 4 years, resulting from stagnant or declining populations, depressed economies, escalating antismoking campaigns, and significant tax and price increases in recent years.

China, the leading manufacturer of cigarettes, reached a new high of 1,062 billion cigarettes in 1984, up 9.7 percent from 1983 and more than triple the 1965 level.

The United States is the second largest cigarette producer with 1984 production of 668.2 billion cigarettes, up slightly from 1983. U.S. output peaked at 736.5 billion cigarettes in 1981 and fell in both 1982 and 1983. The 1984 output level is little changed from the 651.2 billion produced 10 years earlier.

Other major cigarette producers and their 1984 output in billions were Japan, (306), West Germany (162), the United Kingdom (130), Brazil (128), Indonesia (99), Poland (86), India (85), and South Korea (78).

While cigarette output has stabilized in recent years, manufacturing efficiencies have continued to improve worldwide. Less tobacco is needed per cigarette, so that a lack of growth in cigarette output actually means negative growth in leaf utilization in cigarettes in some countries.

Government Involvement

For many countries, tobacco is a major source of government revenue. Taxes can account for as much as 80 percent of the retail price of cigarettes. They range from simple consumption taxes to complicated value-added-taxes and include border taxes, excise taxes, and even the profits from government monopolies retained by national treasuries.

Given the prominence of tobacco in the domestic and export economies of many countries and the importance of tobacco as a cash crop and source of government revenue, it is not surprising that tobacco is subject to a variety of government restrictions and regulations. Government involvement ranges from complete control of the industry to simple taxation. The tobacco industry is controlled by government monopolies in more

than 40 countries.

Additionally, many barriers to tobacco trade have been erected. These take the form of both tariff and nontariff barriers. The tariffs can be either purely revenue tariffs or effective barriers to trade. Nontariff barriers include import quotas, import licenses, mixing regulations, certificate requirements, phytosanitary requirements, foreign exchange permits, artificial exchange rates, labeling requirements, prepayment requirements, or outright bans. Restrictive tariffs can be established to protect leaf producers or the product industry in a given country.

Import Policies of 10 Largest Tobacco-Producing Countries

Country	Tariff Rate	Nontariff Barrier	Imports As % of Consumption
China	50	Gov't monopoly	1
United States	[1]	—	30
India	[2]	Import quota	0
Brazil	85	Effective ban	0
Turkey	50	Gov't monopoly	0
Italy	[3]23	Effective monopoly	30
Greece	[3]23	Cert. of Origin	10
Indonesia	20	Import license	10

[1]Specific duty that varies by item. Examples: Oriental leaf 11.5 cents per pound, stemmed cigarette leaf 26 cents per pound.
[2]Specific duty of 50 Rupees per kilogram.
[3]Rate varies by leaf type and source. Most U.S. leaf is subject to 23 percent ad valorem with a minimum of 28 and a maximum of 30 European Units of Accounts (EUA) per 100 kilograms. The Generalized System of Preferences (GSP) rate is 7 percent ad valorem with a minimum of 13 EUA and a maximum of 45 EUA.

Forestry Around the World

By Vernon Harness, *director, Forest Products Division, Foreign Agricultural Service*

The forest products industry historically has been an important factor in the U.S. economy. Approximately 676,000 people were employed in the industry in 1984, with shipments of wood products, both domestic and foreign, totaling $53 billion. Wood or forest products include logs, lumber, all panel products, moldings and millwork, and miscellaneous material.

More than 20 percent—some 482 million acres—of the U.S. land area is classified as commercial forest land. Nearly three-fifths of this forest land is held by private owners. Federal and other public agencies account for 28 percent of the country's forest base, while private companies account for the remainder. More than two-thirds of the U.S. commercial forest land is in southern and western regions. The harvest and production of forest products is handled by several large corporations, hundreds of medium-sized companies, and more than 20,000 small firms. Large-scale operations are in softwood (coniferous) harvesting and manufacturing, while the hardwoods (nonconiferous) industry is dominated by small firms.

USDA

World Trade in Agricultural Products

World Trade

World trade in wood products, split about evenly between soft-wood and hardwood material, is large and growing, with the 1984 trade estimated at about 175 million cubic meters.

Exporters. The United States is the world's second largest exporter, shipping 25–30 million metric cubic meters of forest products, about two-thirds softwood, valued at $2.7 billion in 1984. The U.S. world market share is about 15 percent. Canada, which accounts for more than one-fifth of the world's forest product exports, ships mostly softwood material—two-thirds of which moves into the United States.

The U.S.S.R. ships about 25 million metric cubic meters, mostly softwood, while Sweden exports about 8–10 million metric cubic meters. Malaysia, the leading exporter of hard-woods, ships about 20 million metric cubic meters.

Importers. Despite its large exports, the United States tra-ditionally has been a net im-porter of forest products. It is the world's largest consumer of

As an exporter of forest products, the United States ranks second in the world behind Canada. (Pennsylvania, logging operation.)

forest products, with domestic supplies accounting for a sub-stantial portion of wood used— some 400 million cubic meters. Imports vary from year to year but recently ranged from 20–30 percent of U.S. consump-tion. By 1995 total consump-tion may be in excess of 500 million cubic meters. Canada is the only significant source of imported softwood material used in basic construction.

Major world import markets for total forest products in 1984 include: Japan, 40 million met-ric cubic meters; the United States, 30 million metric cubic meters; the United Kingdom, about 17 million metric cubic meters; Italy, 15 million metric cubic meters, and West Ger-many, 13 million metric cubic meters. Other major con-sumers of forest products are China and North African and Mideast countries.

Major importers of softwood used primarily for construction include the United States, Ja-pan, the United Kingdom, It-aly, and West Germany.

The leading hardwood im-porters are Italy, Canada, the United States, the United Kingdom, and Japan. Hard-wood material is used primarily for furniture and decoration, such as doors, decorative

paneling, and specialty mill-
work. In some countries, however, large quantities of hardwood are used in plywood for
construction.

The principal plywood markets—softwood and hard-
wood—are the United States,
the United Kingdom, West
Germany, the Netherlands,
France, and Belgium/
Luxembourg.

U.S. Competitive in World Production

The United States is in a favorable position to increase supplies of both softwood and
hardwood. Although in total
productive forest area the
United States ranks behind the
U.S.S.R. and Canada, U.S. forest growth rates are sharply
higher than other major world
suppliers. Moreover, the U.S.
wood inventory, unlike that of
some competitors, contains a
high percentage of commercially usable species in more
accessible areas. The United
States has, for some years,
grown more timber than has
been harvested. U.S. supplies
would likely increase in response to favorable prices for
timber, and overseas demand
will be an important component of U.S. timber prices.

In contrast to the United

States, Canada's exporters of
forest products (mostly softwood) face increased costs as
producers move further inland
for standing timber. Forest re-
generation has not kept pace
with cutting. This will reduce
Canada's ability to compete in
world markets after the turn of
the century. Canada currently
is shipping lumber in large
quantities to the United States.
Competition from Canada over
the next several years will remain intense.

On the other hand, long-
term competition from the
U.S.S.R. is likely to decrease,
despite its large timber base.
Current production is concentrated in western Russia, and
substantially more is being cut
in that region than is being
grown. Expansion into more
remote areas would require a
large distribution system and
shifting of workers. If these
problems could be overcome,
domestic requirements would
probably absorb most of the additional harvest. Since the
U.S.S.R. makes decisions about
trading on the basis of political
considerations, projections of
Soviet trade are especially
difficult.

Few other countries will play
an important role in meeting
future world demand for soft-

woods. Scandinavia has more or less reached a long-term balance between timber growth and removals. A few producers of softwood material, such as Chile and New Zealand, will continue to increase supplies but will not become major factors in international trade for several years.

In recent years, hardwood producers such as Indonesia, the Philippines, and Malaysia have been harvesting more wood than they have grown. Over the long term, this will reduce their ability to continue to export at the current rate. Government policy in these countries encourages exports of processed products, especially hardwood plywood, while restricting shipments of logs. Such a practice will likely increase the value of their exports during the next several years.

Brazil, currently a relatively small exporter, will improve its world position as resources mature. The large U.S. hardwood base puts the United States in a good position to take advantage of future increases in demand.

U.S. Exports

The United States exports a variety of wood products.

Softwood Logs. Shipments of softwood logs, the major U.S. wood export, totaled an estimated 16.1 million metric cubic meters in 1985. Japan purchased more than one-half of the total. China took one-fourth, and its imports are rapidly climbing. Canada and South Korea imported most of the remaining log shipments.

By 1995, these exports are projected to climb to more than 26 million metric cubic meters, with China likely to be the leading buyer and Japan a strong second.

Softwood Lumber. Exports of softwood lumber are expected to total about 4 million metric cubic meters in 1985. Japan, the leading customer, is taking about one-third of these shipments. Other major purchasers include Canada, Australia, Mexico, and Italy. By 1995, these exports could reach nearly 6 million metric cubic meters. The same countries are expected to remain the most important markets for U.S. lumber. But several smaller markets in Latin America and elsewhere are expected to expand rapidly as increased housing requirements put pressure on domestic lumber supplies.

Softwood Plywood. Exports of softwood plywood are estimated at 300,000 cubic meters in 1985, with the United Kingdom being the No.1 market. Belgium, Denmark, Canada, and the Netherlands are other major markets. U.S. shipments could more than double by 1995 if Japan, now a small market, removes import tariffs and other trade restrictive measures and if the EC enlarges its quota of 600,000 cubic meters on plywood imports.

Hardwood Lumber. U.S. exports of hardwood lumber are estimated at nearly 1 million metric cubic meters in 1985. Canada is the leading market, with Japan and Taiwan also taking large quantities. Other major destinations include West Germany, Belgium, and the United Kingdom. Projections for 1995 suggest that

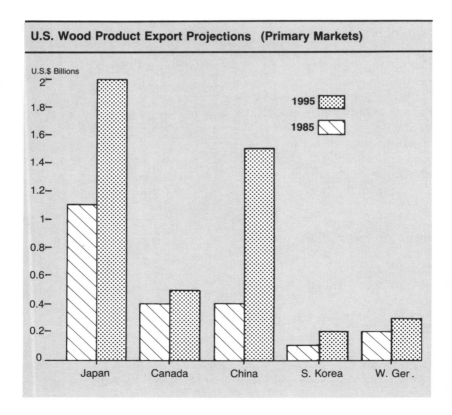

U.S. Wood Product Export Projections (Primary Markets)

these exports could nearly double as competitor supplies tighten and demand increases for U.S. species.

Hardwood Logs. Canada also was the leading destination for U.S. exports of hardwood logs estimated at more than 600,000 cubic meters in 1985. West Germany, Italy, and Japan are major buyers. Exports of more than 1 million metric cubic meters are expected by 1995.

U.S. Export Opportunities

The United Nation's Food and Agriculture Organization has projected that between 1980 and the year 2000, foreign demand for lumber will rise by one-fourth and panel products by more than one-half. Demand for other wood products may increase even more.

Large U.S. Supply. The United States is in a unique position to take advantage of these opportunities. By 1995, the United States could double its export level, with forest product exports ranging between $6 billion and $7 billion.

This country has ample supplies, with increasing supplies of many commercial species. Some competitors will, for various reasons, be unable to take full advantage of the larger world market.

Increased Market Demand. In addition to increased exports to traditional markets in Japan, Canada, and Europe, demand for forest products should step up sharply in other countries over the next decade or so.

China presents an intriguing market opportunity in view of its large population, its relative lack of forest resources, and its booming construction rate. So far, China has purchased mostly softwood logs. A significant shift to lumber and other processed products will require a major effort by U.S. exporters.

South Korea and Taiwan are likely to take increasing amounts, especially hardwoods, to support their booming industrial base.

Most South American countries have large forested areas where hardwoods dominate. The region, however, generally lacks an adequate distribution system to take advantage of large additional demand. The rising pressure for housing opens the door for sales of U.S. softwood building material. A small but worthwhile market also exists in the Middle East and North Africa. Despite rela-

USDA

tively small populations, most countries in these regions have ambitious construction plans over the next decade.

World wood markets will expand in the decades ahead, and the United States is growing more lumber than it is harvesting. (California, redwood forest.)

Trade Barriers

U.S. exports of solid wood products are strongly influenced by business cycles, traditional housing construction methods, consumer preferences, and changing styles. Although supply and demand factors are important, other factors are equally vital in many markets.

Particularly troublesome are a host of governmental trade barriers—tariffs and nontariff restrictions (quotas, product standards). U.S. exporters' success in taking full advantage of new opportunities to significantly increase sales depends, in large part, on sharply reducing current trade impediments.

Tariffs. Japanese tariffs on plywood and panel products are the greatest concern. Although imports of softwood logs and some rough lumber are duty free, plywood and panel products carry tariff rates of 10 to 17 percent. Japan maintains that duty-free imports would seriously damage its small sawmills and plywood plants and adversely affect its forest industry.

U.S. industry and Government representatives have been negotiating with the Japanese to remove their barriers. Open-

ing of the Japanese market would benefit both the U.S. and Japanese industries. Tariffs in other Far Eastern countries are normally higher on processed products than on logs.

Latin America levies extremely high tariffs on forest products ranging from Chile with 10 percent (although it is a net exporter) to Brazil and Venezuela with rates as high as 45 to 160 percent on some items.

Product Standards. Health, safety, and other product standards can be legitimate, but often are used to limit trade. Some standards are applied in situations not clearly related to specific problems, may be changed frequently, and are sometimes interpreted arbitrarily.

Activities are underway now to resolve the following standards issues:

• The United Kingdom requires bark-free softwood lumber.

• German standards on preservatives restrict the types of plywood eligible for import.

• Japanese standards for plywood do not permit the most common U.S. plywood panels to be used for all applications.

• EC standards on U.S. oak logs and lumber require expensive sorting and fumigation treatment.

Quotas. Quotas are sometimes used to limit imports of wood products. The most serious one facing softwood plywood is the EC's quota of 600,000 cubic meters to protect a small-panel industry.

Other Trade Restrictions.

Administrative practices in nearly all countries frequently affect forest products trade by the way in which they are implemented or enforced. Policies that hinder trade include licensing procedures, inspection practices, arbitrary product classification, and arbitrary methods of customs valuation. Sometimes trade is complicated by restrictions on a product's entry to a few specific ports that may be far from where the material is actually needed.

Probably more significant than these barriers are long-standing attitudes toward use of wood in countries that have significant potential for increased demand. Northern Europe and North America have consumption patterns significantly different from those in wood-scarce countries, or in countries where climatic factors cause rapid deterioration of untreated wood. Increasing scarcity, such as that in China,

has turned consumers to other sources of building materials.

If wood-supplying countries develop campaigns to show the cost effectiveness, structural advantages, energy conservation features, and techniques of proper use of wood products, they could help force the removal of tariff and nontariff barriers and bring about greater acceptability of wood as a preferred building material.

Industry and Government Working Together

Over the past several years, leaders in the U.S. forest products industry have become increasingly aware of the worldwide opportunities for sales of wood material and the need for both industry and government to work together to resolve trade problems. The cornerstone of this joint effort in foreign market development is a program by the National Forest Products Association and the U.S. Department of Agriculture's Foreign Agricultural Service. Under this industrywide program, activities aimed at increasing foreign demand for U.S. products are carried out largely by 15 industry associations representing the solid wood sector.

Value-Added Exports Around the World

By Dewain H. Rahe, *director, Trade and Economic Information Division, International Agricultural Statistics, Foreign Agricultural Service,* and Willis G. Collie, *cooperative education, Clemson University*

Value-added exports—products that have undergone some processing or are unprocessed but relatively expensive per unit because of high transportation or storage costs—benefit many sectors of the U.S. economy. For each export dollar increase, an additional $1.68 of business activity is generated. In contrast, bulk commodity exports—those free from processing and having low unit values—are estimated to provide only $1.13 of additional economic activity.

Employment also expands more rapidly with increased value-added exports, compared to gains related to bulk shipments. An expansion of value-added exports by $100 million adds 3,200 more jobs to the labor force than a corresponding growth in bulk exports. Currently, value-added exports account for over 40 percent of the more than 1 million jobs generated by U.S. agricultural exports.

The expansion of value-added exports also provides a more efficient allocation of resources, especially in rural areas, which in turn helps provide high-quality processed products to domestic and foreign customers at attractive prices. Value-added exports

Dana Downie

have been expanding sources of foreign exchange even recently when exports of bulk products have been depressed.

Nevertheless, U.S. exporters find it difficult to take advantage of the rapid growth in world value-added trade because of restrictive trade barriers. Higher tariffs and more restrictions exist in nearly all markets for value-added items than for bulk goods. These measures, along with the large U.S. domestic market, generally discourage many exporters. Also, some markets are relatively small, and there is considerable uncertainty about long-term access to them.

Value-added exports have been an expanding source of foreign exchange. Currently, value-added exports account for over 40 percent of the more than 1 million jobs generated by U.S. agricultural exports. (Norway supermarket features U.S. products.)

U. S. Export Markets

For U.S. agricultural products, value-added exports have shown relatively little change since 1981, while exports of bulk products have declined annually by 5 percent in value and 3 percent in volume, resulting in a larger export share for value-added products.

U.S. agricultural exports totaled $38 billion in 1984, down from the record high of $43 billion in 1981. Value-added products, totaling $14 billion, comprised 37 percent of U.S. agricultural exports in 1984. In 1970 when U.S. farm exports amounted to only $7 billion, value-added products accounted for a 41-percent share.

In 1984, value-added dairy, livestock, and poultry products made up nearly one-third of all U.S. exports in this category. Although cotton, tobacco, and seed products comprised only 11 percent of value-added exports, they have shown the most growth in recent years—increasing an average of 6 percent annually.

A major factor causing the sharp drop in exports of bulk commodities was a substantial production rise in both major exporting and importing countries. In the past 5 years, foreign grain production increased more than 215 million metric tons, or nearly 4 percent annually, and oilseeds by 31 million tons, or more than 6 percent a year. These production gains have led to a tremendous increase in world stocks and severely depressed prices.

Other conditions reducing foreign demand for U.S. farm products included the worldwide recession, a sharp rise in the value of the dollar, especially in developed countries, debt problems in many developing countries, and agricultural policies in many markets that encouraged greater self-sufficiency.

World trade in value-added products—agricultural exports less cereals (excluding wheat flour), raw sugar, coffee, tea, tobacco, cocoa beans, oilseeds, raw cotton, and natural rubber—reached an estimated $128 billion in 1983, versus $134 billion the year earlier. Since 1970, these exports have increased nearly fourfold—about $95 billion. The U.S. share of the world market in the early 1970's and into the early 1980's was 9–10 percent. Some exporters, such as those in the European Community (EC), captured a larger market share because their trade was geared toward processed products. Past commercial ties also gave them advantages in the fast-growing markets of North Africa and the Middle East. Most of this growth resulted from increased petroleum revenues starting in the early 1970's.

1970's Rapid Growth. Much of the increase in both world and U.S. exports of value-added products since 1970 stemmed from sharp economic

World Bank

growth in both developing and developed economies. Higher incomes led to better diets that included more meats, eggs, dairy products, fruit, vegetables, and prepared food products. Often local production could not meet demand—thus, the need for imports. Also, demand increased for value-added products in major markets during the local production off season and, with more two-income families, for con-

Economic growth in developing countries has contributed to the growth of U.S. exports of value-added products. (Brazil, building new port facilities.)

venience foods to ease meal preparation.

Despite the rising U.S. value-added exports, subsidized sales from such competitors as the EC and Brazil have hurt many U.S. exporters. In 1983, the EC exported $1.9 billion of value-added products excluding intra-EC trade. Brazil's exports of value-added items increased 36 percent to $6.4 billion in 1983, up from $4.7 billion a year earlier.

In developing countries, value-added imports generally are tightly controlled. Many development programs in these countries are designed to expand production of value-added products to create more jobs at home. These programs not only restrict U.S. exports to these countries, but also enable some of these nations to compete for many traditional U.S. markets.

Change in Past Decade. A major shift has occurred in the world's value-added exports over the past decade. The Pacific Rim markets (South Korea, Japan, Taiwan, Hong Kong, China, Thailand, Malaysia, Singapore, Indonesia, the Philippines, New Zealand, and Australia), the Middle East, and the newly industrialized countries have increased purchases of value-added products from the United States while Canada, the EC, and other Western European countries have reduced their orders.

Exports to the Pacific Rim, mainly to Japan, Hong Kong, and Singapore, showed the most significant gains in value-added items as sales soared

from $500 million in the early 1970's to more than $3 billion in 1984. The Pacific Rim's rapid economic growth and expanded U.S. trade contributed the most to this phenomenal growth in value-added purchases.

The gains in the Middle East are directly related to increased petroleum revenues generated over the past decade. Recent petroleum price declines, however, have dampened sales in the Mideast and North African markets.

While the EC has become more competitive in the world value-added market, it is still a major importer of these products. In 1983, the EC imported $3.7 billion of value-added products. The U.S. has registered overall gains in value-added exports to the EC during the past decade because of substantial sales to the Netherlands and to Belgium/Luxembourg. The U.S. share of the EC value-added market grew from 6 percent in 1970 to more than 10 percent in 1983, even though exports declined sharply to such large EC markets as West Germany, France, and Italy.

Exports of value-added products to Canada declined during the past decade because of

competition from other suppliers and Canadian support for
domestic production of value-
added items, especially livestock products.

Commodity Review
Grain and Feeds. Although
grain and feed exports of approximately $17 billion in 1984
comprised over 40 percent of
U.S. agricultural exports, they
accounted for only 17 percent
of value-added exports. These
value-added exports have increased at an annual rate of 14
percent since 1970, despite an
average annual decline of 7
percent since 1980.

Over three-fourths of value-
added grain and feed exports
are polished rice, corn gluten
feed, animal feedstuffs, and
wheat flour. Most of these
items are semiprocessed products that are facing increased
competition.

The Netherlands remains the
top market for grain and feed
value-added products, mainly
animal feeds and corn gluten
feed. But animal feeds to the
Netherlands have fallen recently, as a result of the availability of substitutes, such as
feed wheat, and EC limits on
milk production which reduce
demand for animal feeds. By
contrast, exports of corn gluten

feed rose 27 percent between
1981 and 1983.

The Middle East and North
Africa bought 44 percent of
U.S. rice exports in 1984. Modest increases by these markets
have occurred since 1981, but
competition from Thailand has
severely limited the growth in
U.S. rice exports in recent years.

Since 1981, the U.S.S.R. and
Japan have been the top markets for U.S. bulk grain and
feed exports, mostly wheat and
corn, purchasing one-fourth of
the total. Other primary destinations include South Korea,
Taiwan, China, Brazil, and
Mexico.

In 1981–84, U.S. wheat exports to the U.S.S.R. increased
51 percent in value and 87 percent in volume but exports to
China plunged. U.S. corn exports to Japan and Taiwan rose
marginally while those to the
U.S.S.R. increased 78 percent
in value.

Bulk grain exports are larger
than value-added sales because
of high demand for these products to support local livestock
industries, and because of rising food demand in developing
countries. Recent declines in
the U.S. share of these exports
stem from a reduced U.S. competitive position and weak foreign demand.

Oilseeds and Products. In 1984, exports of oilseeds and products, the second largest group, totaled $8.6 billion accounting for 23 percent of U.S. agricultural exports. After increasing about 15 percent annually from 1970 to 1981, total oilseed exports have declined since 1982.

U.S. exports of value-added oilseed products totaled $2.6 billion in 1984, down 20 percent since 1980. Soybean oilcake and meal accounted for nearly 40 percent of these exports in 1984. Nevertheless, other oilcake and meal products processed from corn, vegetables, and sunflowerseed have risen substantially over the period which may indicate a substitution effect. Other value-added oilseed exports include oils processed from soybeans, corn, cottonseed, sunflowerseed, and peanuts, all of which have increased during 1980–1983.

The EC-10 remains the top importer, purchasing more than 40 percent in 1983, but other markets, such as Eastern Europe, South America, and North America, have been expanding rapidly. Important purchasers in these regions include Poland, Hungary, Venezuela, El Salvador, Mex-

ico, and Canada.

The EC and Far East continue as the two leading markets for U.S. bulk oilseed products purchasing two-thirds of the total, although value and volume fell sharply. Before 1975, growth in EC purchases was slightly greater than that of the Far East. Since then, U.S. exports to the Far East have outpaced those to the EC.

Soybeans constitute over 90 percent of bulk oilseed exports, with about one-fifth of these shipments destined for Japan. The Netherlands, a major transshipment point, continues to be the leading EC market for U.S. soybeans. But shipments there have declined substantially since 1980 as a result of competitive gains by Brazil and Argentina, more use of rapeseed in the EC, and increased use of feed grains. About two-thirds of U.S. soybean exports to the Netherlands are used internally, with the rest being transshipped to other countries in both Western and Eastern Europe.

Dairy, Livestock, and Poultry. Value-added products comprise about 98 percent of all dairy, livestock, and poultry exports. While these shipments rose about 12 percent annually during the 1970's, export growth has weakened in recent years.

Value-added exports totaled $4.2 billion in 1984, compared with $3.5 billion in 1980 and $806 million in 1970.

Except for the Far East, most major regional markets have reduced value-added purchases since 1980. By 1984, however, imports by several countries, including Egypt and Mexico, had increased moderately since the late 1970's.

During 1981–83, the Far East increased its share of U.S. value-added exports from 32 percent to 40 percent, while shares in other regions either remained unchanged or declined. Tallow, hides and skins, and fresh and frozen beef accounted for more than half of the 1984 export total.

Egypt, the major tallow market, purchased 27 percent more tallow in 1984 than in 1981. Japan is the leading market for hides and skins as well as fresh and frozen beef products. Japan's purchases of hides and skins have expanded partially as a result of increased demand for leather. Because of the relaxation of quota levels, the value of U.S. exports of fresh and frozen beef to Japan have sharply increased since 1981. Japan bought 78 percent

of U.S. quality beef exports in 1984, valued at $320 million.

The EC, the major competitor for value-added exports of dairy, livestock, and poultry items, has expanded its sales 14 percent annually since 1970 to $450 million in 1983. About half of these EC exports are highly subsidized, driving U.S. products out of such markets as the Middle East.

Dairy, livestock, and poultry products form only a small share of U.S. bulk shipments. The EC, the top market, expanded its purchases by more than 60 percent during 1981–83.

Cotton, Tobacco, and Seeds. U.S. exports of cotton, tobacco, and seed products totaled $4.3 billion in 1984, compared with $3.6 billion the previous year. Although total exports of these commodities declined during the early 1980's, reductions were less pronounced for value-added products. The drop in value-added exports was not felt until 1983 and even then the decline was only 4 percent. By 1984, they returned to previous levels.

Bulk exports began to slip in 1981 and fell nearly 34 percent by 1983, but rose 29 percent in 1984.

Since 1970, the export share of value-added products has risen steadily going from 18 to 36 percent of the total. The largest regional markets were the EC (79 percent to Belgium-Luxembourg), Far East (47 percent to Hong Kong, 28 percent to Japan), and the Middle East (49 percent to Saudi Arabia). Together, these regions purchased nearly three-fourths of all U.S. value-added exports in this commodity group in 1983. Despite an overall reduction in 1983, exports to the Far East and Middle East climbed by 7 and 12 percent, respectively. In contrast, exports to the EC fell 15 percent.

Cigarettes are the largest component of value-added cotton, tobacco, and seed exports. Value-added tobacco exports, which include stemmed tobacco, totaled $1.2 billion in 1984, accounting for 81 percent of all U.S. value-added exports in this commodity group.

Western Europe continued as the major market for value-added tobacco products, but substantial gains have occurred in the Pacific Rim, Middle East, North Africa, and some centrally planned markets. U.S. price increases and the strong dollar have dampened overall export growth in recent years.

Unlike many commodity groups in which only a few products dominate, seed exports cover many commodities. For example, the top five types of seed exports comprised only a little more than 50 percent of the total export value. In 1984, the three leading seed exports were corn seed ($46 million), vegetable seed ($37 million), and grain sorghum seed ($33 million). The ability of the U.S. seed industry to develop new high quality seeds that increase yields and are disease resistant has spurred foreign demand for U.S. seeds. Nearly half of these exports go to developing countries trying to increase domestic food production.

For bulk products, raw cotton and unstemmed tobacco leaf comprised nearly 100 percent of the export total. Japan (25 percent) and South Korea (19 percent) were the leading buyers of U.S. cotton, and Japan (19 percent), West Germany (12 percent), and Spain (11 percent) were the top buyers of U.S. tobacco.

Since 1980, Japan expanded its cotton purchases 15 percent as South Korea reduced its imports 3 percent. During 1980–84 U.S. tobacco exports to Japan rose 45 percent; those to Spain skyrocketed 177 percent;

and shipments to West Germany declined 17 percent.

Horticultural and Tropical Products.

Exports of value-added horticultural products stood at $2.6 billion in 1984, little changed since 1980. Value-added items accounted for almost all of U.S. horticultural exports, which rose steadily through 1981. Since then, these exports have declined.

The United States is at a comparative disadvantage in exporting fresh fruit and vegetables because of high transport and handling costs. In addition, U.S. labor costs are high making it difficult for U.S. producers to compete with domestic producers in countries protected by tariff and nontariff barriers.

Three main groups—citrus and noncitrus fresh fruits, shelled tree nuts, and fresh and chilled vegetables—account for over two-fifths of these exports.

The United States shipped half of its value-added horticultural exports to the Far East (Japan, 16 percent; Hong Kong, 6 percent) and North America (Canada, 26 percent) in 1983. During 1981–83, exports to the Far East were up slightly while sales in North America decreased.

U.S. exports of fresh citrus fruits went mainly to Japan (48 percent) and Canada (24 percent) in 1984. More than 40 percent of noncitrus fruits and nearly 77 percent of fresh and chilled vegetables were exported to Canada. West Germany and Japan together purchased one-third of U.S. tree nut exports.

Marketing

The Foreign Agricultural Service (FAS), which is responsible for export promotion in USDA, has put more emphasis on value-added exports in recent years. The Washington staff and worldwide FAS network of agricultural attachés, counselors, and trade officers gather and corroborate detailed and accurate trade and market information for value-added products, vital to successful market development.

The Agricultural Information and Marketing Service (AIMS) of the FAS operates as a liaison between U.S. companies and foreign buyers seeking U.S. food and agricultural products. Its services are designed to help U.S. companies introduce products, especially value-added items, in foreign markets as well as expanding current sales.

Transportation: Linking Buyers and Sellers Together

By Wesley R. Kriebel, *deputy administrator, Office of Transportation*

The trip begins at harvest time. Trucks roll down rural roads and super highways filled with the American harvest. A single barge, among thousands, moves through inland waterways full of wheat harvested from 1,333 acres of Kansas farmland. A single ship loaded with corn harvested from 18,692 acres of U.S. farmland sails toward a foreign port. In 1984, 78 million acres of U.S. grain was moved to international markets. Together, these movers of literally mountains of grains can ship everything the American farmer can grow.

The process of finding and knowing the best way to move the product, however, is complex. A bushel of grain could see the inside of a truck, a barge, a railcar, a ship, and several grain elevators before it is processed, moved again, and consumed at one of many international locations. When the product is highly perishable and needs to be quickly delivered, air transportation is needed. In 1984, $848 million worth of livestock, flowers, fish and other products were flown to markets around the world.

Almost every country in the world has transportation experts whose ongoing commitment is finding the best and

Larry Rana

Barges loaded with grain move down the Mississippi River as a helicopter with State grain inspectors on board prepares to land and take grain sam- *ples. One barge can carry all of the grain harvested from 486 acres of corn, 1,333 acres of wheat, or 1,857 acres of soybeans. (Illinois, shipping grain.)*

Corn Exports by Port Area

/Dot ● 10,000 Acres

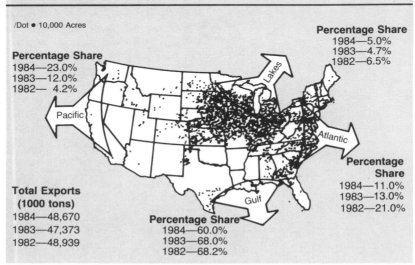

Percentage Share
1984—5.0%
1983—4.7%
1982—6.5%

Percentage Share
1984—23.0%
1983—12.0%
1982— 4.2%

Lakes

Pacific

Atlantic

Percentage Share
1984—11.0%
1983—13.0%
1982—21.0%

Total Exports (1000 tons)
1984—48,670
1983—47,373
1982—48,939

Gulf

Percentage Share
1984—60.0%
1983—68.0%
1982—68.2%

most cost-effective method of moving the product from farm to national and international markets.

Agricultural economists have calculated that exports provide nearly 25 percent of farm marketing income, and that each dollar earned by sales abroad translates into additional business activity in the general economy. To a large extent, the U.S. farm and food system has been, and continues to be, part of a complex, interdependent world economy.

Brian M. McGregor

Selecting the Right Modes

Transportation links buyers and sellers of agricultural commodities throughout the world. All methods of transportation, called modes, participate in the movement of agricultural products. Trucks move fruits, vegetables, dairy products, meats, and food preparations from the

Transporting commodities by container, overland and overseas, can reduce shipping costs. (Florida, getting ready to ship.)

AERO-PIC

packaging, processing, or distribution points to the ports. Bulk grains and oilseeds are transported by rail, barge, or ocean vessel to storage, processing, or export facilities. Air cargo service is used for time-sensitive, high-valued commodities, such as live animals, cut flowers, and gourmet fruits and vegetables, which are shipped great distances. Intermodal operations combine truck, rail, and ocean movements through moving containers of fruits and vegetables between the United States and foreign markets. The transfer of unitized containers between modes of transportation can reduce total costs by using the lowest cost method of transport for any given part of the trip.

Vigorous competition of firms within each mode and between modes have helped to moderate cost increases to buyers and sellers. This competition is in the form of adopting new transportation technologies and marketing practices in light of Federal economic deregulation in the transportation industries.

Innovations in transportation

Containerization permits superbarges to carry as many as 512 trailers, 20-40 feet in length, loaded with farm products. (From Florida to Caribbean ports.)

technology and equipment, such as dedicated unit trains hauling a single commodity between two points, have increased efficiencies and reduced costs. Such innovations coupled with the benefits of the interstate highway, waterway, and railway system have increased the ability of U.S. farmers and ranchers to keep existing markets, compete for new foreign markets, and to expand farm income.

Transportation Resources

The United States, the world's largest agricultural exporter, in 1984 exported an estimated 137 million metric tons of farm products. Transportation represented as much as 30 percent of the total marketing costs of some of those products. The transportation cost is affected by the method used, the handling characteristics required, and the intrinsic value of the product.

Ocean-Going Vessels. As much as 60 percent or more of the total production of some major farm commodities—mostly bulky, relatively low-valued products such as wheat and rice—is exported by ocean-going vessels. Dry-bulk cargo vessels of the 35,000- to

50,000-ton capacity range carry most of the export grain and oilseed. Usually these vessels are supplied by unit trains consisting of 100-ton covered hopper rail cars or tows of 15 or more 1,500-ton covered barges traveling from inland terminals.

One barge on average can accommodate 486 acres of shelled corn, 1,333 acres of wheat or 1,857 acres of soybeans. The large number of acres of grain that fill one vessel reveals the enormous capacity of modern ocean-going ships.

A second world market for U.S. agriculture has developed in recent years requiring somewhat more specialized transportation facilities. This relatively new and lucrative market is for highly processed, semi-processed, and certain unprocessed farm products. Examples of high-value farm products are fruits, vegetables, food preparations, meats, processed grain, and oilseed products.

Liner services consisting of regularly scheduled ocean vessels plying fixed trade routes provide timely, reliable service in transporting high-valued products to overseas customers. Cargo ships, containerships, roll-on-roll-off (ro-ro) ships and other special combination ships are used. In contrast, charter service provides irregular, although reliable, transportation and offers all, or a part of, the vessel for hire by shippers. Grain exports are usually transported under a charter agreement.

The world's supply of ocean transportation capacity is quite large and exceeds demand. During 1960–1980, the carrying capacity of the world fleet increased 350 percent or 504 million tons. Since 1980, world demand has not kept pace with this enormous growth in capacity despite record U.S. marketings in 1981.

Although the U.S. merchant fleet shares in the total world carrying capacity, today only 622 privately owned vessels are available, or about half the number that were available in 1950. The reasons for most of this decline include higher costs of constructing vessels in the United States and operating them with U.S. crews. U.S. maritime interests are attempting to overcome the decline in the U.S. share of world commerce. Several initiatives have produced a slight growth in the number of ships although the percentage share remains un-

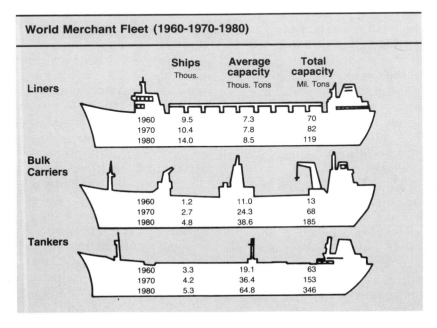

World Merchant Fleet (1960-1970-1980)

	Ships Thous.	Average capacity Thous. Tons	Total capacity Mil. Tons
Liners			
1960	9.5	7.3	70
1970	10.4	7.8	82
1980	14.0	8.5	119
Bulk Carriers			
1960	1.2	11.0	13
1970	2.7	24.3	68
1980	4.8	38.6	185
Tankers			
1960	3.3	19.1	63
1970	4.2	36.4	153
1980	5.3	64.8	346

USDA

der 5 percent. Their objective is to continue to produce a new, modern, and fuel-efficient merchant fleet as evidenced by containerization, a concept pioneered by American industry which has been revolutionizing world commerce. Worldwide container capacity has increased from 180,000 twenty-foot equivalent units (TEU) in 1970, to a projected 2.3 million TEU in 1985.

Air Transport. In contrast to bulk commodity movements by low-cost water transport, most air cargoes consist of fragile or perishable, high-value products. With the advent of jet aircraft and its greater lift capability and speed, air freight has been attracting more and more farmers whose commodities re-

The U.S. merchant fleet consists of 622 ships, about one-half the number available 35 years ago. (Port of New Orleans, loading grain for export.)

quire timely service. For instance, live animals, and, recently, embryo transfers are being airlifted in hours to remote locations throughout the world. Air transportation is supplying the best genetic stock to foreign customers. Strawberries, picked at their prime stage of maturity in California fields and flown in the cargo compartment of a jet passenger plane, are routinely available in marketplaces like Frankfurt, Germany, the next day.

Air transportation plays a small, yet important part in U.S. agricultural exports. In 1984, air carriers received reve-

Air Cargo Exports—1984

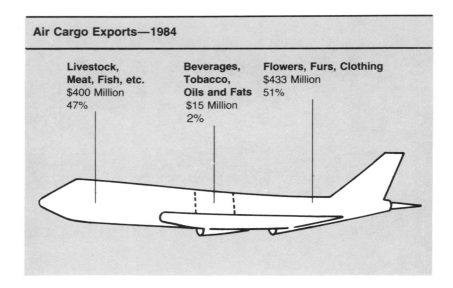

**Livestock,
Meat, Fish, etc.**
$400 Million
47%

**Beverages,
Tobacco,
Oils and Fats**
$15 Million
2%

Flowers, Furs, Clothing
$433 Million
51%

Flying Tiger Line

Air transportation is the primary way animals are shipped to foreign markets. Specially equipped jetliners, sometimes called "flying barnyards," move high value animals safely, quickly, and comfortably. (New York, exporting brood cows to Europe.)

nues of $848 million from an estimated $33.5 billion of farm exports. Higher freight rates are charged to reflect higher costs of air service handling and shipping. Although these rates may seem high relative to ocean rates, the air freight cost of total marketing costs of high-value products is quite low.

Agricultural Transportation in Transition

Almost one-third of the value of U.S. agricultural exports is now going to markets generally located in the Far East. As a consequence, the demand for transportation of some important farm products is shifting to port areas along the Pacific Coast. For example, from 1982–84 a dramatic upward shift in corn exported through Pacific coast ports relative to other port areas has occurred. The increased demand in Far East markets, plus attractive unit train freight rates from the western area of the Corn Belt, contributed to this situation. The gain in the share of corn exports of nearly 20 percent in 2 years has had a significant positive economic impact for the railroads and other marketing firms who took advantage of an opportunity. Conversely,

the decline in market shares along the Atlantic and Gulf ports adversely impacted the nonfarm economy in those areas.

Government Policies

Government policies also have a direct impact on the transportation industry. Because U.S. farm exports are now a factor in foreign diplomacy, agricultural transport demand has taken on added importance. The year-to-year uncertainty of foreign demand and crop production with resulting wide traffic fluctuations has created problems of forecasting the capacity needs for international agricultural transportation. A future concern is how markets can be stabilized to be consistent with U.S. production and distribution capacity and to avoid abrupt shocks that strain the farm and food system. Merchant vessels that provide regularly scheduled services and operate in the U.S. trades are subject to U.S. shipping laws. The current regulatory framework embodied in the Shipping Act of 1984 was designed to improve the competitiveness and productivity of U.S. liner firms. Its recent enactment resulted in substantial changes in the regulations governing the operation of the carriers,

Transportation—The Vital Link in Export Expansion

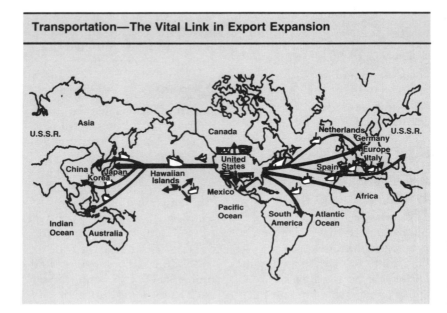

such as updating U.S. maritime regulations and providing for innovations like the intermodal carriage of cargoes.

Specifically, the Shipping Act of 1984 granted carriers and rate conferences (regional price-setting organizations of ocean liner firms) greater antitrust immunity. This law also provided new incentives for shippers of agricultural commodities. It permits the formation of shipper associations that consolidate or distribute freight on a nonprofit basis for the members of the group in order to secure more favorable terms.

Challenges in International Transportation

Several challenges to maximizing transportation's contribution to the competitiveness of U.S. farm products include better management of the export transportation functions and moderating the trend toward increased trade protectionist policies.

Improved Management. Today, most U.S. agricultural exporters are reluctant to become involved in the full international transaction. They are usually satisfied to be financially responsible for delivery of the shipment to a port of export. Unfortunately, they fail to understand that they may still have to bear unnecessary risks because of the buyer's inefficient management. The challenge to sellers of U.S. farm products is to exercise greater control over the transportation services performed by taking a more active role in selling and arranging the transportation to the foreign customer.

By working in cooperation with other shippers and other business entities, sellers can exercise greater control over transportation functions. Two methods of achieving cooperation are through shipper associations and export trading companies. The Export Trading Company Act of 1982 allows separate competitive and complementary U.S. businesses to join together for the purpose of exporting. Export Trading Companies can include producers, processors, and providers of services like transportation and banking as partners. International business managers must achieve greater leverage in order to negotiate more economical freight rates with the carriers and to provide for better coordination of export sales.

Protectionism. A second challenge to U.S. trade expansion is how to moderate rising protectionist initiatives. A number of countries, mostly the emerging nations, are advancing plans designed to favor their merchant vessels in liner shipping relations. Their most recent endeavor was an October 1983 Code of Conduct for liner conferences. A major provision of this Code, which is a part of the United Nations Conference on Trade and Development (UNCTAD), included a 15-month freeze on freight rates. Also, a method was developed and agreed on to allocate or reserve a specific amount of cargo in a particular sale for the vessels of each country participating in the transaction.

The United States has resisted placing limitations on the open marketplace for ocean shipping services because restrictions tend to increase rates and decrease services in the long run. For this reason the United States has not ratified the UNCTAD agreement. Even so, the Code could adversely affect U.S. shippers who seek to trade with a nation that has signed the treaty. For example, countries which have ratified the Code may pressure nonsignatory countries to implement some type of cargo reservation plan.

It is likely that the push to adopt protectionist measures in international shipping will continue, and moderating this trend will be a key challenge to agricultural exporters.

Transportation Vital to U.S. Agriculture

Over the years various national laws and regulations have been enacted to protect carriers and shippers, for reasons of national defense and security. For example, Federal programs specific to transportation have been available through subsidies to operate and/or build ships, or through government guaranteed loans, tax deferrals, and the like.

Further, some of the variability in U.S. agricultural exports and imports has been blunted by Government-supported programs for developing nations. The steadfast commitment of Congress and efforts by the USDA and others to develop export markets for agricultural commodities through the P.L. 480 Food for Peace Program have had a stabilizing impact on agribusinesses and derived-demand industries such as transportation. Also, commer-

cial export programs under the Commodity Credit Corporation which provide for short-term financing of U.S. agricultural commodities, have enabled U.S. exporters to expand markets.

As time goes by, more and more U.S. agribusinesses and transportation executives are recognizing their mutual interdependencies. Adequate transportation capacity and service at reasonable prices are basic to sustaining the viability of U.S. agriculture. In the long run, productivity increases can partially offset high production costs and enable U.S. farmers to remain competitive in world markets.

It is difficult to predict what set of international transportation policies will arise over the next few years. The achievement of a worldwide free trade system is unlikely, and, on the other hand, unrestrained protectionism is not likely either. It seems that agriculture, trade, and transportation policy should be aimed toward long-term international market development, not cyclical or short-range business transactions. Transportation, the vital link, provides the means for future U.S. agricultural export expansion.

Part IV.
THE POLICY
ENVIRONMENT

The Effect of Monetary and Fiscal Policy on Agriculture

By Robert L. Thompson, *assistant secretary for economics, USDA*

Macroeconomic policy—monetary and fiscal policy—probably has a greater effect on world agriculture today than those policies which are conventionally viewed as farm policy. Through both the interest rate and the exchange rate, macroeconomic policy heavily influences the farm sector.

Interest and Exchange Rates

Agriculture is very sensitive to interest rates. Many believe the interest rate is the single most important factor affecting the farm sector today. First, the capital-labor ratio in U.S. agriculture is twice that in the economy as a whole, and the capital-output ratio is three times that of the economy as a whole. Second, the interest rate is the opportunity cost of carrying inventories and maintaining livestock herds. Third, when interest rates rise, land prices tend to fall. Fourth, farmers spend about half their gross returns on purchased intermediate inputs—often purchased with operating credit. Finally, total farm debt today is about $215 billion, and each 1-percent point increase in interest rates lowers net farm income by more than 10 percent. For all these reasons, the well-

being of farmers is strongly dictated by the interest rate.

The second means by which macroeconomic policy affects agriculture is through the exchange rate. Agriculture, which generates 25 percent of its gross sales from exports, and is one of the largest export sectors in the U.S. economy, is very sensitive to macroeconomic policy in an environment of floating exchange rates. Budget deficits in the face of tight monetary policy bid up interest rates. So, when the United States attracts net international capital inflows because of favorable interest

Agriculture is sensitive to interest rates. Many believe the interest rate is the single most important factor affecting the farm sector today. (Washington, DC, Federal Reserve.)

rates, as has occurred, the exchange rate moves up. The dollar rises which stimulates larger imports and reduces exports. Agricultural exports suffer in such an environment. Under floating exchange rates, unstable macroeconomic policy imposes substantial adjustment shocks on traded goods sectors of the economy.

Because the United States is such a major power within

global capital markets and world trade, macroeconomic changes are quickly transmitted throughout the world economy. Many U.S. farm exports are used to produce livestock products in countries where demand is responsive to changes in income. These exports include grains and soybean meal in particular. The United States' fastest growing export markets in the 1970's were the more rapidly growing developing countries. Macroeconomic policies that alter the rate of economic growth in export markets, in turn, affect the demand for U.S. farm products. To the extent that high interest rates and the strong dollar compound the debt problems of Third World countries, they further limit growth in U.S. farm exports.

Other Macroeconomic Influences

Macroeconomic policy also can cause other shocks in the agricultural sector.

Prices. Agricultural commodity prices tend to be more flexible in the short run than manufactured goods' prices. In response to any given monetary shock, agricultural prices can be expected to adjust more quickly than other prices. In fact, a large price adjustment, in response to monetary shocks, is likely in the short run, subjecting agriculture to larger stocks than sectors in which prices are less flexible.

Loans. In periods when inflationary expectations are built up, farmers have an incentive to borrow heavily to pay more for land than its agricultural earning potential can justify. If inflation continues long enough, the asset value appreciation makes the loan a bankable investment. When inflation is brought under control—as it inevitably must be—those investors who jumped on the bandwagon late, and got heavily leveraged, can easily find their collateral worth less than their loans. This type of investment is not good for the health of the farm sector.

Taxes. Inefficient investment decisions also are encouraged by the laws which facilitate creation of farm tax shelters. The farm sector as a whole now shelters more nonfarm income through tax losses than it generates in taxable

Macroeconomic policy can cause shocks in the agricultural sector. Agricultural commodity prices tend to be more flexible in the short run than manufactured goods' prices. (Chicago, Board of Trade.)

USDA

profits. Tax policy clearly distorts the investment incentives in agriculture. Further, uncertainty about future changes in the tax laws imposes greater uncertainty on agriculture.

International Economic Policy

International economic policies also have become an important source of uncertainty and instability in U.S. agriculture—particularly as U.S. exports have grown. Trade policy and international monetary institutions are two dimensions of this source of instability.

Trade Policy. The world agricultural trading environment is dominated by nontariff barriers to trade—such as quotas, variable import levies, and variable export subsidies. By cutting the link between world and domestic prices, nontariff barriers stabilize internal prices but at the cost of passing all the adjustment onto the world market. In times of large global supplies, the necessary downward adjustment in world

Unstable global monetary conditions impose instability on traded agricultural goods. (World Bank President A.W. Clausen.)

World Bank

prices is magnified since many countries have isolated their internal prices by use of nontariff barriers. And, since the United States is the largest supplier of the world agricultural market, U.S. farm exports suffer accordingly.

A major source of uncertainty about future farm exports lies in future import demand by developing countries. Their economic growth is a necessary condition for rapid U.S. farm export expansion. If those countries are to grow and, in turn, to increase their demand for U.S. farm exports, they will have to be allowed to export the goods in which they have a comparative advantage to the industrialized countries. Unless the developing countries find an open trading environment for their exports— whether these are shoes, shirts, sugar, steel, or whatever—the United States is unlikely to experience rapid growth in farm exports. We are finding more and more cases in which continued U.S. purchases of developing country exports of labor-intensive manufactured goods is made a necessary condition by those developing countries to purchase our farm products.

International Monetary Institutions. Unstable global monetary conditions impose considerable instability on traded goods sectors such as agriculture. A number of proposals for reform of the international monetary system have been advanced. One proposal recognizes that the world is, in effect, on a dollar standard, and that the United States is effectively the central banker to the world. It finds this role is not an unmitigated blessing and suggests expanding the responsibilities of the International Monetary Fund (IMF). Another proposal calls for greater coordination of macroeconomic policies among countries.

But whatever the solution, from the perspective of U.S. agriculture an essential element of international monetary reform is to seek greater monetary stability to reduce variability in exchange rates and, in turn, in commodity prices.

U.S. Agricultural Policy

While one of the principal objectives of U.S. farm policy is to mitigate uncertainty by reducing market instability, farm policies themselves have evolved as a source of uncertainty. In recent times, commodity program provisions have changed annually, if not more often, adding to uncer-

tainty and inefficiency in resource allocation.

Loan rates and acreage adjustment programs have provided some price stability at a
higher price level than would
otherwise have prevailed in the
world market. This stability is
provided to other countries,
however, at no cost to their
taxpayers, and at the cost of reduced U.S. exports. When
world market prices fall to our
loan rates, we withdraw sufficiently from the export market
to support the world price at
our loan rates. Our producers
sell instead to the Commodity
Credit Corporation or the
Farmer-Owned Reserve. When
stocks become burdensome, we
have a Payment-in-Kind or a
similar program to reduce
them. This policy approach
makes the United States the
residual adjuster in the world
market. Other exporters appre-
ciate our doing this, but this
approach damages U.S. prospects as a commercial exporter.
Even more damaging are the
large year-to-year changes in
the volume of U.S. export sales
which this causes.

Modern U.S. agriculture involves large capital investments
in specialized types of equipment that have few alternative
uses. The average commercial

farm has an investment in
land, building, and machinery
of more than $1 million today.
The value of the land and specialized equipment reflects the
expected future earning capacity of those resources. Instability in market prices and uncertainty about future market
trends also leads to instability
in the value of agricultural
resources.

If government policies are
the source of instability, the
most efficient solution is to
modify them. Negotiating a
more liberal trade policy, in
particular reducing nontariff
barriers, would be an important
start. Greater stability in monetary policy and maintenance of
a balanced Federal budget also
would help.

Market instruments such as
futures markets and commodity futures options make it possible to insure against some
relatively short-run price instability. No insurance markets,
however, extend several years
into the future. To sustain a vi-
able, high productivity export-
oriented agriculture, some public policies and institutions
need to be redesigned to reduce this uncertainty or to
minimize its adverse effects on
U.S. agriculture. To reduce on-
farm uncertainty as much as

possible may involve agronomic research to breed more drought-tolerant and disease-resistant varieties of crops as well as research on optimum farm business management under uncertainty.

The 1981 farm bill mandated a study of farm revenue insurance to be offered possibly as a rider on a farmer's crop insurance policy. Several analyses suggest that the idea has sufficient merit to try a pilot project. Other observers have looked north of the border at Canada's Western Grain Stabilization Scheme as a possible prototype for smoothing out interannual variation in farm revenue and helping to reduce the boom and bust cycles in the land market that accompany export expansion and decline.

Still others have suggested focusing on the land market itself. One proposed approach would create low-interest-rate farm mortgage instruments in which the bank would share in any asset appreciation or depreciation. A similar proposal for low-interest-rate farm mortgages would have the principal indexed to the value of farmland. Some think that it is too disruptive to rely mainly on debt refinancing in agriculture with the whole farm business

being refinanced every generation. If so, more equity financing or greater reliance on land rental is suggested.

A different class of proposals addresses the possible role of buffer stocks in reducing market price instability. The Farmer-Owned Reserve was designed for this purpose, but the rules have probably been changed too often for it to serve this stabilizing function well.

Stabilization Needed

Modern American agriculture is a highly capital intensive, export dependent industry closely linked to the rest of the American economy. Some amount of instability is inevitable because of the effects of weather conditions on crop yields here and abroad. American agriculture, however, also is buffeted by instability from macroeconomic, trade, and agricultural policies. Excessive market price instability complicates the formation of price expectations and makes efficient resource allocation difficult.

This may justify some price and income stabilization—particularly if we are unsuccessful in reducing the instability originating in macroeconomic, trade, and agricultural policies.

Domestic Policies and International Trade Rules

By Dale Hathaway, *vice president, The Consultants International Group, Inc., Washington, DC*

The General Agreement on Tariffs and Trade (GATT) is the world organization set up by member nations in 1947 to provide a forum to develop rules on world trade. GATT is not a trade court that interprets and enforces trade law. It is a negotiating forum in which member nations reach political agreements on international trade rules and work out trade disputes. Agricultural trade policy needs to be understood in this context.

Agricultural trade is treated differently in GATT because it is treated differently by most member countries. Several basic underlying factors lead to this different treatment, and until those factors change it is unlikely that the treatment of agricultural trade will come under the same rules that are supposed to apply to trade in manufactured items.

Government intervention in agriculture is greater than for most other industries, regardless of the form of government

Most policies that encourage agricultural output are established to increase or maintain producers' self-sufficiency, and income and price supports are one of many programs used. Sixty-eight percent of U.S. corn producers participate in the price support program which maintains an orderly market. (Maryland, corn farm.)

The Policy Environment

Tim McCabe

or its philosophy. One reason is the political power of farm producers in many countries, which results in programs to reduce the economic adjustments farmers might face from producers in other countries. Another reason is the extreme political sensitivity of urban consumers to food price changes, especially in economies where food prices are a major component of living costs. In many countries an obsessive desire for food security has resulted in government programs to reduce dependence on food imports by increasing domestic production and self-sufficiency.

Three basic types of policy instruments affect trade flows directly or indirectly: domestic production subsidies which 1) offer price incentives or use government programs to reduce production costs; 2) restrict the flow of imports or raise the price of imports; and 3) increase exports, usually by reducing their price to below the domestic market price.

Production Subsidies Distort Production

Most of the policies which encourage agricultural output are established to increase or maintain farm producers' income or food self-sufficiency, or both. Almost every country has such programs; they include price supports, direct farm income payments, production credit at below market rates, government purchases of commodities at above world market prices, fertilizer prices at below market rates, irrigation water from government projects, etc. Whether intended or not, these various programs encourage higher output and distort production in countries with them. The magnitude of the distortion depends upon the extent of subsidies, the supply elasticity of the products in the country, and the way the subsidy is operated.

GATT rules prohibit the use of such domestic production subsidies for manufactured products entering into international trade. Much less has been made of the production subsidies in agriculture, and the attempts made to bring domestic agricultural subsidy programs under GATT review have been futile. Most countries take the position that it is a nation's own business to determine how and how much it subsidizes its domestic agricultural industry to support farm incomes. The United States has been interested in discussing domestic programs in

GATT, but there has never been serious political support in the United States for such negotiations.

Import Controls Destroy Competition

The most widely used domestic policy instruments in international agricultural trade are import controls. Tariffs are used on agricultural products, but most countries have sought other methods to reduce competition from imports. The most pervasive and distorting mechanisms are quotas on imports.

There are two major methods of implementing import controls for agricultural products. The one often overlooked in discussions of trade barriers, yet the most common, is the use of a state-controlled import agency. It is estimated that as much as 90 percent of world imports of wheat are handled by government buying agencies. They are used in such widely differing economies as the U.S.S.R., Japan, and Brazil. GATT rules do not prohibit state buying agencies. They say that where they exist they should act in the same way as the private sector. This, of course, does not happen. In fact, state control of import agencies is set up precisely to avoid some of the instability found in agricultural markets.

These government buying agencies distort trade in several ways. They generally do not pass on higher or lower world prices to internal consumers. They do not respond to world prices by buying more when prices are low or less when prices are high. Their buying is political by definition, because governments are political and act for political as well as economic reasons.

The second method of import control is quotas. Whereas quotas are prohibited under GATT rules for industrial goods, they have been authorized for agriculture under certain conditions. At U.S. insistence, import quotas for agriculture can be used if a domestic production control program is in effect for the product. In addition, the United States has for many years had a special GATT exemption which allows it to use import quotas on agricultural products if imports threaten to undermine the effectiveness of government agricultural price support programs. This GATT waiver allows the United States to maintain import quotas on products such as sugar and dairy products which would

World Bank

otherwise be illegal because we do not have domestic production control programs for these products.

Despite the GATT rules and without the special rights enjoyed by the United States, a number of countries still have import quotas on agricultural products. Japan, for example, still maintains quotas on some products, the most notable being beef and citrus.

Another form of import pro-

A major method of implementing import controls on agricultural products is the use of state-controlled import agencies. Estimates are that up to 90 percent of world imports are handled by government buying agencies. (Brazil, unloading U.S. cotton.)

tection is the variable levy. It is widely used by the European Economic Community as its border protection for domestic agricultural products. The levy changes so that it automatically amounts to the difference between the lowest import offer price at the border and a predetermined internal price target. This device is designed to give domestic producers an absolute preference over imports in the domestic market regardless of the efficiency of the foreign producer.

Another method of barring imports is through health and sanitary measures which prohibit certain kinds of products or products from certain areas. While many of these measures are legitimate efforts to protect the importing country from introduction of insects or organisms harmful to plants, animals, or humans, many are covert methods of barring unwanted imports.

A closely related set of measures imposes certain standards upon imported products such as requiring that they be sold in certain kinds or sizes of containers or be labeled in certain ways. These standards also may be used as barriers to imports because they may make the exporters' costs prohibitive.

Import quotas, variable levies, state import agencies and other measures all have a single common feature. Regardless of how efficient an exporter is, these devices do not allow foreign products to offer

price competition to internal producers. They distort the fundamental precepts of low-cost foreign producers being able to compete in a market and ignore the idea of comparative advantage. It is precisely because these devices offer absolute protection against lower cost producers that they are so widely used in agricultural trade.

Export Subsidies Distort Trade Patterns

Whereas GATT rules prohibit export subsidies for industrial goods, this is not the case for agricultural products. Article XVI says that a country may use export subsidies for agriculture as long as they do not result in more than an equitable share of the world market for that country. This relatively vague statement has led to a series of GATT cases and is the major point of contention between the United States and the European Community (EC).

GATT rules prohibit export subsidies, except for primary products. This means that two issues are contended—when is an agricultural product a primary product and what is an equitable share?

The use of export subsidies

arises when a country or trading bloc has a system that maintains its internal prices at above world prices but is still determined to export some of these products. Several mechanisms can be used to achieve this outcome. In the case of the EC, there is a specified export restitution whereby private exporters are reimbursed a specified amount per unit of product exported. In the cases of Japanese rice in the late 1970's and of U.S. dairy products in the 1980's, the Governments purchased the products at a high internal price and then sold a portion of them at a fraction of the internal price to foreign buyers.

As countries have followed a practice of maintaining high internal prices as a device for maintaining farm incomes, they have found export subsidies an increasingly attractive way of disposing of production in excess of domestic requirements. If the excess is only a modest fraction of the total production, export subsidies generally cause less direct budget expenditure than would other methods of disposing of surpluses not consumed domestically.

Agricultural exporters have been especially critical of the EC's Common Agricultural Policy (CAP) which has export subsidies as an integral feature. Through the use of its subsidies, the EC has become in the 1980's the largest exporter of dairy products, beef, and sugar, second in wheat and poultry, and subsidizes almost every agricultural product from wine to eggs.

Using subsidies in exporting basically removes the cost of product and comparative advantage from competition in world markets. Market share becomes totally dependent upon the willingness of a government to spend money on export subsidies.

Since producers in countries using export subsidies usually receive the higher domestic price on all their production, they get more than the real value of their products in international trade. The incentive is great to produce output in excess of world market needs. Some argue that the U.S. target price system, which also is paid on all output of many farm products when the market price falls below a predetermined price target, constitutes an export subsidy. While it is true that a target price system has the same output-increasing effects as does a high internal support price, it does not result in a two-price system with lower prices for exports than in the domestic market.

Another widely used form of export subsidy is the provision of government credit at below-market interest rates to foreign purchasers of agricultural products. These practices can take an infinite variety of forms, but in the end they provide the import buyer the commodity at a lower cost.

The United States has provided "blended" credits, a combination of no-interest, direct government credits and market-rate guaranteed credit. Other countries use similar credit devices, many of which are difficult to document because they are not openly announced.

So What?

The combination of domestic and trade policies clearly distorts agricultural output and trade flows. With so many instruments of intervention, it is impossible to determine where comparative advantage lies for many agricultural products. Without question, the various policies result in more resources employed in agriculture, with fewer markets available to low-cost producers who

find themselves not only barred from competing in many markets, but also competing with subsidized products in third-country markets.

The distortions in resource allocation are so numerous that it is not possible to judge accurately what their effects are on a single commodity or country. For some products such as sugar, EC import controls, export subsidies, and the U.S. import quotas have clearly denied the lower cost producers in developing countries their comparative advantage in producing sugar. For most products, estimating comparative advantage is much more complex, given the web of domestic and export subsidies.

As long as governments maintain domestic programs designed to prevent their agricultural industries from having to adjust to world market forces, substantial distortions in world resource use and international trade in agricultural products will occur. There is no way that the trade aspects of agriculture can be dealt with in the absence of substantial revision of many national agricultural policies. It appears unlikely that most governments will be willing to undertake the changes necessary.

Domestic Farm Programs and World Trade

By Philip L. Paarlberg, *assistant professor of agricultural economics, Purdue University, W. Lafayette, Indiana* and Jerry A. Sharples, *agricultural economist, International Economics Division, Economic Research Service*

At the economic summit in Bonn in early 1985, the Reagan Administration proposed that new trade liberalization talks begin in 1986. Agricultural issues are high on the priority list. Previous trade talks have done little to reduce barriers to farm trade. These barriers are hard to reduce because of countries' tight linkages between domestic agricultural programs and world trade.

All countries have their own farm and food programs. Depending on how the programs are run, they may create food surpluses or shortages. Countries look to the world market to absorb their surpluses or cover their shortages. But, at the same time, they shape their domestic programs to protect their farmers and consumers from world market swings. Attempts to liberalize world trade conflict with the sovereign power of countries to pursue their own production and consumption interests.

Domestic agricultural policies of the United States and other countries do affect agricultural trade in a major way. They affect the volume, the prices at which goods are traded, and the volatility of the world market. Various countries have many different kinds of

The White House

President Ronald Reagan, Secretary of State George Shultz, and Secretary of the Treasury James Baker at the 1985 economic summit in West Germany proposed new trade liberalization talks. Agriculture was high on the priority list.

programs that can be grouped into two general categories: producer-oriented programs and consumer-oriented programs. One protects farmers and usually leads either to surplus production that is dumped on the world market or to protection from cheap imports. The other favors consumers, fixing farm and food prices at low levels that lead to domestic food shortages and the need to increase imports. Developing countries typically favor the consumer, industrialized countries the farmer.

Policies of Developed Countries

The developed countries over the last 50 years have had relatively poor farm sectors, so they have focused on policies that support farm income, often at the expense of taxpayers and consumers.

Farm Support Prices. Farm support prices are frequently set at levels higher than the market will bear, thereby encouraging production, and discouraging consumption. If the country is an exporter, its exports fall and supplies increase. It then must subsidize exports or cut production to reduce burdensome stocks. If the country is an importer, increased production and reduced consumption thwart imports. If the price supports are high enough above world market prices, the importing country can become an exporting country. The effect of these types of policies on world market prices is to lower their level but make them more unstable. Lower world prices occur because the producer-oriented policies reduce imports and encourage exports. Price instability grows because domestic price supports above market-clearing levels inhibit production and consumption adjustments.

A wide variety of producer-oriented policies are used by the developed countries, and the effects vary greatly. Japan sets both consumer and producer prices for wheat and rice well in excess of world prices, with the producer price being higher than the consumer price. As a result, wheat imports are lower, and rice production and stocks are higher than otherwise would be the case. The imbalance in rice has become so great that on occasion Japan has subsidized rice exports and feed use at considerable taxpayer expense.

The European Community (EC) also has set price supports well above market clearing levels. The result has been to encourage the displacement of grain with imported nongrain substitutes, such as manioc, corn gluten, and soybean meal. Grain production in the EC has been encouraged. Until the middle 1970's, subsidies for wheat feeding were used to control stock levels. Since the middle 1970's, the EC has been increasing its subsidized wheat exports and is now a major net exporter. Recently, the use of export subsidies for barley also has enabled the EC to become a net exporter of feed grains.

Argentina and Brazil, major competitors with the United States in world grain and oilseed export markets, generally rely on producer support prices set below world market levels to support their agricultural sectors. Consequently, these support prices add to supply only when prices fall to support levels.

Marketing Boards. Canada and Australia use marketing boards and price pooling to assist their agricultural sectors. Although the basic orientations of their policies are similar, the operational details differ between countries and by commodity. In both countries producers receive a first advance

NFB Canada

from the marketing boards, serving as a guaranteed price for producers on grain delivered to the board. In Australia all grain moving off the farm is sold to the board. Canada's delivery quotas generally restrict how much producers can sell to the board. Canadian grain not delivered to the board is either sold at lower prices for feed within the province, or stored on farms. The grain de-

Grain marketing in Canada is governed by a centralized marketing board system that has a broad impact. (Canada, government train and grain elevator.)

livered to the boards is pooled and sold. If pool receipts exceed board costs, then the difference is returned to producers in subsequent payments. If there are net losses, producers receive the first advance only. Centralized marketing in Canada and Australia has the potential to increase and stabilize producer returns. Despite numerous studies comparing U.S., Canadian, and Australian prices, however, no consensus has emerged about whether prices are higher and more stable through board marketing.

U.S. Farm Programs

Like other high-income countries, the United States has many programs to help farmers. All affect world trade to some extent. Taken together, they have an especially large impact upon agricultural trade because of the U.S. dominance in global production, consumption, and world market share.

Cotton and Grains. The United States exports the most cotton, wheat, and feed grains, and next to the most rice. Farm programs for these commodities have similar impacts upon world trade—they support and tend to stabilize the world price because the United States holds its surpluses in the form of government controlled stocks. As a result of the artificially high price, foreign producers increase production and foreign consumers use less. Consequently, U.S. exports fall, stocks accumulate, and eventually production must be controlled.

The accumulated U.S. stocks tend to add stability to the world market by being available to use when someone in the world runs short. But the stocks can become burdensome. The Payment-in-Kind (PIK) Program in 1983 was a dramatic example of a program both to cut production and reduce the record stock surplus.

Supporting world prices, reducing U.S. exports, and adding stability to the world market are unintended side effects of programs to help U.S. farmers. But these side effects have more of an impact upon world trade than many trade policies specifically pursued for that purpose.

Tobacco. The United States also exports the most tobacco. As with grains and cotton, the tobacco program supports the domestic and world price of tobacco using Government accumulation and production controls. But the tobacco program does not restrict imports. In fact, the high domestic price support discourages tobacco exports and encourages imports. In recent years this has caused U.S. losses in both the world and domestic markets. For example, in 1970 the United States imported less than 1 percent of domestic use of flue-cured or burley—the main types of tobacco our farmers grow. But by 1982, imports were 20 percent of consumption of these types even though the United States was still the world's leading exporter.

Sugar and Dairy. Domestic sugar and dairy programs support farm prices well above world prices. The United States is a net importer of sugar and dairy products, but imports are limited by quotas that protect U.S. producers. Without the protection of these programs, the United States would produce less sugar and dairy products and import substantially more. Unlike the other farm programs, these tend to decrease the stability of the world market. The quotas insulate the U.S. from shortages or surpluses abroad, forcing all the adjustment on unprotected countries.

Indirect Subsidies. Indirect subsidies, such as special breaks for suppliers to farmers, are designed to lower the cost of farming thereby stimulating output and, ultimately, exports, and lowering world prices. Several policies subsidize farmers' inputs. Various programs provide credit at below-market interest rates. Examples include short-term commodity loans, grain storage facility loans, long-term loans to high-risk beginning farmers, and disaster loans. Barge transportation of grain also is subsidized because the Federal Government maintains the waterways. The largest input subsidy in recent years was the control of energy prices. Another type of input subsidy is the preferential treatment of agriculture in the tax code. The general effect is to stimulate investment and expand agricultural production. The impact is larger in years when producers' incomes are high.

Policies of Developing Countries

The food and agricultural policies of developing countries tend to favor urban consumers at the expense of farmers.

Price Ceilings. Consumer-oriented policies hold down the price of major commodities through price ceilings. Prices below world market levels discourage production and encourage consumption. These internal adjustments encourage imports, or discourage exports, raising world market prices. Price ceilings also inhibit internal adjustments to altered market conditions. They keep in-

World Bank

The food and agricultural policies of developing countries frequently favor consumers at the expense of farmers. (Brazil, grain farmer.)

ternal prices from fully responding to changes in world market prices. As a result, these policies force greater adjustments elsewhere and increase world price swings.

A consumer-oriented policy initially pays high political dividends by transferring resources and income from rural areas to politically vocal urban groups. Because of the sensitivity of consumers to food price increases, removal of consumer-oriented policies entails considerable political risk. In the long run, however, increased imports at higher world market prices can place an ever-increasing burden on government expenditures.

Country Variations. As is the case for the developed countries, types of domestic policies used vary greatly from country to country. Brazil, Pakistan, Mexico, Egypt, and India sell grain at prices below free market levels, but Egypt and India also allow a parallel free market. South Korea and Taiwan are more concerned about price stability. For example, wheat imported into South Korea is sold at a government-established import price. If actual import prices exceed the government price, flour millers are subsidized. When actual import prices are below the government price, millers are taxed.

Since rice is a particularly important food grain for developing countries, government price controls are common. Indonesia controls prices through government sales when retail prices exceed price ceilings by a specified amount. Many countries in Africa and the Middle East control rice prices. Easing price controls in recent years in some of these countries—Tunisia and Sri Lanka—led to considerable political problems for governments, including food riots.

Even countries with policies favorable to producers will frequently insulate consumers. Although rice prices paid by consumers in South Korea are above world market levels, they are not as high as producer prices. The South Korean Government sells rice at prices below those on the free market.

Domestic Policies Affect World Trade

Producer-oriented policies, as in developed countries, tend to lower world prices and increase their variability. Consumer-oriented policies, as in many developing countries, raise world market prices and also increase their variability. Countries with producer-oriented policies appear to dominate the wheat and coarse grains market. Rice prices in world markets are probably higher because consumer-biased policies in two major exporting countries — Thailand and Burma—and in African and Middle Eastern markets appear to have been more important than producer-oriented policies in the United States, Japan, South Korea, and Taiwan. Markets for soybeans are relatively free of such distortion. Support prices in two major exporting countries—the United States and Brazil—are set low enough that they rarely encourage surplus production. Although Asian countries have high price supports for soybeans, their production is small.

Whether the myriad of domestic policies has raised or lowered world prices is subject to debate, but these policies do inhibit domestic market adjustments to changing world market conditions, and thereby increase world price swings. Further, these policies clearly affect trade. Negotiation of trade barriers implicitly includes negotiation of domestic agricultural policies as well. That is why trade talks can get so prickly.

U.S. Marketing Practices Around the World

By Melvin E. Sims, *general sales manager and associate administrator, Foreign Agricultural Service*

The reduced competitiveness of U.S. farm products in world markets in recent years is a serious problem not only for U.S. agriculture but also for the entire national economy. The problem was created and compounded by a strong dollar, large world supplies, increased competition and weakened financial conditions in many importing countries.

In addition, U.S. farm programs have inhibited efforts to compete on price, while unfair trading practices of competitor countries are threatening the U.S.'s ability to maintain some traditional markets, let alone expand into new ones. As a result, U.S. agricultural exports have declined for the past 5 years. As long as these conditions persist, maintaining and expanding markets for U.S. farm sales will be tougher than ever.

Export Promotion

The economic health of U.S. farming is undeniably linked to exports which already account for one-third of harvested cropland and about one-fifth of farm income. Demand increases will come only from growth in overseas markets. The United States will have to work harder for export markets

World Bank

and can expect them to be even more competitive for the remainder of this decade than perhaps they have ever been. The current exporting climate makes the job of export market development a difficult and crucial one.

Market Development Cooperators. The Foreign Agricultural Service (FAS), U.S. Department of Agriculture (USDA) has the leading governmental role in developing

U.S. farm income is linked to exports. Agricultural exports account for one-third of harvested cropland and one-fifth of farm income. (Brazil, unloading shipment from United States.)

farm markets abroad. An important part of the FAS export expansion effort is overseas promotion work carried out jointly with agriculturally oriented nonprofit associations, called market development cooperators. Today, more than 56 of these groups are working with USDA on a continuing ba-

sis. Virtually every U.S. product going to overseas buyers is
promoted by one of FAS's market development activities,
which cover 138 countries.

The big advantage of the cooperator program is that it permits government and private
industry to pool expertise and
funds, so that each gets more
mileage out of its market development efforts. In 1985, USDA
will spend some $30 million on
cooperator programs. Overall,
the cooperators and the foreign
groups that join them in market promotion match USDA
contributions on a 2-to-1 basis.

FAS and the cooperators
work to identify opportunities
likely to generate the greatest
returns for dollars invested. As
a result, resources are being re-
directed from Japan and Western Europe—where the pro-
gram now focuses primarily on
aggressive trade servicing to
maintain sales—toward the
Middle East, Africa, Latin
America, the Caribbean, and
Southeast Asia—where there is
greater growth potential.

Lamb Program. One of the
most successful cooperator programs has been the heavy
lamb program conducted in
several countries by the U.S.
Feed Grains Council. The program encourages producers in

foreign countries to adopt cost-
effective methods of feeding
lambs to higher slaughter
weights, including early wean-
ing of the lambs, balanced rations utilizing feed grains and
high protein meals, and improved flock management.

The program began about 15
years ago in Spain, and was instrumental in the development
of a Spanish lamb feedlot industry, which now consumes
large quantities of U.S. feed
grains and protein meal. An
evaluation of the program
found that, for each dollar
spent under the cooperator program, $320 in U.S. feed grain
sales was generated. Furthermore, the Council has introduced the heavy lamb program
to at least 12 countries in
southern Europe, the Middle
East and North Africa, allowing
these countries to modernize
their lamb-fattening technology
and increasing the demand for
U.S. agricultural exports.

Rice and Wheat Markets.
Another example of successful
market development is in Iraq.
Cooperators for rice and wheat

*A lamb program conducted in several
countries by the United States Feed
Grains Council involved the use of U.S.
feed grains, protein meals, and improved flock management techniques.
(Syria, milking sheep.)*

World Bank

U.S. Marketing Practices

have been working in Iraq for 10 and 8 years, respectively. Persistent, personalized market development servicing, combined with the extension of GSM-102 credit guarantees, is paying off for U.S. rice and wheat growers as Iraq has become their fastest growing market.

Exports of U.S. rice to Iraq in 1984 totaled nearly 448,000 metric tons, valued at $182 million. These shipments to Iraq were critically important to the U.S. rice industry, since they came at a time when total U.S. rice exports were down in the face of stiff price competition from other exporters.

U.S. Wheat Associates began similar work on behalf of the wheat industry in 1978. Since then, purchases of U.S. wheat have continued to grow, and for 1984/85 Iraq is expected to import roughly 850,000 tons. U.S. shipments to this market reached a record of just under 1.3 million tons in 1983/84.

Other Market Development

In addition to working with the cooperators, FAS has other tools for market development. These include trade exhibits and sales teams, as well as Agricultural Trade Offices (ATO).

These are one-stop service centers for U.S. exporters and foreign buyers seeking market information. During 1985 new ATO's were opened in Istanbul, Turkey; Baghdad, Iraq; and Guangzhou, China, bringing the number of trade offices to 14, of which 12 will be serving developing countries.

AIMS Project. Modern electronic technology has been introduced to bring timely market information to producers and traders. In 1984, FAS initiated an 18-month project called the Agricultural Information and Marketing Service to expand and improve the trade leads and export marketing services offered to U.S. exporters of food and agricultural products. It encourages U.S. exporters to assume a more active role in pursuing export opportunities.

To do this, AIMS has contacted about 70,000 firms to inform them of, and to encourage them to use, their services to pursue new export opportunities. As a result of the various educational media used, the number of AIMS' client companies has grown from roughly 300 at the start to more than 1,100 and continues to rise. During 1984, AIMS supplied trade lead clients with almost

USDA

6,000 sales leads submitted by foreign buyers seeking U.S. food and agricultural products.

Buyer Alert Program.
USDA has initiated the Buyer Alert Program, which electronically transfers information about products that U.S. firms would like to sell to targeted foreign buyers in London, Manama, Tokyo, and Seoul. The service soon will be expanded to 15–20 posts, which collectively account for approximately 75 percent of all U.S. value-added exports.

Agricultural Intelligence System. In addition, USDA maintains a worldwide agricultural intelligence gathering system, based on a network of Agricultural Counselors and Attachés covering over 100 countries. They provide the kind of information needed for

USDA's Foreign Agricultural Service uses many tools in market development including sales teams, agricultural trade offices, and trade exhibits. (Spain, U.S. livestock exhibit.)

rapid responses to changes in market and credit situations.

Credit Programs
The Office of the General Sales Manager (GSM) uses financing programs to help counteract economic problems faced by many customers who offer longer term potential. Without credit, some countries would have had to go without needed foodstuffs. In other cases, credit has enabled U.S. exporters to make sales that otherwise would have gone to competitor nations. Agricultural credit also frees up foreign exchange for badly needed industrial supplies for many develop-

ing nations, allowing them to maintain economic growth. That growth, in turn, helps long-term growth of agricultural markets.

In 1985, USDA's export credit and food aid programs will provide the resources to support up to $7.3 billion of U.S. farm commodity exports to foreign countries. Additional exports will be provided through direct sales of Commodity Credit Corporation (CCC)-owned commodities, including the special sales program for African countries, Section 416 commodity donations, and wheat and wheat products provided from the Food Security Wheat Reserve.

In 1984, these programs helped to move close to 16 percent of U.S. agricultural exports and in 1985 they will cover up to an estimated 20 percent if the resources are fully utilized. GSM sales activities are backed by an extensive support system that includes direct access to almost the entire range of government and private sector trade information and expertise.

Public Law 480. Over 30 years old, Public Law 480 is the oldest USDA credit program. It started out as a program to dispose of surplus commodities. P.L. 480—or the Food for Peace Program—allowed the United States to sell its surplus commodities to friendly nations abroad and accept those nations' local currencies in payment. It also included authority to donate commodities in cases of emergencies or disasters.

Over the years, however, P.L. 480 has evolved into something far more than a commodity supply management tool. It also has been a vehicle for developing commercial export markets, for meeting humanitarian food needs, and for spurring economic and agricultural growth in the developing world. Roughly $34 billion in agricultural commodities have been shipped overseas under P.L. 480, which provides two types of assistance.

Title I. Under Title I, long-term concessional sales are made to friendly countries for terms up to 40 years' repayment, with a 10-year grace period, at low interest rates. One of the lesser recognized benefits of Title I has been the hands-on experience it has offered foreign participants in the business of importing U.S. agricultural commodities. As a result of buying U.S. products through P.L. 480, the sophistication of many developing countries as importers from the U.S. market has increased.

In the long run, the P.L. 480 purchasing experience was de-signed to encourage buyers to turn to the United States for their commercial imports of agricultural products. Of the 10 largest U.S. customers, 8 were former P.L. 480 recipients.

The Title I concessional sales program has been effective in economic development and in the creation of commercial markets for U.S. farm products. It has been expanded in recent years, growing from a total of just over $800 million in 1982 to $1.1 billion in fiscal year 1985.

Efforts have continued to accelerate the signing of agreements under the Title I program and to speed up the Title I process even further. Ideally in coming years, the initial steps will take place even before the fiscal year begins. Besides benefits for U.S. agricultural marketing, recipient countries can then prepare for shipments and for more orderly purchasing.

Title II. Under the Title II donations program, the United States gives commodities to needy people and also pays for shipping them. For example,

USDA has provided special assistance to drought-stricken African nations. In recent years, the United States has provided almost half of all the food aid received by countries in sub-Saharan Africa. P.L. 480 assistance to that region during fiscal 1985 exceeded the 1984 total.

CCC Programs. The workhorse of USDA's marketing effort has been the Export Credit Guarantee Program (GSM-102). A relatively new program, GSM-102 was created to cover nonpayments for any reason by any CCC-approved foreign bank. Credit guarantees protect U.S. exporters and financial institutions against loss from nonpayment because of commercial and noncommercial risk. Transferring that risk to the CCC has facilitated U.S. exports and has helped meet competition from other exporters. This short-term credit program requires no budget outlays except for nonpayment by foreign banks. Private U.S. banking institutions provide the day-to-day operating funds.

In recent years, USDA has provided record levels of CCC export credit to help expand foreign sales of U.S. farm products. During fiscal years 1982 through 1986, USDA will have made available some $22 billion in export credit guarantees, and an all-time high of $5 billion in guarantees was authorized for 1985.

A new approach, combining credit guarantees with interest-free government credit, was begun in 1982 to move more U.S. agricultural products into foreign markets. But the blended credit program was suspended earlier this year, when a Federal court ruling found that blended credit sales commodities were subject to cargo preference, in effect crippling the program and rendering sales uncompetitive.

Direct export credit—GSM-5—is another commercial tool used to reinforce and complement a variety of other market development activities.

These programs have been valuable tools in market development efforts. Again, Iraq is a good case in point. Iraq was approved for CCC credit programs with $435 million in U.S. sales covered in fiscal year 1983. Coverage jumped to $681.8 million in 1984 and to $710 million for fiscal 1985. In tandem with these increases, direct U.S. agricultural sales to Iraq, which were about $135 million in 1982, reached an estimated $700–800 million in 1985. Not only has the availability of financing helped to boost commercial sales, but the expanded trade may have helped re-establish diplomatic relationships between the two countries.

The focus has been on developing countries because that is where the greatest market growth potential lies. The United States is working to support growth in these countries and to establish open two-way trading relationships with them.

The greatest risk of credit programs is that of failure to pay what is owed. Fortunately, this problem has not occurred often. Even the repayment performance of P.L. 480 recipients, often weak financially, generally has been quite respectable.

In the credit guarantee program, the CCC is obligated to make payment to U.S. banks when a borrower fails to repay for any reason. In most cases, the debt is rescheduled. Thus far, nine countries have been rescheduled. In terms of government outlays, if 20 percent of the debt under the credit guarantee program had to be rescheduled, and if the terms of rescheduling continue as they are now, the net cost would be negligible. It does, however, have a negative short-term impact upon cash flow, and complicates the budget deficit.

Overall, there are strong indicators that the risks are well worth taking when the full range of expected benefits is considered. For example, a recent—and conservative—benefit-cost analysis supported the GSM-102 credit guarantee program. Benefits included increased federal tax revenues, farm program storage cost savings, and CCC credit guarantee fees. The cost analysis took into account the risk of rescheduling, principal write-offs in high risk categories, the costs of rescheduling and other key factors. All things considered, the credit program looks like a sound investment with an effective cost-benefit ratio.

Export Role of Cooperatives

As farmers' incomes depend more and more on foreign customers, cooperatives have moved increasingly into the international arena. Today, more than ever, cooperatives are a marketing arm of the farm. Cooperatives are direct exporters to foreign buyers, assembling commodities from member

farmers for shipment to port locations. For many U.S. commodities, cooperatives have been responsible for increasing U.S. exports through innovative market development techniques.

1980 Sales. In 1980, 63 cooperatives had direct export sales of $3.2 billion, or roughly 8 percent of total U.S. agricultural exports. Grain was the largest export commodity for cooperatives, with direct sales of $1.3 billion, about 7 percent of total U.S. grain exports. Cooperatives had their largest export shares in nuts and fruits, 35 and 31 percent, respectively. That year, more than 50 percent of U.S. fresh citrus exports were from cooperatives.

Commodity Differences. But sales volume and market share comparisons do not give a total picture of the cooperative role in U.S. agricultural exporting because of the differences among commodity groups regarding shipping and other export functions.

For example, grains and soybeans are shipped in bulk, whereas many other commodities are containerized and traded in smaller volume lots. Local cooperative elevators provide interior assembly of a substantial volume of export grain—receiving about 41 percent of total U.S. off-farm sales. Noncooperatives moved roughly half this amount into domestic and export channels.

Regional and interregional grain cooperatives operate port elevators along the Gulf of Mexico, the Great Lakes, and the West Coast. Although their port elevator capacity has declined in recent years, cooperatives are significant participants at both interior origination and port elevator points in the U.S. grain export system.

Commodities other than grain often permit product differentiation and opportunities for promoting specific qualities or brands in the international marketplace. Rice has a bulk handling system similar to grain and soybeans, but is also exported in bags and often identified by brand names. Cooperatives have port elevators for rice exporting in California and along the Gulf Coast. Cooperatives such as Riceland and American Rice, Inc., also have established their brands as the preferred rice in many foreign markets and in competition with other exporting nations.

Cotton is another commodity with substantial direct exports by cooperatives. In 1971, four regional cotton cooperatives, covering a range of varieties and qualities, organized AMCOT as a marketing agency for representing their different cotton varieties in all major world textile markets.

Cooperatives are major exporters of many varieties of U.S. fruits, vegetables, and nuts. Food products virtually unknown in Asian markets until the past two decades were first introduced overseas by U.S. cooperatives, often with assistance from the FAS. For example, the California Almond Growers Exchange is largely responsible for popularizing the American almond in Japan. Fruit juices such as cranberry, grape, and apple have had several export markets developed by the Ocean Spray, Welch Foods, and Tree Top cooperatives.

In 1982, the Central Bank for Cooperatives began offering export financing services, providing cooperatives with all the major financing techniques used in international trade. It participates in the credit guarantee programs of the USDA and the Foreign Credit Insurance Association. The Central Bank's participation in these latter programs has allowed

U.S. agricultural exports to several high-risk countries that would probably not have occurred otherwise.

Cooperatives have a unique role in exporting because of their exclusive involvement in U.S. commodities and their ownership and control by U.S. farmers. These characteristics enable cooperatives to build a link between the producer and the foreign buyer. This link is becoming more important as increased foreign exporter competition and the expansion of more sophisticated consumer markets overseas require more adaptations in product quality and form. Cooperatives are an efficient mechanism for improving the communication of world market price signals to the U.S. farmer.

Trade Two-Way Street

Among world exporters is a growing tendency to circumvent the free market process through the use of export subsidies, dual pricing schemes, and other trade-disrupting practices. In addition, U.S. exporters encounter a wall of quotas, tariffs, and nontariff barriers all designed to keep out foreign imports. The European Community's variable import levies and Japan's import quotas are only a few of the multitude of controls that impair the international movement of agricultural goods.

As efficient producers, U.S. farmers stand to benefit from a trading environment geared as closely as possible to market forces, and pressure will continue to be applied to liberalize international trade. Because of a belief in an open system of world trade, the United States is prepared to bring its programs and policies to the negotiating table in an effort to resolve trade differences. A similar commitment from other world traders is needed, however, if progress is to be made.

While the climate of agricultural trade will improve in the long run, it will only come at a price. If the United States expects access to other countries' markets, it must be willing to give access to its markets. Every country in the world faces protectionist pressures which are often particularly acute for agriculture. The United States is one of the world's largest trading nations. If it is not willing to live by the premise that trade is a two-way street, it will encourage the erection of many more "Do Not Enter" signs in markets overseas.

Trade Negotiations— Past and Future

By Clayton Yeutter, *United States trade representative, Executive Office of the President, Office of the United States Trade Representative*

The history of U.S. participation in trade agreement negotiations is a long one. The first reciprocal trade treaty negotiated by the United States was with the German Zollverein (Customs Union) in 1844. It never became effective, however, because of failure to receive Senate ratification. Eleven years later, a trade agreement with Canada was ratified.

1890 Trade Act
It was not until Congress passed the Trade Act of 1890 that the President was given authority to enter into trade agreements not requiring subsequent approval of either the Senate or the House of Representatives. Even then, this authority was narrowly defined. In the 1890 Act, in order to put pressure on several countries to enter into these agreements, the President was empowered to impose penalty duties on certain duty-free articles (coffee, tea, hides, sugar, and molasses) whenever the supplying country's treatment of imports from the United States was deemed "to be reciprocally unequal and unreasonable."

1897 Tariff Act

In the Tariff Act of 1897, the President was not only given the authority to impose penalty duties on certain products, but for the first time was permitted to reduce duties on certain products in return for concessions by other countries. At this time, most negotiations were conducted on a conditional Most-Favored-Nation (MFN) basis, such that different levels of duty would be applied to different countries. That policy changed beginning in the 1920's as it was found that discriminatory duties created economic distortions and foreign policy problems, as well as breeding retaliation against U.S. exports from unfavored countries.

Multilateral Negotiations

During World War II, various interdepartmental committees, composed of U.S. Government officials and experts in negotiating foreign trade policies, considered how to re-establish world trade after the war and how to eliminate the arbitrary restrictions, discriminations, and barter arrangements that had grown up in that period and during the 1930's depression. Also, a source of congressional complaint with bilateral

agreements was that because of the Most-Favored-Nation policy many third countries got a "free ride" when the United States and a trading partner negotiated tariff concessions. One way to solve this problem was to hold the negotiations in a multilateral context.

In December 1945, the United States invited 15 countries to prepare projects for a general international conference on trade and employment and to negotiate both with the United States and each other for the reduction of tariffs and elimination of tariff preferences on specific commodities. The results of the negotiations were included in the 1947 General Agreement on Tariffs and Trade (GATT), which also included general provisions—or articles—to safeguard the tariff concessions made in the agreements. On January 1, 1948, nine countries including the United States agreed to apply the Protocol of Provisional Application of the GATT. Today, 90 countries are members of the GATT.

Trade Rounds

The first of seven major tariff-cutting rounds in the GATT was held at Geneva in 1947. The others were: Annecy,

Trade Negotiations

1949; Torquay, 1950; Geneva, 1956; Dillon Round, 1960–61; Kennedy Round, 1964–67; Tokyo Round, 1974–79.

Roughly the same amount of attention was given to agricultural tariffs in the early rounds of negotiations as was given to tariffs on industrial products. Starting in 1961, however, when the European Community (EC) withdrew concessions on those commodities to be covered by the variable levy system, agriculture's participation began to lag. This lag was further exacerbated in the Kennedy and Tokyo Rounds when industrial tariffs were negotiated on the basis of formula cuts for most countries while agricultural tariffs continued to be negotiated on the basis of requests and offers. When negotiating on a request and offer basis, countries easily protected certain sectors by simply not offering their tariffs as candidates for reduction.

Despite the request and offer procedure, the extensiveness of U.S. participation in tariff reductions on agricultural products was evidenced by the concessions granted on 90 percent of U.S. agricultural tariffs, whereas the average for 10 other industrialized countries was only 60 percent.

Starting with the Kennedy Round of multilateral trade negotiations, the United States began in earnest to seek improved rules covering nontariff barriers to trade in agricultural products, an elusive goal since from the beginning the GATT permitted exceptions for trade in agricultural products.

GATT Articles

With two important exceptions, the 38 GATT Articles apply equally to trade in agricultural products and industrial products. The two exceptions are with regard to import quotas and export subsidies. Quantitative restrictions or quotas are prohibited for industrial products (unless justified for balance of payments reasons or, in the case of developing countries, to protect infant industries) but are permitted for agricultural products under certain conditions, e.g., if necessary to enforce a domestic support program which restricts domestic production or marketings in the same proportionate degree as the import quota. Similarly, export subsidies on manufactured products are prohibited, but export subsidies on primary products, basically farm products, are permitted under certain circumstances.

In practice, the conditions for imposing agricultural quotas have been loosely respected. The existence of a special U.S. waiver for Section 22 quotas or fees is one reason countries may not feel compelled to live closely by the GATT obligations on quantitative restrictions for agricultural products. In 1955 the United States asked for the waiver because our domestic price support programs for certain commodities did not require production controls. At the time the waiver was granted, a number of countries continued to apply quotas for balance of payments reasons even though the original balance of payments rationale no longer seemed justified. Some trade experts feel the U.S. waiver was granted because of the abundance of quantitative restrictions at that time. Also, it was envisioned that the waiver would be temporary.

The number of U.S. restrictions under the Section 22 waiver has declined over the years, but the United States retains in principle the right to take Section 22 action.

Kennedy Round
A principle U.S. objective was to obtain improved disciplines on nontariff trade barriers to agricultural trade, in particular, the EC's system of variable levies. The United States hoped to treat the variable levy as it would the traditional import duty—that is, to reduce and make it binding against future increase. The United States proposed that there be no distinction between agricultural and industrial products in the Kennedy Round negotiations— that if fixed tariffs were the only barrier, they should be cut; and if barriers other than fixed tariffs existed, protection should be reduced by a comparable amount.

The EC, however, proposed to base negotiations on domestic support programs. For products subject to variable levies and other forms of internal price or income support, they proposed to bind the margin of support. Variable levies could be changed to make up the difference between the bound internal price and the actual world price. Exporters would bind existing subsidy levels. If no subsidy existed, the exporter would be bound not to institute one.

The United States and other exporters found the EC proposals unacceptable principally because they would eliminate price as a mechanism for adjusting production and trade patterns and therefore discriminate against more efficient producers. Since the EC subsidized far more products than did other countries, the EC proposals on export subsidies were similarly unacceptable.

Tokyo Round

During the Tokyo Round the United States focused upon obtaining greater discipline on export subsidies on agricultural products. A Subsidies Code that sought to interpret GATT's Article XVI was negotiated, and as of April 1, 1985, 21 countries had signed it.

In the Code, export subsidies on nonprimary products were prohibited. For primary products, export subsidies were permitted as long as the subsidizer did not obtain more than an equitable share of world trade or materially undercut prices of other suppliers to the same market. "More than equitable share" was defined to include displacement of another exporter in a third country market.

U.S. experience with resolving agricultural disputes under the Code has not been satisfactory. A panel appointed to review EC export subsidies on

wheat flour reported that it could not determine whether the EC had obtained "more than an equitable share of world trade" because the term "equitable share" was not precise enough.

A panel that reviewed EC export subsidies on pasta found that pasta was a nonprimary product and, therefore, export subsidies on it were prohibited. The panel decision was blocked, however, by the EC and other European countries who maintained that such export subsidies should be permitted to the extent the subsidy only compensated for the high cost of durum wheat in the EC.

Future Trade Negotiations

A new round of multilateral trade negotiations is expected to begin in 1986. A major U.S. objective will be to bring greater discipline to the rules which govern trade in agricultural products and provide greater opportunities for expanding trade on the basis of comparative advantage.

The productive capacity of world agriculture exceeds demand for a number of commodities, and implementation of new technologies is likely to further aggravate surpluses. This scenario is far different from what has generally existed when past trade negotiations have taken place. There seems to be a growing recognition that domestic agricultural policies have been inordinately successful in increasing domestic agricultural production. As a result, government costs for these programs have grown enormously. There also is a growing sense that reducing government incentives for production and introducing greater market orientation to domestic production decisions is now needed.

GATT Committee on Trade in Agriculture

In preparation for the new round, a Committee on Trade in Agriculture has been created within the GATT. In the fall of 1984, the Committee made several recommendations for liberalizing trade in agricultural products. In the preamble to the recommendations, the Committee explained that it was seeking to reinforce the linkages between national policies and the GATT articles on quantitative restrictions and subsidies in such a way as to more clearly define the extent to which domestic agricultural

policies can affect trade. The Committee recommended that:

1. All measures affecting access (variable levies, quantitative restrictions, minimum import prices, and voluntary restraint agreements) be subject to improved GATT disciplines.

2. All subsidies be subject to strengthened GATT rules. For export subsidies and other forms of export assistance two approaches should be developed at the same time: 1) improvement of existing rules and disciplines and 2) a general prohibition with exceptions.

Work has been slow in the Committee as governments wrestle with the changes in domestic legislation and prices which are necessary to bring greater market orientation to domestic programs. But every step that governments take in their efforts to reduce incentives to production is one additional step in the direction of liberalizing trade in agriculture. At last, it might be possible to reform the rules not so much because of a greater orientation to free trade but simply because the root of the problem, high governmentally induced price supports, is simply overburdening national treasuries.

World Organizations Make an Impact

By Martin Kriesberg, *senior assistant to administrator, Office of International Cooperation and Development*

Many international institutions influence world economic development by improving world agricultural production, distribution, food security, and trade. Most of those providing assistance for agricultural development in low income countries are autonomous organizations associated with the United Nations (U.N.) system. In addition to those agencies which specialize in food and agriculture matters, many U.N. agencies have a peripheral interest in and influence on world food, e.g., *The World Health Organization (WHO)* and the *United Nations Children's Fund (UNICEF)*. Most commodity organizations are not part of the U.N. but work closely with the *U.N. Conference on Trade and Development (UNCTAD)*. The United States provides leadership for the work of these organizations and, as the world's largest economy, is often the largest contributor to their resources.

What International Organizations Do

The *Food and Agriculture Organization (FAO)* of the U.N. is perhaps most widely known for its work to improve the technology of agriculture in developing countries and to provide

FAO

training and technical assistance for over 100 country members. In carrying on its work, FAO gets about 40 percent of its resources from quota payments by member nations, 35 percent from the United Nations Development Program (UNDP) and other U.N. agencies including the World Bank, and also administers funds from donor member countries for ad hoc program activities. FAO's resources have increased fivefold in the past decade, and its overall budget for 1984–85 is now about $1 billion for the biennium.

The FAO and the U.N. share paternity for the *World Food Program (WFP)* which uses food aid to further development in needy countries and also

The Food and Agriculture Organization of the United Nations is representative of international organizations which provide agricultural development assistance to low-income countries. FAO provides assistance to over 100 country members of the organization.

provides food in emergency situations. Countries contribute both surplus commodities and cash to WFP for its disbursements to meet country needs and programs. The United States contributes less than 10 percent of its P.L. 480 commodities to the WFP; this is about 25 percent of actual WFP operating levels. The pledge amounts agreed upon among countries comprising WFP's governing council have not been fully met in recent years.

The *International Fund for*

International Organizations Affecting World Agriculture

Agricultural Development (IFAD) is a relatively new U.N. agency, established pursuant to a recommendation of the 1974 World Food Conference. IFAD engages in project and program financing, principally for the poorest developing countries, often doing so in cooperation with the World Bank and other financial institutions. Funding of projects has been on very concessional terms, and commitments were $300 to $380 million a year during 1979–82. New commitments have fallen in subsequent years.

The *World Bank (IBRD)* has been the largest provider of lending for development projects in low income countries. Moreover, during the past decade the World Bank has allocated a major share of its total resources to agriculture and rural development projects. Annual funding in 1981–83 was about $3.7 billion for the agricultural sector. The World Bank operates through three financing mechanisms: 1) regular bank loans on interest just above the bank's own borrowings; 2) concessional loans through its affiliate, the International Development Agency, and 3) equity investments to private enterprise by its International Financial Corporation.

Also, regional development banks patterned after the World Bank make project loans, and they too have given highest priority to food and agriculture development projects. The *Inter-American Development Bank,* the *Asian Development Bank* and the *African Development Bank* reached their highest level of lending for agriculture in 1982; at that time the three banks committed $1.6 billion to the agricultural sector.

The U.S. share in the Banks varies from about 20 percent of the World Bank's capital subscriptions to somewhat more for the Inter-American Development Bank and less for the Asian and African lending institutions. Only a small proportion of the capital subscriptions are paid in. The banks borrow in the world money markets for most of their lending, and the backing of all member governments earns the banks good credit ratings and borrowing terms.

The *International Monetary Fund (IMF)* is concerned principally with maintaining stability in world monetary matters; it helps countries borrow credits for short periods to meet problems in their balance of payments; i.e. maintain international solvency and pay for imports of goods and the servicing of foreign debts. It was largely the IMF, working with the U.S. Government, the World Bank, and the private banks (at considerable risk on their loans to developing countries in 1983–84) that arranged for debt servicing by developing countries deepest in debt.

A number of international agencies pursue studies and publish papers designed to foster better understanding and contribute to more enlightened international agricultural policies. Some also organize forums for harmonizing national policies to improve the workings of the world food and agricultural system.

The U.N. *World Food Council (WFC)* convenes annual meetings of the agricultural ministers from 36 member countries. Membership to the council is by annual election (the United States, China, and U.S.S.R. have been on the council since its formation 10 years ago). The WFC is oriented toward the needs of developing countries and the agricultural trading problems of all countries. Papers prepared by the WFC Secretariat set the direction of discussion for the

FAO

annual ministerial meeting.

The *Organization for Economic Cooperation and Development (OECD)* is comprised of Western European countries, the United States, Japan, Canada and Australia and seeks to advance their economic well-being. Among operating committees are ones on agriculture, trade, and developing country assistance. The secretariat develops studies in line with member country requests, and these papers become the subject for technical discussions and annual meetings at the ministerial level. Member

Five years of drought in Ethiopia have caused devastating famine to 10.5 million people. International organizations have food reserves to meet these kinds of emergencies but are often faced with obstacles that prevent many of the victims from receiving supplies.

country policies and performance in agriculture and other economic sectors are critiqued within the context of each substantive committee.

Another policy-oriented international agency is the *International Food and Policy Research Institute (IFPRI)* which is a unit of the *Consultative Group on International Agricultural*

Research (CGIAR). IFPRI conducts studies on policies and publishes papers conducive to improving production and distribution of food and which may be of special benefit for developing countries.

IFPRI, located in Washington, DC, is unique within the CGIAR system in that most of the dozen research centers comprising the system are located in developing countries and are engaged in agronomic research directed at producing higher yields to increase food supplies in low income countries. Each of the research centers focuses on several food crops, e.g., wheat, rice, potatoes, cassava, that are indigenous to the region's farming system and important in their people's diets. The CGIAR system is funded by national governments (mostly the Western donor countries) several international organizations, and charitable foundations. Contributions are voluntary and agreed upon at annual donor meetings.

Major U.S. charitable foundations such as Ford, Kellogg, and Rockefeller have been major contributors to worldwide agricultural research. They were instrumental in organizing the CGIAR system and

have played a major role in its funding since. Several foundations carried on major agricultural development programs in some individual countries, e.g., The Ford Foundatiion in India from the mid-1960's to the mid-1970's.

What They Have Accomplished

The impact of international organizations on world food and agriculture has grown significantly during the decade since the 1974 World Food Conference. The Conference was convened by the U.N. to deal with widespread shortfalls in food production which affected the U.S.S.R., large parts of Africa, and countries in Asia as well. The U.S. Secretary of State as well as the Secretary of Agriculture participated in the meeting, and the United States joined the consensus for a wide-ranging group of resolutions aimed at avoiding a repetition of serious world food shortages. A major part of the responsibilities was lodged with existing international organizations and several newly formed U.N. agencies. Some of the principal priorities set by the Conference for international agencies supported by the assembled governments were to:

● Provide more assistance to
developing countries to improve their food and agriculture
systems

● Expand agricultural re-
search and spread the adoption
of high yield technologies for
food crops

● Increase food production,
particularly in low-income food-
deficit countries

● Promote national policies
and strategies to link increased
production with improved
consumption

● Strengthen world food security and open up trade in agricultural commodities

Although resources increased
to improve food and agriculture

systems in developing countries since 1974, 1982–85 contributions to the multilateral
development organizations
have leveled off in the
aggregate.

The growth in agricultural
research and the transference
of high-yielding crop technology has been particularly
marked. Since its beginning in
1972, the Consultative Group
for International Agricultural
Research has grown from a
few research centers to 10 and
it supports major programs in
other research institutions.
Budgets have grown from some
$15 to $200 million a year, including those of institutions

Trends in Development Assistance Funding

	1973–74[1]	1978–79[1]	1982–83[1]
	—Million dollars—		
Specialized food and agriculture organizations (FAO, WFP, IFAD, and CGIAR)	272	986	1,434
International banks and UNDP providing financing for food and agriculture projects	1,563	4,787	5,638
Bilateral agencies of DAC member countries [2]	1,425	4,335	4,300
	—Percent—		
Multilateral organizations	.56	.55	.62

[1]The figures in this column are for each year and should be doubled for the 2-year period.
[2]DAC is the Development Assistance Committee of OECD and is comprised of the major donor countries providing foreign aid to developing countries on a bilateral and multilateral basis.

FAO

concerned with improving national food policies and the transfer of new knowledge to national research centers in developing countries.

Gains in food production in most regions of the world have been significant—with the obvious exception of sub-Saharan Africa. There have been dramatic *per capita* increases in the production of food grains in China, India and in South Asia where well over half the world's population lives. While the numbers of hungry and malnourished are estimated to be no less than there were 10 years ago, almost a billion more people are now on earth. Most

Food grain production has dramatically increased in China, India, and South Asia. Recent estimates predict further gains in those countries. China has been successful in developing small-scale farm technology to run farm equipment and electric generators. The FAO has sent technicians to China to export this useful agricultural technology to other developing countries.

of these people live in developing countries, and there has been enough food grown for them. Estimates for the year 1984 indicate further gains by Asia and continued production setbacks in Africa.

While the international organizations can be credited with helping to create and spread improved technology for raising

FAO

production, progress in improving the food consumption of the poor has been limited. There is more food self-reliance in many countries and regions considered almost hopeless a short decade ago. But production has not led to adequate diets for many. Rapid population growth, high unemployment, and uneven income distribution have contributed to hunger and malnutrition for tens of millions. This situation has led to new international policies on food aid and national policies on linking food production and distribution to better consumption.

The WFP, the food aid arm of the U.N. system, has received increased resources for its work and has distributed foodstuffs to meet emergencies and chronic cases of hunger and malnutrition. Food aid has gone particularly to meet the needs of vulnerable groups in the poorest countries. It has also used an increasing propor-

A section of dried-up earth in the Niger river bed in Mali is being planted with bourgou, a local name for animal fodder, in anticipation of the rain season. When the waters rise the plants will grow, and when the waters recede the plants will be harvested. The food supply outlook for the sub-Saharan African region remains critical because of the lack of rain.

FAO

tion of its resources to foster economic development as in food-for-work projects and for policy improvements.

But the international organizations have had neither the resources nor the authority to deal with fundamental problems of poverty and income distribution in many developing countries. National food strategies that were worked out for numerous countries in Africa remain useful blueprints for increasing production and improving food consumption, but shortcomings at both the national and international levels have constrained constructive efforts in those countries.

Thus, another goal of the in-

Food for work is a means of allowing the needy a means to feed themselves after World Food Program (WFP) aid stops. A knitting workshop in Peru set up on a cooperative basis provides training and work for mothers. Strict quality standards are required for export.

ternational organizations, namely, to improve world food security, has been only partially successful. Increased worldwide production of food and feed grains has led to adequate reserve stocks to meet shortfalls that might occur. But political as well as economic and logistical problems in the countries and regions most in need have sometimes meant that available supplies did not get to the hungry. That has been the sorry story in some African countries.

Another area in which international institutions have had limited success is in efforts to open up and increase agricultural trade. U.N. agencies like UNCTAD, the World Food Council, and the OECD as well as commodity organizations like the International Wheat Council, have urged freer trade, but protectionist tendencies have grown since the early 1980's. Faced with worldwide recession, governments have sought to insulate their economies and particularly their agricultural sectors. In many developing countries and some EEC countries, economies remain stagnant and the protectionist tendencies persist despite the good offices of international agencies. Nevertheless, the weight of international organizations has probably kept protectionist tendencies from worsening and has had an influence on improving market access for the low income countries. The U.S. Caribbean Basin Initiative and the EEC Lomé Convention are examples of enlightened self-interest, helping low income countries improve their trade with the industrial world.

But the successes carry with them the danger of complacency and near-term cutbacks in production and stocks and the underlying support structure of agricultural research, soil and water management. Reductions in the support for international organizations that have given impetus to overcoming hunger and malnutrition also may follow.

U.S. Benefits

Increased worldwide production of foodstuffs has meant declining real prices for consumers and this, in turn, has meant better real incomes for many so they can improve their diets and buy many other products from the United States and other industrial countries. This is the kind of economic development we have experienced in the United States. The pattern seems likely to be followed in developing countries with gains for them and us. The record on agricultural trade between the United States and developing countries shows increased agricultural imports from the United States as the economies of developing countries grow. U.S. policies toward international organizations and leadership seem to be sound for long-term self-interests.

Global Food Security

By Cheryl Christensen,
*agricultural economist, Economic
Research Service (ERS);*
T. Kelley White, *director,
International Economics Division,
ERS;* and
Paul P. Kiendl, *agricultural
economist, Program Analysis
Division, Foreign Agricultural
Service*

Global food security—assuring that food is accessible to the world's population—remains an elusive goal. Although world food production over the past decade has outpaced global population growth, a large portion of the world's inhabitants remain undernourished.

In 1974 the World Food Conference resolved that within 10 years, no child should go hungry; no person fear for their daily bread. Yet, during 1984 and 1985, famine in Africa claimed thousands of lives in Ethiopia, Mozambique, Chad, and Sudan, despite record food aid shipments to the affected countries. Millions of other people in Africa, Asia, and Latin America are still undernourished, even though world grain supplies are far more abundant than a decade ago.

As world population continues to grow rapidly from a current 4.8 billion to an estimated 6 billion by the year 2000, the challenge of providing enough food where it is needed most becomes even more formidable.

Food security is primarily a concern of poor people and poor nations. At the global level, the primary problem is food distribution. Countries and individuals that lack purchas-

FAO

Food security is a major concern of poor people and poor nations. Food distribution is the primary global problem. Countries lacking purchasing power are unable to buy food even when supplies are abundant. (Nigeria, World Food Program shipment.)

ing power cannot buy the food they need, even when supplies are abundant. Supplies are not always abundant, however, and coping with production variability is a key part of food security. When food supplies become scarce—because of production shortfalls or price variability—the poor generally suffer first and hardest.

A relatively small portion of the world's total productive resources would be required for the additional production to provide adequate diets. USDA estimates that approximately 20 million tons of cereal imports would currently be required to bring per capita consumption up to minimally adequate levels in poorer African, Asian, and Latin American countries. This figure is only 8.5 percent of total world cereal trade, and only 1.2 percent of total world grain production.

National and Global Approaches

Nations, individually and collectively, have tried to provide food security in a variety of ways. National approaches include increasing domestic food production, building national food security stocks, and relying on international markets, either through holding monetary reserves or relying on food aid to supplement regular commercial purchases. Some countries, such as the Asian members of the Association of Southeast Asian Nations, have instituted regional food security programs. Suggested international approaches include global food stocks, financing facilities for food imports such as the International Monetary Fund (IMF) Cereal Facility, and food assistance programs.

Food Self-sufficiency. Many countries have tried to promote food security by increasing their domestic food production, in order to eliminate the need for food imports. Some governments enunciated self-sufficiency strategies as a response to their own food emergencies and the uncertainties of global markets in the 1970's. Many African countries followed this pattern. In other instances, such as the case of many Middle Eastern oil exporters, policies were enunciated in response to political concerns about their dependence on international food markets.

A decade later, these efforts have shown mixed results. A variety of Asian countries—including India and China—have dramatically increased domestic food production and substantially cut imports. In other regions—such as sub–Saharan Africa—capita food production has fallen and import dependence increased.

Food self-sufficiency can be a costly approach to food security, especially when countries attempt to produce commodities that are cheaper in international markets. Saudi Arabia's self-sufficiency in wheat—achieved at a cost of $1,000 per metric ton, seven times the international market price—is an extreme example. Similarly, countries that produce food at the expense of export crops, which would earn more than enough foreign exchange to purchase required food, are using resources inefficiently. As a consequence of attempting to achieve food security through self-sufficiency, they sacrifice a potential national product and consumption suffers.

Even so, increased food production, leading to greater self-sufficiency, can be an important component of food security. While food security is not a global production problem, it is, in some cases, a regional or national problem. One clear example is sub–Saharan Africa, where a decade of declining per capita food production has left countries with inadequate diets, extreme vulnerability to weather-related production variability, and import needs well beyond what they can afford. Increased food production is an indispensable element of food security in most of these countries.

FAO

Increased domestic production also may be an important element of food security where transportation problems make it risky and expensive to rely on external food supplies. Many landlocked countries, with poor transportation systems, find increased local production essential. The same is true of more isolated areas within developing countries.

Finally, increased domestic production may be a beneficial although costly way of insuring against trade-associated risks. The sources of risk may be economic (tariffs, trade restric-

Increased domestic production also may be an important element of food security where transportation problems make it risky and expensive to rely on external food supplies. (Swaziland, farm woman.)

tions, price variability), political (embargoes, export restrictions, policy-related conditions) or logistical (transportation bottlenecks).

Increased national food self-sufficiency may not mean improved food security for all segments of society, however. Whether increased production contributes to broadly based food security depends both on the direct impact of producing more (whether the rural poor benefit through increased employment and income) and the indirect impacts on prices and employment in other sectors (real urban wages). India, for example, now produces enough food to provide a nutritionally adequate diet for the entire population; yet undernutrition persists among both the rural and urban poor.

Food Stocks. Even with increased domestic production, countries must offset production variations to guarantee a stable food supply by 1) accumulating national stocks or 2) relying on international stocks and trade to offset more extreme variations.

Global production is less variable than national or regional production. For this reason, holding grain stocks at the national or regional level requires larger total reserves than holding them globally. In addition, holding stocks can be expensive, particularly if storage is prolonged and carrying costs are high. Management of the stocks is a major factor in determining waste and loss and in determining stockholding cost. There are offsetting benefits, however, including more timely response to changes in

USDA

Few countries, other than the United States, maintain grain reserves to meet international crises. (Kansas, inspecting wheat for storage.)

production and savings of foreign exchange.

There have been periodic proposals for internationally held and managed grain stocks to meet emergency shortages.

No such emergency stocks currently exist. Major grain-exporting countries including the United States, Canada, and the European Community (EC) currently hold large stocks, which serve as *de facto* global stocks, although the ultimate disposition of these stocks is still a national decision, leaving food-short countries potentially vulnerable.

Countries that have based food security strategies on increased domestic production have frequently developed national stocks to offset domestic shortfalls. Again, India provides a good example; national stocks, while expensive to hold, have enabled India to offset most production shortfalls with its own resources. In sub-Saharan Africa, on the other hand, stock levels are low, and production variability translates more directly into reduced consumption, and import or aid requirements.

Trade and Monetary Reserves. Relying on international trade is an alternative to self-sufficiency policies. Self-reliance strategies seek to maintain food imports at a level that can be financed without international aid, using trade to improve diets and to cover national variability in production.

In practice, many developing countries have taken this approach, even when their policy statements emphasized self-sufficiency. This approach permits a country to specialize in the production of commodities in which it has a comparative advantage, reduces the cost of holding and managing expensive stocks, and permits flexibility in responding to changing conditions.

Recent economic conditions demonstrate the limitations inherent in this approach to food security, however. General economic conditions may prevent countries from having access to global food markets. Debt crises and falling export earnings have weakened the foreign exchange position of many developing countries in Latin America and Africa, as well as several planned economies in Eastern Europe.

In addition, unstable food markets may create uncertainties which limit their effectiveness in guaranteeing food security. During the early 1970's, when global food supplies were periodically tight, stocks often perilously low, and markets extremely volatile, most discussions of food security focused on measures to increase supplies, and create institutional mechanisms to moderate market variability. Many of these concerns are less pressing now. Global food supplies are abundant, cereal stocks are large, and most production variability could be absorbed without forcing down consumption levels.

The IMF Cereal Facility was designed to reduce developing countries' vulnerability to price variability by providing a global financial facility that could be used to finance food imports. Few countries have taken advantage of this facility, since it provides only short-term relief from balance of payments difficulties.

Food Aid. For countries facing severe emergencies or long-term food deficits and inadequate foreign exchange earnings, food aid provides a supplement to commercial imports. As domestic food production faltered and foreign exchange constraints grew, poorer countries in sub–Saharan Africa became more dependent on food aid. Hence, in 1984, food aid accounted for almost half of their total imports, up from about a third in 1982.

Food aid, while a practical short-term necessity, has serious weaknesses as a basis for food security. Food aid is often difficult to deliver quickly and requires extensive approval processes within donor countries. In addition, it is subject to changing political and economic priorities within donor

Food aid, while a practical short-term necessity, has serious weaknesses as a basis for food security. (Canada, handling U.S. food aid shipment.)

FAO

countries, which may affect both its availability and its allocation. Commodity availability generally reflects the surpluses of major donor countries such as the United States and the EC and may not match consumption patterns or preferences in recipient countries. Food aid tends to be least available when the need is greatest—when global supplies are short and prices high.

U.S.Food Aid

The concept of U.S. food aid developed in the years immediately following World War II when the United States implemented the ambitious Marshall Plan aimed at initiating economic recovery in war-torn Europe. This highlighted a fundamental shift in U.S. foreign policy strategy from one of reticent involvement to one of active leadership in global affairs.

The post-World War period also witnessed an unparalleled technological revolution in agricultural production. Through modern chemical fertilizers and hybrid seeds, agriculture flourished and surpluses became a growing problem. Despite this plentiful supply, hunger was a widespread problem in nations too destitute to purchase or produce food for their own in-

creasing consumption. It was in this climate that the U.S. Congress enacted Section 416 of the Agricultural Act in 1949, which permitted the Commodity Credit Corporation to donate surplus commodities to needy countries. This Section provided the basic structure for the Food for Peace (Public Law 480) Program.

Food for Peace. In an effort to bolster international trade, the Agricultural Trade and Development Act (P.L. 480) was enacted in 1954 as the primary mechanism for channeling food aid to foreign nations. The objectives were to provide humanitarian assistance, foster economic development in developing countries, establish and expand markets for U.S. agricultural commodities, and support U.S. foreign policy. Since its inception about 300 million tons of food, valued at over $35 billion, have been exported to needy countries around the globe.

P.L. 480 is composed of three program titles. The most prominent is title I which offers qualified friendly countries long-term, low-interest loans for the purchase of U.S. agricultural commodities. Currencies generated from local sales of these imports are then used

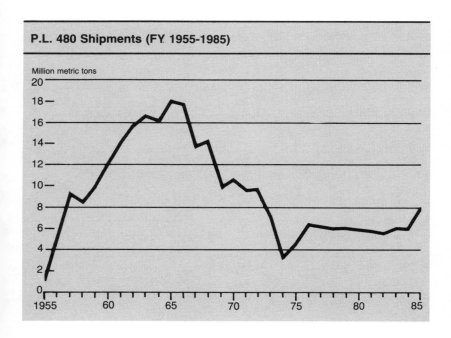

P.L. 480 Shipments (FY 1955-1985)

Million metric tons

for developmental activities specified in the P.L. 480 agreements. The end-result is an economic boost for the recipient country and a marketing foothold for U.S. agricultural products in a potential growth market. Such countries as Brazil, South Korea, Japan, Taiwan, and Spain, which have evolved from P.L. 480 recipients into major cash markets, attest to the success of this strategy.

Title II is a humanitarian program providing food donations to meet famine or other emergencies and a developmental program promoting economic and community development. U.S. private voluntary agencies, such as CARE and Catholic Relief Services, through the World Food Program, and government-to-government programs distribute title II food aid.

The title III Food for Development Program, authorized by Congress in 1979, is carried out through a title I agreement providing a longer term grant up to 5 years to support development goals. On successfully

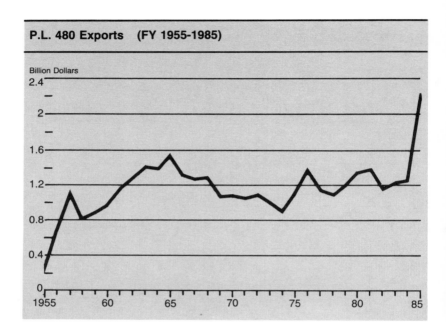

P.L. 480 Exports (FY 1955-1985)

completing the development goals, the title I debt is forgiven, resulting in a grant.

Current U.S. Efforts. The introduction of high-yielding crops in the 1970's created the possibility of a "Green Revolution" in some developing nations, raising hopes of a solution to the hunger problem. Although there has been astonishing progress in countries such as India, today over half a billion people in the world remain undernourished—mostly the young or the elderly. Nations now realize that hunger

is a long-term problem requiring the joint efforts of developing and developed countries to solve.

The P.L. 480 programs remain a major component of U.S. efforts to improve nutrition and to encourage economic development in developing countries. In fiscal 1985, an overall program of $2.2 billion will provide more than 8 million metric tons of farm commodities including food donations of over 3 million tons to help meet the needs of drought-stricken Africa.

The U.S. commitment to food aid is underscored by participation in international organizations such as the World Food Program (WFP) and the Food Aid Convention (FAC). During 1985–86 the U.S. pledge to the WFP totals $250 million, mainly from the P.L. 480 title II program. This alone accounts for 25 percent of all donor pledges. In the case of the FAC, over the past 5 years the United States has consistently provided food in excess of its minimum annual pledge of 4.47 million tons and often provides more than half the total FAC target of 10 million tons of grain.

Another important tool in combating world hunger is USDA's Office of International Cooperation and Development (OICD). This agency transfers technical knowledge to help developing nations in agricultural and scientific projects. Since 1950, more than 72,500 agriculturalists from these countries have received training and education in agricultural and rural development.

Development Basis for Food Security

Difficult financial straits, political instability, natural disasters, and a need for expanded trade are all handicapping developing nations striving for higher living standards. This is particularly true of Africa which has recently become the focus of renewed worldwide attention. As in the past, the U.S. food aid program can be expected to continue its role in helping solve these problems.

But in the long run, increased food security depends heavily on patterns of economic development, both within and across nations. Countries stand to gain most from pursuing self-reliance strategies in a global environment which provides both well-functioning international food markets, and opportunities for trade growth between developed and developing countries. Trade gains will not, in and of themselves, ensure adequate purchasing for poorer people within countries, however. National development strategies which are narrowly based, and have the effect of excluding significant portions of the population from employment and earned income will perpetuate undernutrition, even with substantial growth in national income, trade and food availability. Food security at the household and national level depends ultimately on widely shared economic growth.

Impact of Technology on Agriculture

By Orville G. Bentley, *assistant secretary for science and education, USDA,* and
Paul F. O'Connell, *staff assistant to the deputy chief for research, Forest Service*

"**T**he capacity to develop and to manage technology in a manner consistent with a nation's physical and cultural endowments is the single most important variable accounting for differences in agricultural productivity among nations." (Ruttan, Vernon W., *Agricultural Research Policy*), Minneapolis, University of Minnesota Press, 1982). As Ruttan's statement implies, technology policies for the food, fiber, and forestry sectors are of crucial importance if these sectors are to be productive.

Past U.S. technology policies have had a substantial degree of success because of the diversity and efficiency of the food and agriculture system. American consumers spend only 16 percent of their disposable income for food, and the sale of American agricultural and forestry products represents 24 percent of total U.S. exports, contributing substantially to the balance of payments. As an industry, American agriculture since World War II has had a high rate of growth in productivity—a rate more than three times as high as that of the nonfarm industrial sector.

Past achievements will not automatically assure continued future growth in productivity and industry well-being. Vast changes are underway in the social and economic fabric of our society.

● There is a supply and demand imbalance in U.S. agriculture, causing a severe pinch on profitability.

● Rate of technology adoption in other agricultural countries of the world has increased significantly in recent years, creating more competition for U.S. farmers.

● There are continuing concerns about agricultural and forestry production practices and the environment.

● The knowledge of molecular genetics and cellular biology is increasing rapidly, creating and expanding opportunities in improving agriculture worldwide.

● There is increased public awareness of the relationship between personal well-being and diet. Changing life styles and the increasing average age of U.S. citizens has led to questions about nutritional needs.

Research and education programs can help in providing options for these and other issues facing agriculture. The long-term answer to farmers' financial squeeze is improved productivity and higher quality

products. Environmental and human health goals can be enhanced by developing safer chemical systems. Human nutrition requirements can be better linked to agricultural production by developing plant and animal products that meet changing market demands. Technologies have had a major impact on agriculture in the past and will likely have greater impact in the future.

Productivity and Technology

When a society's resources are being fully used, the real income status of both producers and consumers can be improved only through productivity gains, in periods of commodity surpluses as well as in periods of shortages. Yet one source of uncertainty about what constitutes appropriate productivity and technology policies is confusion about the meaning and use of the term *productivity*. When used accurately, it always refers to the ratio of output per unit of total input. In this measure, the several inputs used in the production of goods and services— land, labor, buildings and equipment, energy, and others—are value-weighted and aggregated so that changes in output can be related to changes in total input. If such a total productivity measure is constructed carefully, it can be interpreted as a reasonably accurate depicter of technical efficiency and used to measure changes in efficiency over time.

From the beginning, improving productivity has been a prime motive for agricultural science and education programs. From the Civil War to World War I, the change from human power to horse power and continuous inventions and improvements in farm implements heralded the first phase of productivity increases. These innovations resulted in an almost twofold increase in labor productivity. During this period, the United States made a commitment to scientifically based agriculture institutionalized in the land-grant college system and the U.S. Department of Agriculture. The period between World Wars I and

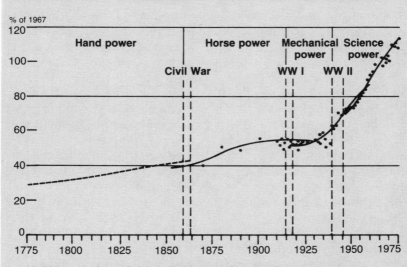

U.S. Agricultural Productivity Growth During the Past 200 Years[1]

SOURCE: Lu, Yao Chi and Quance, Leroy, "Agricultural Productivity: Expanding the limits," AIB 431, U.S. Dept. Agr., Econ. Res. Serv., 1979

II saw the second phase of productivity increases in agriculture, based primarily on internal combustion tractors powered by cheap fuel. Along with the increased use of fertilizer, massive water projects, and a cooperative extension service to transfer this new knowledge, productivity doubled again. Both labor and land productivity increased tremendously in the post-World War II period, because of the application of technologies stemming from the first full phase of scientific agriculture. The key factors were the use of hybrid crop strains, widespread use of pesticides and herbicides, improved nutritional and medical practices in animal husbandry, and the increased use of energy and fertilizers.

Examples of Improved Productivity

The evolution of a science-based agriculture has led to many spectacular changes.

Hybrid Corn. From 1929 to 1933, before the commercial use of hybrids, corn yields averaged 24 bushels per acre. In 1958, hybrid corn varieties accounted for 94 percent of planted corn acreage and U.S. average corn yields exceeded 50 bushels an acre. Twenty

Jack D. Lake

With the introduction of hybrid corn in 1958, corn yields have rapidly increased. The U.S. average is almost 5 times greater than it was 50 years ago. (Michigan, corn bin.)

years later the U.S. average yield broke the 100-bushel mark. These yield increases were made possible by genetic plant improvements which permitted intensive planting practices (high plant populations, better drainage and moisture control, and higher levels of fertilizer and pesticide use) and by the reduction of harvest losses through improved harvesting and drying technology.

The success of hybrid corn also has stimulated the breeding of other crops, such as sorghum hybrids, a major feed grain crop in arid parts of the world. Sorghum yields have increased 300 percent since 1930. Approximately 20 percent of the land devoted to rice production in China is planted with hybrid seed, reported to yield 20 percent more than the best nonhybrid varieties. And many superior varieties of tomatoes, cucumbers, spinach, and other vegetables are hybrids. Today virtually all corn produced in the developed countries is from hybrid corn.

Broiler Chickens. Changes in the broiler chicken industry have been phenomenal over the past 30 years. U.S. broiler production quadrupled, and annual consumption of chicken meat jumped from 23 pounds to over 54 pounds a person in

Technology changes in the broiler chicken industry have been phenomenal over the past 30 years. U.S. broiler production has quadrupled and annual consumption of chicken has increased to over 50 pounds per person. (Mississippi, broiler farm.)

George A. Robinson

1984. The farm price of broilers fell from 36¢ per liveweight pound in 1948 to 33¢ in 1984. After adjustment for inflation, the real price of broilers has fallen even more dramatically.

Improvement in the efficiency of broiler production owes much to public-supported research and to the employment of university-trained geneticists by breeders. In addition to genetic improvement in feed conversion efficiency and quality of meat, there were accompanying changes in housing, feed and waste handling systems, and disease control methods. Over the past 30 years the structure of the industry also has changed significantly. The size of broiler farms has increased while the total number dramatically declined. These larger units employ forward contracting and obtain large scale infusions of credit from feed suppliers.

Farm Management. Farm management specialists devote the great bulk of their farm-oriented research toward developing information and guides for farmers choosing enterprises and methods of production. The largest single group of studies deals with enterprise costs and returns. Production studies are devoted to providing

USDA

Farm management specialists are providing producers with information and alternatives for producing crops and livestock using cost-effective methods, materials, and new technologies. (Colorado, computer specialist and farmer—controlling an irrigation system.)

cost information on alternative ways of producing crops and livestock using alternative irrigation systems, fertilizer combinations, fertilizer and seed, labor-machinery-equipment combinations, alternative rations, and dryland versus irrigation farming. Given this nation's economy, rich in alternative farm technologies and highly dynamic in developing new technologies, it is not surprising that a great deal of effort is devoted to providing guidance in choice of production methods. Nor is it surprising that the choice of enterprise is regarded as the most important decision problem, because comparative advantage shifts as technologies, prices, and institutions change.

The impact of farm management research cannot be measured as easily as the results of biological and physical sciences, but anyone having knowledge of the farm enterprise realizes its importance. In contrast to farmers in controlled economies, U.S. farmers operate as free, independent business managers, controlling their means of production, making their own decisions, and receiving the results of their own labor and management abilities. Helping these

independent farmers make the best decisions possible, given the circumstances facing them, has been a major factor in the success story of U.S. agriculture.

Need for Improved Technologies

The urgency of short-term needs of the agricultural sector, such as credit, should not obscure the continuing need of producers and the agricultural support system for scientific knowledge. Continued vigor of the food and fiber industry calls for improved productivity and higher quality goods and services—including more value-added products for the export market. The combination of traditional research methods and the new biotechnology techniques offers tremendous potential for improving the competitive position of U.S. agriculture.

Animal Technologies. New and improved animal technologies point to faster growth rates, less feed per unit of output, increased disease resistance, and more offspring per animal. Animal diets can consist of more forages and crop byproducts, and be supplemented with minerals, vitamins, amino acids, and other nutrients.

Plant Technologies. Using biotechnology techniques and conventional plant breeding, crops will have increased resistance to disease, insects and nematodes. Variation in temperature, water availability, and competition from weeds will have less effect on new, more resistant varieties of tree crops, potatoes, corn, soybeans, and grain sorghum. Genetic engineering can alter plant structures and shapes to improve harvesting and maturing processes with a potential reduction in production costs and improvement in quality.

Nutrition. Plant and animal scientists need a better understanding of the results of human nutrition studies, and nutritionists should become more aware of the realities of agricultural production. Producers need help in adjusting to changing markets. They have made large investments and will resist changes until they can see reasonable options. Scientists and educators are in a good position to provide this help. Nutritious food cannot be provided without the cooperation of the farmer and other performers in the food system.

Future Challenges

Forces creating a need for im-proved technologies include the following:

• Concerns are increasing about the continued availability of the natural resource base. Improved resource-saving technologies need to be incorporated into current production practices. What resource use patterns are consistent with sustained agricultural uses over time?

• During the past century, converging scientific, economic, and technological developments have led to growing public concern over the effects of these developments on human health and quality of life. Such changes have prompted vigorous debate over the enforcement and adequacy of our laws and regulations. How can the wholesomeness and safety of the nation's food supply be effectively monitored? How can the safety of genetically engineered microbes which may be used in food processing or production be properly evaluated? And how do we evaluate low-level carcinogenic risks from multiple sources?

• The United States has extensive acreages of forest and range resources (71 percent of total land area). These resources provide jobs, wood, wildlife, water, forage, and energy—and a varied array of recreation opportunities. As with annual crops and domestic farm animals, improved forest and range technologies can increase yields, better protect the resource, reduce input costs, and enhance quality of outputs—all to meet changing demands of domestic and foreign customers.

● The United States is still competitive in world markets for most of its agricultural and forest exports, but its future position and comparative advantage are in question. Comparative advantage is affected by investments in human and natural resources and in research and development of technology as well as by policy and the marketing and transportation system. Understanding the interactions and trends of these variables and then acting on that knowledge is critical for the future of U.S. agriculture.

To meet these challenges, the agricultural science and education system must attract and train scientists and specialists with needed skills in molecular genetics, human nutrition, soil and water sciences, international marketing, systems analysis, agricultural engineering and other specialties.

Some other concerns are: 1) Low salary levels and lack of promotion opportunities in the USDA/State system, which make it difficult to retain highly qualified people in the high-tech fields; 2) Graduate and undergraduate education programs that are not attracting enough students in critical fields; and 3) Obsolete scientific equipment.

The technology development process must continue to consider the incentives of final users. Before new or existing techniques are adopted by an owner, manager, or consumer, many questions need answers. Will an alternative approach be more cost-effective? Can the farmer afford the additional cost when the prices of wheat, corn, or stumpage are so variable? What financial plan best fits a given farm or household? USDA's Cooperative Extension Service has a primary responsibility in this area, but it needs help—especially in the more advanced technical areas such as integrated management systems and technologies resulting from biotechnology. The private sector is becoming more active in the technology transfer process, but scientists also will need to provide more assistance.

Part V.
LOOKING
AHEAD

Agriculture in the Next 20 Years

By Dennis Avery, *senior agricultural analyst, Bureau of Intelligence and Research, U.S. Department of State*

A recent surge in world agricultural output has been powered by new technologies, broader use of incentive-oriented farm policies, and additional investments in agriculture. This progress is almost certain to continue—and the rate of growth may actually increase—over the next two decades.

Agricultural production in the world rose 25 percent between 1971 and 1982—a huge increase. Farm output in the developing countries rose an even more impressive 33 percent. Per capita food production improved in every major region except Africa (though some non-African countries suffered per capita declines). Moreover, the rate of farm output increase in developing countries was higher in the last half of the period (3.3 percent) than in the first half (2.7 percent). The progress in food production could have been even better except for policy-induced failures in a number of countries with good agricultural resources—including Nigeria, Tanzania, Ghana, Ethiopia, Sudan, Colombia, Nicaragua, Guatemala, and the Dominican Republic.

Given the current dizzying pace of change in the world

USDA

generally—and the rapid changes in farming particularly—world agriculture is certain to change radically in the next two decades.

Potatoes normally grow in cool climates, but they soon may be produced in regions of high temperature and humidity. (Georgia, potato experiment.)

Better Farming Technology

Advances in agricultural technology are occurring on a broader base today than ever before. The most powerful changes have probably resulted from plant genetics—the Green Revolution wheat and rice vari-

eties, short-season corn, rust-resistant wheat, and more recently the powerful new sorghum varieties now emerging for the Third World. Important contributions also have come in engineering (such as center-pivot irrigation sprinklers and electrostatic sprayers that give farmers in developing countries more effective pest

USDA

control), animal nutrition (doubled poultry feed efficiency), pest control (antibiotics and the new genetically engineered vaccines), institutions (the worldwide network of international agricultural research centers), communications (satellites, computers, word processors, microwave relay), transportation (from outboard motors to containerized

As ground water dwindles, high-tech irrigation becomes a high priority prospect. ARS scientists are developing a traveling trickle system that takes the guesswork out of irrigating and saves valuable water. (Maryland, irrigation experiment.)

freight), conservation (minimum tillage, trickle irrigation), effective weed control (herbicides), and forestry (fast-growing, leguminous trees that are now producing firewood, retaining soil, fertilizing crops, and feeding livestock through-. out the Third World).

In the 1950's, perhaps 50 percent of the world's arable land was in countries that could make broad use of high-technology agricultural methods. Today, more than 90 percent of the world's arable land is located in countries making relatively broad use of high-technology methods, and these nations' proportion of high-technology farmers continues to rise.

The Green Revolution is not a one-time occurrence. Improving agricultural technology is a process—and once it starts it does not stop. In 1984, the European Community's (EC) wheat crop was the largest on record—by a whopping 20 percent—primarily because of a high-yielding new winter wheat. The EC, of course, has one of the most highly developed agricultures in the world. U.S. agricultural output rose 33 percent between 1971 and 1982—and technically it could have increased even more. Agricultural output is becoming less and less the result of natu-

Increased grain yields are possible through major advances in soil tillage techniques and equipment. (Maryland, checking experimental grain field.)

USDA

- A new class of feed additives called isoacids have recently been approved for use by U.S. dairy producers. They increase bacterial action and protein synthesis in cows' stomachs. The immediate result is likely to be an increase of 15–25 pounds of milk per cow per day in U.S. dairy herds—or an equivalent feed savings. Approval for bovine growth hormone treatments is expected soon, and should stimulate milk production per cow by another 10 percent, at least.

- Short-season hybrids have moved corn grain production 250 miles nearer the earth's poles in the last decade. The northern border of the Corn Belt is now in central Canada. East Germany is moving into corn grain production with a new hybrid, and plans to shift its hog feed from imported corn to domestically produced corn/cob. Chinese corn production is up sharply in recent years, and Argentina is looking at short-season hybrids for its southernmost croplands.

- Chinese agricultural production rose more than 40 percent in 5 years—one of the most dramatic surges in agricultural history—after China scrapped its communal farms in 1979. The land was leased back to families and small work groups, and incentive prices offered for farm products. More and more of the world's farmers are being offered such broad-based price incentives, and in virtually all cases they are responding with higher output.

- Saudi Arabia is the world's newest wheat-surplus nation—by spending billions of petrodollars on high subsidies for Saudi-grown wheat. Saudi business producers have drilled wells and installed center-pivot irrigation systems that literally turn the desert green. Saudi wheat output has risen from 150,000 metric tons a year a decade ago to a projected 2.3 million tons for 1985.

- Hybrid corn was a major breakthrough for world agriculture in the 1930's and 1940's. Recently, plant breeders have developed the world's first practical hybrids for wheat, rice, and cotton. Hybrid alfalfa and rapeseed are at the field test stage. Triticale, a hybrid of wheat and rice that is sterile when it occurs in nature, has been made fertile. Researchers say the new hybrids have not yet produced radically higher yields, but not for lack of genetic potential. Rather, these newly hybridized plants were designed for self-pollination, and require more extensive re-engineering before their hybrid vigor can be fully tapped.

• Genetic engineering has produced the first fully safe vaccine against foot-and-mouth disease and a vaccine against a major form of malaria (an important farm labor constraint in developing countries). The Volta River valleys in West Africa have been cleared of river-blindness. Other new insect control techniques promise to open up millions of acres in Africa where agriculture is currently constrained by fly- and tick-borne diseases.

• Until recently, traditional farming methods produced an adequate food supply for most of Africa, so little food research was done there. Moreover, little of the research done in other regions has been usable under Africa's unique conditions. Recently, however, several highly promising research developments appear to offer Africa major increases in farm production—including high-yielding new varieties of corn, sorghum, cassava and peanuts; improved pest control; alley cropping between rows of leguminous trees; and better soil and water conservation. The policies of the African nations are currently the most serious constraints on increased African food production. African governments have consistently failed to offer price incentives to farmers, while their bureaucracies have swollen the cost of inputs and marketing, and overvalued their currencies.

• In Ghana, the staff of the Cocoa Marketing Board soared from less than 10,000 at independence to more than 103,000 recently—while the quantity of cocoa marketed dropped from 600,000 metric tons to about one-fourth of that level. Ghana's currency at one point was overvalued by 3,000 percent, making food imports seem vastly cheaper than they really were, and sharply increasing farmers' costs for fertilizer and pesticides.

ral factors, and more and more a matter of assembling cost-effective technology, inputs, and systems.

In fact, the current breadth of agricultural development is reinforcing the technological trends. Decades ago, West Africa developed high-yielding strains of oil palm. Indonesia then borrowed the oil palm and imported the Cameroon weevil (which improves pollination and yields). Indonesian tissue culture experiments have recently produced varieties with a higher proportion of oil in the kernels. These varieties and the weevil are now being introduced in Colombia, which has perhaps 600,000 acres that could be planted to oil palm.

Farm Investment Increases

Capital continues to become relatively cheaper than labor over time, and countries all over the globe are continuing to invest in their agricultures.

● Saudi Arabia has invested billions of its oil dollars for the food security of home-grown wheat.

● Indonesia has invested heavily in rice self-sufficiency, but also in tree crops such as oil palm, cocoa and rubber.

● Brazil has increased its ag-

ricultural exports recently, sharply expanding production of such new exports as soybeans, frozen orange juice, and cocoa as well as such Brazilian economic mainstays as coffee and sugar.

● Eastern India is beginning to invest in tube wells to tap shallow underground water flows for dry-season wheat production; two Indian states had wheat crop increases of more than 40 percent in 1984.

● Thailand continues to clear about a million acres a year for production of rice, corn, and other export crops.

● Turkey is building three big dams in the upper Euphrates Valley, an economic development effort similar to the U.S. Tennessee Valley Authority. The project will provide electricity for homes and industries in addition to irrigating more than 16 million acres of farmland.

● In Europe, Japan, and the United States, individual farmers continue to invest in higher agricultural output in response to attractive government support prices.

Importance of Farm Policies

Government policies have been among the most serious constraints on food production in many developing countries. Prices of farm products were kept low to placate urban consumers. Exchange rates were overvalued, making food imports seem cheaper than they really were. Farm support functions were monopolized by government agencies or parastatals. Much of Africa focused its agricultural investment on big state farms which absorbed money but achieved little productivity. Small farmers retreated into subsistence. Kenya's government marketing boards have been so expensive that farmers received only 40 percent of the consumer price. Developed countries have been all too willing to export their surpluses, depressing prices for farmers in developing countries.

Progress in World Agricultural Policies. Some progress has been made, however, in the world's agricultural policies. The debate about the most apropriate agricultural policies for development has been ended by the near-universal success of one policy model—offering real price incentives to a broad group of family-sized farmers, and then supporting them with access to better technology and inputs.

The dramatic success of China's recent family farming policy simply underscores a broad pattern of developing country success on every continent—when the energies and enthusiasm of small farmers care harnessed through incentives and technological opportunities.

Policy Problems Remain. Major policy problems, however, still constrain agricultural output in nearly every developing country. Many of these are strongly entrenched politically. It is possible to be optimistic about technology and pessimistic about the policies needed to encourage its broad adoption.

The most likely outcome for the next two decades is that Africa and the other poorest countries will be pushed toward somewhat more effective support for their farmers by necessity and the success models of other developing countries. Hunger emergencies are still likely but they should become smaller in scale and less frequent. Increasingly, they will be due to failures of government (e.g., wars, policy mistakes), and less and less often to inadequate agricultural technology. Africa will continue to be the major hunger risk, locked in a crucial race between population growth, agricultural development and the next major drought. The total amounts of food needed to meet hunger emergencies is not large, however. Food aid shipments to drought-stricken Africa in 1984 totaled less than 12 million tons, compared with world grain carryover stocks of nearly 200 million.

Agricultural Constraints Not Severe

The physical constraints on agriculture—which some had feared would limit world farm output and bring on a population and food crisis before the year 2000—have turned out to be far less severe than almost anyone foresaw.

Limited Cropland Offset. Little additional cropland can be created, but things can be done which have the effect of creating more cropland. New corn varieties from the international research center in Mexico are ready to double yields for small farmers in Central America and in West Africa. In fact, high-yielding varieties are raising yields and improving fertilizer response in all types of crops. Shorter-season varieties mean more double and even triple cropping. A new growth-regulating chemical shortens the

soybean growing season by up to 2 weeks, and will permit expansion of wheat/soybean double-cropping. Irrigation is being expanded. Wet areas have been drained. Brazil is opening up more than 100 million acres of acid soils on the Cerrado plateau; lime and phosphate make the area productive and competitive. New ways are being found to farm the world's 700 million acres of black, sticky Vertisol soils—most of them in India, Australia, and the Sudan.

Soil Erosion Countered. Soil erosion has been less severe and detrimental to the world's crop yields than many expected. Conservation tillage and minimum tillage techniques have spread rapidly under the double impetus of soil conservation and lower fuel costs. Surveys indicate that perhaps a third of the Corn Belt is currently farmed with some form of conservation tillage—probably including most of the land at serious risk. At current soil loss rates, irreplaceable soil fertility losses in the Corn Belt over the next 100 years would cut crop yields less than 8 percent below the levels they would otherwise achieve, according to the University of Minnesota Soil Science Department. Moreover, the odds are strong that improved conservation methods will continue to be found, and it is almost certain that improved agricultural technology will dwarf such losses over the next century.

Some regions of the world, of course, have higher erosion risks than the Corn Belt. But high productivity on the world's best acres makes it possible to return many fragile lands to forage, pasture, and forestry. New England and West Virginia, for example, have moved strongly in this direction in recent decades. Africa's soil conservation problems can be solved with higher productivity on its best lands, better soil conservation methods, and better range management. Lack of cropland and soil erosion problems need not prevent adequate nutrition for the world's expected population in the next 20 years.

Oil Prices Reduced. Oil prices have constrained agriculture less severely than expected. Real oil prices have declined a full one-third from their 1981 peak. More efficient techniques are being developed for such energy needs as crop drying. The prices of nitrogen fertilizers never rose as much

as oil prices because of relatively cheap gas feedstocks produced in association with oil. Indonesia has increased its fertilizer production from a tiny 30,000 metric tons a year a decade ago to 1.2 million tons in 1984. Such major oil producers as Iran and Nigeria are still flaring off large quantities of their associated gas, although Nigeria is now building one modest-sized urea plant.

Demand Growing Slowly
Demand for farm products has been growing less rapidly than agricultural output in recent years. The vast majority of the world's population is already consuming enough calories for at least minimal nutrition, and much of it is well fed indeed. Foreign exchange constraints have pushed the developing countries, which were increasing food imports in the 1970's, to explore their own farm potential in the 1980's, and they are increasing productivity. Now, even Africa seems poised for higher agricultural productivity with new seed varieties and better incentives for broad groups of small farmers.

The other major element of farm market growth in the 1970's was rising demand. Petrodollars were being recycled, many of them to developing countries and Eastern Europe, which used them to import farm products. Real incomes also were rising in many countries, enabling more people to add meat, milk, and eggs to their diets. Farmers helped demand by delivering protein foods at declining real costs through improvements in grain productivity and poultry efficiency. In the 1980's, however, protein demand has proven surprisingly sensitive to relative prices and incomes. Economic growth rates have slumped. Eastern Europe, which was borrowing money in the West to finance its feed imports, ran out of credit. World feed grain consumption, which rose nearly 100 million metric tons in the 1970's, has increased only about 20 million tons in the first half of the 1980's. An unknown part of the slowdown has been due to low-fat diet consciousness.

Trend Toward Self-Sufficiency

Increased farm productivity clearly offers more countries more opportunity for agricultural self-sufficiency, and many of them are using it:

• Taiwan is solving the problem of the rice surplus created

through its high support prices by diverting 300,000 tons of rice a year into livestock feed. The substitution has cut imports of feed grain by an even larger amount; the rice diversion has been financed by taxing grain imports, while imports of untaxed tapioca pellets have jumped from zero in 1983 to 200,000 tons in 1985.

• Saudi Arabia will probably begin shifting its irrigated farms away from surplus wheat toward barley, which it still imports.

• China has already shifted from a major cotton importer to a significant exporter, and has achieved net self-sufficiency in grains.

• The EC has raised its per capita agricultural output by more than 15 percent in the past decade, shifting it from the world's largest farm import buyer to the world's second-ranking farm exporter. Even if the Common Agricultural Policy were eliminated, EC crop yields would remain high and most of its farmland would remain in farming.

Implications for U.S. Agriculture

For the future, conventional markets for farm products will rise less rapidly than the potential for farm output. And the world already has structural surpluses of cereals, oilseeds, sugar, coffee, cocoa, dairy products, red meat, poultry meat, wine, tomato products, and cotton.

The United States cannot evade the impacts of rising world farm productivity. Inevitably, the productivity and politics of other countries are intruding on U.S. farm policies. The price-based farm subsidy regimes of the developed countries are becoming more expensive. Almost nowhere can additional surpluses be sold at virtually any price.

Nor can U.S. agriculture afford to give up its exports—which have recently contributed about 25 percent of U.S. farm income. Turning away from farm exports would eliminate hundreds of thousands of U.S. farm and farm-related jobs.

Even farm programs oriented to protecting a country's farmers from imports, such as the EC's and Japan's, will come under heavier pressure. Japanese farmers, for example, will have to fend off not only U.S. export pressures but also those from Pacific Rim trading partners. Many of these nations cannot afford balance-of-pay-

ments deficits so Japan has a strong, direct interest in taking imports from them. Some are already winning relatively favorable access to Japanese farm product markets.

Lower Production Costs.
The future of American farming will turn on the relative costs of producing farm products in the United States or somewhere else. It is unlikely that the United States can adapt to the higher productivity trends in the agricultural world without significantly revamping its farm programs, and without at least some economic difficulty for its farmers. The strategy for U.S. farmers must be to invest only in those things that will significantly lower per unit costs. This will often mean output-increasing technology.

Obviously, land values are not likely to rise in this situation. U.S. farmland values rose 50 percent in real terms with the cheap dollars, low interest rates, export expansion, and inflationary expectations of the 1970's, but they have already lost much of that gain. One of the key questions now is whether a weaker dollar and high interest rates will help farmland hold even its current value. It also is questionable whether high land values are good for U.S. farming, since they are a cost element just as surely as machinery and chemicals.

Key Question—Price Supports? Another key question today is the best type of farm policy for the U.S. to follow. The two major elements of U.S. farm policy over the last 50 years have been price supports and land diversion. The last few years, however, have demonstrated the enormous difficulty of administering price supports in a period of volatile exchange rates. Moreover, both our price supports and our land diversion have encouraged competing producers to expand their production and aim for a larger share of the world market.

There also has been a strong tendency for the benefits of farm subsidies to become capitalized in land values. Over the long term, higher land values mean higher prices which, in turn, mean high farm production costs, just as surely as do higher prices for tractors or chemicals. U.S. farmers have always tended to see their fine cropland and its climate as a major part of their competitive advantage. The competitive advantage of U.S. farming today, however, lies less in its land

and climate than ever before. Technology and investments are rapidly overcoming the constraints of other, less expensive cropland in other countries.

U.S. Farmers' Advantage. The U.S. farmers' advantage today lies increasingly in their own high productivity, and in the off-farm systems that enhance the efficiency of their farms—research and extension institutions, input manufacturing and distribution, and the marketing system that moves huge volumes of farm products from farms to consumers at unit costs foreign farmers can only marvel at. Developing countries' farmers are still at a strong disadvantage in these off-farm functions—with rutted roads, poor storage facilities, overstaffed government marketing boards, and severe credit shortages.

The Long Term

In the long term, the current trends are likely to force a rationalization of world agriculture. Self-sufficiency will become less attractive when its costs become clearer (as has already become apparent in such places as the EC and Southeast Asia). Costs of production will regain their importance in determining buyers and sellers.

In the meantime, adverse impacts on U.S. farmers are likely to be moderated by several positive factors. The world's population is continuing to grow, and the world will add 1.5 billion people by year 2000, many of whom will be in middle-income countries with good economic growth rates. They will be more affluent, with high standards of living, supported by more productive, efficient, and specialized farms all over the globe. Billions of people will be seeking better diets, many of them buying additional farm products with more value added. A decline of the dollar also would remove some of the protection that U.S. prices supports have been giving to producers in other countries.

New markets also will develop for new and existing farm products. Just as the soybean rose from a specialty crop to occupy more than 100 million acres of the world's cropland in the past few decades, other new crops and new uses will add important new demand for farm products by the end of the century. As one example, researchers have discovered that a particular bacterium, fed on sugar, produces a plastic with many of the properties of polypropylene. Polyhydroxibutyrate (PHB) has the additional advantage that it is biodégradable in the soil and in the human body. Experts expect PHB can be used for such high-value specialties as surgical sutures, plates to mend broken bones, and wound dressings. In addition, big PHB plants in sugarcane-growing regions could profitably make such high-volume items as irrigation pipe and bags for flour, salt, and sugar. Although PHB was a scientific curiosity just 3 years ago, a British company has now put together a financial package to assist developing countries to build major PHB plants.

Genetic engineers believe they are close to being able to design woody plants to produce a wide variety of complex organic chemicals with useful properties.

It is impossible to predict the details of the world's future agriculture, or even American agriculture's exact role in it. It is possible to predict confidently, however, that as long as American agriculture remains on the cutting edge of technology and productivity, it will continue to make an important—and well-rewarded—contribution to the Nation and the world.

Credits

Photography

Yuen Gi Yee, better known as Bernie, served as visual coordinator. He researched, acquired, and edited the photographs for the chapters. Bernie is a public affairs specialist with the Food Safety Inspection Service where he handles all photographic chores.

Because of the international nature of the Yearbook, Bernie visited scores of embassies and international organizations seeking appropriate photos. He tapped into the photo files at the State Department, the Agency for International Development, U.S. Information Agency, and National Aeronautics and Space Administration. Within USDA, Theodosia Thomas, head of the Photography Division, was most helpful.

Credit for each photograph is given when the source is known. Prints of duplicate slides of photographs taken for or by USDA are available for a nominal charge from the Photography Division, Office of Information, Room 4407-S, U.S. Department of Agriculture, Washington, DC 20250.

Design, Printing, Editing

Art Direction: George Baka, Design Division, Office of Information
Design and Production: William J. Kircher & Associates, Inc.
Printing Coordinator: Warren Bell, Publishing Division, Office of Information
Editor: Larry B. Marton, Special Programs Division, Office of Information
Technical Editor: Grace I. Krumwiede, consultant
Proofreader: Janet G. Baker, Agricultural Stabilization and Conservation Service
Typography: Typehaus

Index

Italicized numbers refer to tables and charts.

U.S. GOVERNMENT PRINTING OFFICE: 1982   O—484-628: QL 2

For sale by the Superintendent of Documents, U.S. Government Printing Office
Washington, D.C. 20402

LC 85-600627